★ CAPITAL ★
HOMESTEADING
For Every Citizen

Published by Economic Justice Media
P.O. Box 40711, Washington, D.C. 20016, U.S.A.
(Tel) 703-243-5155 • (Fax) 703-243-5935
(Eml) thirdway@cesj.org • (Web) www.cesj.org

International Standard Book Number: 0-944997-00-7
Library of Congress Control Number: 2003113509
First Edition
Design, layout and illustrations by R.L. Brohawn

★ CAPITAL ★ HOMESTEADING

For Every Citizen

A Just Free Market Solution
for Saving Social Security

Norman G. Kurland • Dawn K. Brohawn • Michael D. Greaney

www.cesj.org

★

"All men are by nature equally free and independent, and have certain inherent rights, of which they cannot, by any compact, deprive or divest their posterity; namely, the enjoyment of life and liberty, *with the means of acquiring and possessing property*, and pursuing and obtaining happiness and safety."

> George Mason
> ("Father of the American Bill of Rights")
> Article 1 of the *Virginia Declaration of Rights*,
> adopted June 12, 1776

★

"Power naturally and necessarily follows property."

> Daniel Webster
> Address, Massachusetts Convention, 1820

★

"I take it that it is best for all to leave each man free to acquire property as fast as he can. Some will get wealthy. I don't believe in a law to prevent a man from getting rich; it would do more harm than good. So while we do not propose any war against capital, we do wish to allow the humblest man an equal chance to get rich with everybody else."

> Abraham Lincoln
> Campaign Speech in New Haven, March 6, 1860

★

★

"Over one hundred years ago, Abraham Lincoln signed the Homestead Act. There was a wide distribution of land and they didn't confiscate anyone's already owned land. They did not take from those who owned and give to others who did not own. We need an Industrial Homestead Act."

Ronald Reagan
Speech to the Young Americans for Freedom, July 1974

★

"Tax policy alone may not be adequate if expanded ownership is ever to become a reality. It seems to me that we will have to do something on a monetary side as well and I am speaking here in terms of using the government powers through the Federal Reserve Bank and others to see to it that loans are made available on more reasonable terms that help workers acquire capital."

Senator Russell B. Long
(Longtime chairman of the Senate Finance Committee and political champion of the Employee Stock Ownership Plan)
Keynote address at Harvard University, April 17, 1982

★

"[The challenge is] to make the world work for 100% of humanity in the shortest possible time through spontaneous cooperation without ecological offense or the disadvantage of anyone."

Buckminster Fuller
(Philosopher, world design scientist and inventor of the geodesic dome)
Attributed to *The World Game*, mid-1970s

★

CONTENTS

ACKNOWLEDGMENTS

The authors express our deepest thanks to former U.S. Ambassador Curtin Winsor, Jr. and the William H. Donner Foundation. Their generous support made possible the publication of this work. We are also profoundly grateful to Dr. Norman A. Bailey for his long support of Capital Homesteading and expanded capital ownership. During his tenure as chief economist for the National Security Council during the Reagan Administration, Dr. Bailey commissioned the drafting of the "Capital Homestead Act" and the strategy paper that led to the formation of the 1986 Presidential Task Force on Project Economic Justice. Dr. Bailey's innovative concept of a "Federal National Capital Credit Corporation," an enhancement to the original Capital Homestead strategy, attracted the attention of the W.H. Donner Foundation and led to the grant that funded this project.

In presenting this new policy thrust, we look back with gratitude to former **President Ronald Reagan** who called for an "Industrial Homestead Act" in 1975, and to the late **Senator Russell Long,** who championed worker ownership in America, overcoming the opposition of naysayers. In winning a place for the Employee Stock Ownership Plan (ESOP) in U.S. law, Senator Long proved not only his political brilliance but his moral courage. A true statesman, Senator Long based his support for a politically unknown idea not on "who's right," but on "what's right."

This proposal owes a great intellectual debt to the expanded ownership philosopher, lawyer and economist, the late **Louis Kelso.** The late philosopher Mortimer Adler, his coauthor of *The Capitalist Manifesto* and *The New Capitalists,* credited Kelso as having conceived "the most revolutionary economic idea of the 20th century." Kelso laid out the principles, theory and institutional mechanisms of a socio-economic system that reconciles humanity with technology by making every person an owner of capital. Kelso's conceptual breakthrough in "binary economics" continues to be disseminated worldwide by his wife and coauthor **Patricia Kelso** of the Kelso Institute for the Study of Economic Systems, and by such leading binary economists as **Professor Robert Ashford** and **Rodney Shakespeare**.

Along with Kelso, we must acknowledge other seminal thinkers whose "post-scarcity" concepts comprise a new global vision and paradigm for economic and social problem-solving: the late **Rev. William J. Ferree, S.M., Ph.D.**, a leading Catholic philosopher on Social Justice and Social Charity who cofounded the Center for Economic and Social Justice (CESJ) a year before his death; the late **Buckminster Fuller**, the world design scientist who challenged all of us to "make the world work for 100% of humanity in the shortest time possible through spontaneous cooperation without ecological offense or the disadvantage of anyone;" and the late **Rev. Dr. Martin Luther King , Jr.**, whose universal message of "peace through justice" inspires this book and the concerted actions of many courageous people around the world.

We also thank CESJ's board of directors, counselors and members worldwide, for their dedication to economic and social justice for all. Special mention goes to CESJ Counselor **Rev. William Christensen, S.M.**, known to his Muslim friends and coworkers at the Institute of Integrated Rural Development as "Brother Bill." A former student of Fr. Ferree, Fr. Bill labors tirelessly in Bangladesh among the poorest of the poor. Exemplifying "the act of social justice," he is organizing with others to launch, as part of IIRD's successful economic development program, a model of "Justice-Based Management[SM]." CESJ board member **Joseph Recinos**, an international development economist and counselor to President Reagan's Task Force on Project Economic Justice, has shown similar courage and dedication over the years introducing Capital Homesteading to Latin America and other regions. We are also grateful for the extraordinary initiatives of CESJ members **Norbert Hermes** and **Bishop Herbert Hermes**, identical twins from Shallow Water, Kansas. Norbert has been working relentlessly among the farmers of Kansas to promote Capital Homesteading as an economic agenda for a "Culture of Life" that would address the problems of rural America. Herbert Hermes, Bishop of Cristalandia, Brazil has been opening doors for CESJ to get its "Just Third Way" message to his network of visionary politicians and Catholic leaders in Brazil.

Among the political leaders laboring to bring economic and social justice to the poor and disenfranchised of America, **Illinois State Representative Wyvetter Younge** deserves special mention. Over the past thirty-five years, Rep. Younge, who is working closely with CESJ, has kept alive within East St. Louis, Illinois a bold dream of a 21st Century city, incorporating the genius of Bucky Fuller, Louis Kelso and Martin Luther King, Jr. A fellow visionary, and genius in his own right, is CESJ Counselor **Dean Price**, former master planner and *architect emeritus* of Georgetown University (Washington, D.C.). Dean, who today heads Equitech International, LLC, a professional consortium of scientists and engineers, is working with leaders like Rep. Younge to introduce and commercialize advanced, hydrogen-based waste-to-energy systems that could provide the technological foundation for a new ownership economy. Promoting CESJ's Just Third Way message in America and Africa, are former **Congressan and Rev. Walter Fauntroy**, and **Rev. Virgil Wood**. They are carrying the human rights mission of their colleague, Martin Luther King, Jr., to the next stage, that of economic democracy through property rights for all. Two other intrepid "paradigm shifters" are CESJ Counselors **Steve Nieman** and **Richard Foley**, who are organizing OU® Union as a vehicle for transforming the traditional wage-system-based labor union into an ownership union.

Finally, we are deeply grateful for the editorial contributions to this book made by **Dan Parker** and **Harriet Epstein**. Dan, a leader in Canada's Social Credit Movement, is introducing Just Third Way concepts to his network and the world through his superb website (GlobalJusticeMovement.org). He helped refine the terminology in this book regarding concepts of interest and pure credit generated through the central bank. Harriet, a longtime CESJ member and leading national spokesperson on retirement policy, combed through the manuscript and pointed out sections and passages needing clarification.

It is through the persistence of such courageous individuals, working together with others sharing their vision, that we may realize within our own times the far-reaching wisdom of Abraham Lincoln's Homestead Act, through a Capital Homestead program for every citizen.

EXECUTIVE SUMMARY

- The proposed Capital Homestead program would offer a private property and free market oriented alternative for saving the Social Security System as a national retirement income maintenance plan, while introducing a new national policy to foster "capital self-sufficiency" as a means to achieve true economic independence for all Americans.

- Following the precedent of Abraham Lincoln's Homestead Act of 1862 that democratized the ownership of frontier land, this economic policy would universalize access to capital credit — the 21st century equivalent of the 160 acres of land — to every citizen. This would provide access to the means for every citizen to accumulate over his or her lifetime an independent income-producing capital homestead in the ever-expanding technological frontier.

- Based on four pillars of a free and just market economy — (1) expanded capital ownership, (2) limited economic power of the state, (3) restoration of free and open markets, and (4) restoration of the rights of private property — the Capital Homestead program would strengthen the political constituency for linking supply-side with demand-side economic policies. It would add social justice and compassion to conservative principles. It would also reduce the political pressures for redistributive, anti-growth and protectionist policies.

- Capital Homesteading would introduce basic reforms in the monetary and tax systems, geared toward maximizing private sector growth without inflation, shifting from a debt-backed to an asset-backed currency, while systematically building a nation of owners.

- Capital Homesteading would reduce pressures on the present pay-as-you-go Social Security and Medicare systems, while leaving in place a social safety net for those individuals whose capital homestead accumulations were insufficient to generate an income to meet their basic needs.

- The Federal Reserve would revive its existing money-creating powers under Section 13 of the Federal Reserve Act, opening its discount window to provide sufficient money and capital credit to finance the estimated $2 trillion needed annually for new plant and equipment, new technology, new rentable space, and new infrastructure. Channeled through each citizen's Capital Homestead Account (CHA), Fed-monetized credit would be allocated by the competitive banking system to financially sound investments and irrigated through mechanisms that systematically create new owners of the new wealth, without taking old wealth from existing owners.

- Five central banking innovations would be introduced: (1) a two-tiered Federal Reserve credit policy that favors broadly owned private sector growth over nonproductive government and consumer borrowing; (2) a shift to the Federal Reserve's discount mechanism from its Open Market Committee for controlling the money supply, thus freeing growth from its current dependency on past savings; (3) 100% reserves (the "Chicago Plan") to replace fractional reserve banking; (4) the Federal Capital Credit Corporation (FCCC),[1] a Fannie-Mae-type "bundling" operation to facilitate Capital Homesteading loans and establish national standards for lenders; and (5) the Federal Capital Insurance Corporation (FCIC),[2] to provide an alternative to traditional forms of collateral, thereby eliminating a major barrier to widespread citizen participation in significant capital ownership.

- Capital Homesteading would offer an economic growth model based on access to private property as a fundamental human right, encouraging other countries to emulate America by lifting themselves into economic prosperity, thus building a more free, just and unified global market, the economic foundation for enduring political democracy and peace around the world.

INTRODUCTION

Social Security is a system built to collapse. While the horrific events of September 11, 2001 wrenched the nation's attention away momentarily from retirement security to national security, the economic costs of this one terrorist assault on America, coupled with an already ailing economy and the "bursting of the bubble" of publicly-traded securities, placed an even greater burden on America's public retirement system, hastening its day of bankruptcy.

Prior to the September 11 attacks, according to the *Washington Post,* congressional estimates projected that the government would drain almost all the Social Security surplus to operate at current levels through 2011, "imperiling the retirements of the baby-boom generation."[3] In the face of massive layoffs and economic displacement caused by the attacks, Congress must now consider in its budget debates the billions needed to cover the replacement of destroyed property, insurance losses, homeland security, rebuilding postwar Iraq and Afghanistan, and other related costs. In the long-term, Federal Reserve Chairman Alan Greenspan warned that the demand for added security will force firms to cut back on employment and productive activities such as research and capital investment.[4]

The bipartisan Presidential Commission on Social Security issued its final report, *Strengthening Social Security and Creating Personal Wealth for All Americans*, on December 11, 2001. The report concluded: "Social Security is in need of an overhaul. The system is not sustainable as currently structured.... (p.7)" While the commission members agreed on the use of Private Savings Accounts (PSAs) to allow Americans to invest in the stock market a portion of their Social Security funds, they were unable to offer a unified set of recommendations. There was no consensus on what percentage of Social Security assets should be put into publicly traded securities. It was also assumed that there was no better way for workers to invest than to place their wages and savings in the stock market (mainly via mutual funds). Even more important, as many commentators observed, the commission failed to recommend any significant structural reforms for maintaining the long-term viability of Social Security.

Flaws in the Foundation

At the inception of the Social Security program in 1936, the United States Government promised explicitly, "What you get from the Government plan will always be more than you have paid in taxes and usually more than you can get for yourself by putting away the same amount of money each week in some other way."[5] Unfortunately and predictably, however, the increase in benefit obligations over time has made the original promise unsupportable, even though today 76 percent of Americans pay more in payroll taxes than they do in federal income taxes.[6]

Most people are living longer than age 65, the life expectancy projected when the Social Security program was born, and they are getting higher benefits than the system had originally expected to pay out. As the population growth rate in the U.S. declines, there will be a shrinking pool of working Americans paying higher taxes to cover Social Security benefits for a growing pool of retirees. As the *Wall Street Journal* summed it up in 1988: "Baby boomers and their children will pay more for their own retirement and get less in return."[7]

Some analysts have warned that, calculated at present value, projected Social Security deficits combined with those of Medicare could reach $43 *trillion*.[8] This dwarfs the projected $3.5 trillion in federal budget deficits that the government officially reports as its current level of public debt. In contrast to credit extended to private enterprises, there are no productive capital assets standing behind public sector debt.

Part of the reason for the present crisis is that shortly after its creation, Social Security abandoned its original purpose as a social safety net/insurance program to ensure every working American a minimally adequate income after retirement. It is now expected to provide the bulk, if not all, of a person's retirement income. If Social Security collapses, many retirees will be left economically vulnerable and dependent on their families, public welfare or charity.

Society's great expectations, and the efforts of policymakers to satisfy them, rest on a shaky edifice erected on a flawed foundation. Three of the most serious structural weaknesses are:

1. Social Security is a pay-as-you-go system and has no productive assets, but rather government debt in the form of government bonds and Treasury bills to stand behind the government's mounting promises. Nobel economist Paul A. Samuelson even proclaimed the system "the greatest Ponzi game ever contrived."[9] The problem with pyramid schemes, however, is that they eventually leave someone "holding the bag." It is anticipated that by 2020, Social Security could begin to pay out more than it collects, forcing the Federal government to reduce benefit levels, tap into general revenues, or print money to meet the deficits.[10]

2. An unhealthy generational political split is inevitable between younger workers and aging Social Security recipients. Potential beneficiaries are growing larger in number. 75 million baby boomers will soon join their ranks. The working population who pay into the system (and whose payrolls are taxed from dollar one) is shrinking in proportion to the recipient population. In 1940, soon after the program was launched, most Americans died before reaching the eligible Social Security age of 65, and the burden ratio was roughly 42 to 1. Now the burden ratio is about 3 to 1, putting the weight of more and more dependents on fewer and fewer backs.[11]

3. The rich are largely exempted from sharing in this mounting burden. Not only is there a cap on salaries taxed for the so-called trust fund,[12] but also there is no tax on incomes from dividends, interest, and capital gains to support Social Security. The payroll tax is extremely regressive, placing the greatest burden on the working poor who must pay into the system from the first dollar of earnings. Thus high-income workers and the wealthiest Americans escape the responsibility to meet the nation's promises to poor and middle-class workers.

Social Security and Enron

Wall Street debacles such as Enron, Global Crossing and WorldCom are certain to have an impact on the Social Security system and its reform. Were these corporate disasters merely aberrations or do they reveal a fundamental flaw in the present system upon which the Bush administration and other policymakers hope to build a privatized retirement system?

Analysts such as Daniel Yergin have characterized Enron's collapse as the inevitable outcome of a system driven by the "quarterly stampede" of investors to companies whose quarterly performance is able to meet the "consensus forecast" of stock analysts:

> The name of the game was to keep those earnings coming. Not because they meant dividends, which went out of fashion. The whole system depended on rising stock prices. Who was calling the shots? To a considerable degree, it was all of us — and our $11.5 trillion fortune of retirement savings. The quest for 'share-holder' value and higher returns was the guarantee that our re-tirements would be okay, and we expected our money managers to deliver. Their compensation and even jobs depended on their performance.[13]

Companies that do not show a quarterly rise in stock prices and earnings risk being dumped by pension fund managers who have invested huge sums of retirement funds in them. Such outflows of investment dollars drive a company's share price even lower, making it a prime target for such "serial acquirers" as WorldCom.

Further motivating company executives to show increased quarterly earnings is the shift in the bulk of executive compensation from fixed salaries to option packages. Stock options (frequently mis-identified as ESOPs, which are employee stock *ownership* plans) were hailed as a way of aligning the interests of management with those of shareholders. Yergin points out, however, that options became an attractive means for executives to "have their cake and eat it," at the expense of shareholders:

> Unlike shareholders, executives suffered no out-of-pocket penalty if the share price went down. Moreover, the options, which could

eventually be worth tens or even hundreds of millions of dollars, were not charged as an expense, masking their real cost to shareholders.[14]

Share prices can also be manipulated, as Enron and WorldCom proved, through improper accounting practices. In those cases, accounting firms serving the companies' board of directors as both auditors *and* consultants (which should have been seen by regulators as a conflict of interest), had an incentive to hide information from shareholders through questionable adjustments to financial reports.

Are Enron, Global Crossing and WorldCom reflections of a financial system that is inherently prone to the sorts of speculative bubbles and "irrational exuberance" of which Federal Reserve Chairman Alan Greenspan spoke in December 1996 when the Dow was at 6,437?[15] Does today's financial system of trading in secondary issuances even constitute real investment, or is just another form of gambling? Should the retirement security of Americans be governed by the "Greater Fool Theory,"[16] or should we seek to connect systematically more citizens as owners to real growth in the economy?

As a result of Enron there has been a further deterioration of pubic confidence in corporate governance and credibility, and the institutions that are meant to oversee them. How long the public's "malaise" will continue before the stock market is "pumped up" by the next temporary stimulus (such as tax cuts or higher defense spending for the war on terrorism), is anyone's guess.

What is clear is that our institutions, and the values and systems that govern their operation, will have a profound influence on the culture and value systems of our society as a whole. For companies driven by Wall Street's incessant demands for higher share values, delivering quality and value to customers has given way to hype and buzz as the business strategy of choice. The property rights of small investors are virtually non-existent. Executives and boards of directors are largely non-accountable and company financials, non-transparent. Workers are viewed as assets, or even worse, as commodities to be dumped if necessary to boost corporate "productivity" measurements.

Social Security and the Wealth Gap

The inherent weakness of the present Social Security system and a possible solution to its ills, become even more clear when viewed against the backdrop of another dangerous social phenomenon: the growing "wealth gap." While a few commentators like P.J. O'Rourke might argue that the widening economic differential between rich and poor is an unavoidable or even a healthy consequence of our "free market system,"[17] growing evidence challenges that position. [*See* Appendix 5.]

Contrary to President Kennedy's dictum that "a rising tide lifts all boats," not only are all "boats" *not* rising together, a great many are sinking — while a few others have lifted into the stratosphere.[18] As political thinkers from George Mason to Abraham Lincoln to Ronald Reagan recognized, America's political democracy requires an economic counterpart to sustain it. Furthermore, gross disparities in wealth and economic power merely fuel world-wide resentment against America and globalization of the marketplace. As September 11th reminds us, America is not an island unto itself.

Addressing the Social Security Problem
from a Systems Perspective

The proposals contained in this report focus primarily on addressing one problem in our economic infrastructure — the impending collapse of our Social Security system. Other problems that will affect the future of our nation's retirement income system include:

- A looming crisis in the health system
- So-called "overcapacity" in the economy
- Displacement of jobs by advancing technologies
- A growing wealth and income gap
- Enormous and rising consumer and government debt
- Huge budget deficits in our largest cities and states
- Loss of basic industries
- The continuing U.S. trade deficit
- Wage arbitrage and flight of jobs to lower wage countries

The problem with piecemeal solutions is that they often breed problems of their own. What policymakers have yet to consider is a comprehensive economic strategy for (1) stimulating sustainable, noninflationary private sector growth and (2) connecting more and more people to the ownership of that growth. Such a strategy would offer the opportunity and access to the means for every American citizen, particularly the poorest of the poor, to acquire, share the rights and status of first-class shareholders, and enjoy the fruits of productive equity.

This long-range agenda would involve major restructuring of our laws and economic policies to foster more equitable distribution of future corporate capital, more robust rates of private sector investment, and a shift in the source of mass purchasing power from inflationary increases in wages and welfare payments to increased profit sharing and dividend incomes.

Our top business schools continue to preach Wall Street capitalism as the model for America and the world. Yet we ask, can a system that promotes short-term thinking and gambling, and encourages greed, cheating, and non-accountability, produce an ethical, justice-based business environment necessary in the long-run for sustainable economic development?

Contrary to the claims of its most ardent advocates, the Wall Street model, through defective financial, tax, and legal institutions, has helped create barriers to a truly free and just market economy. We see instead gross concentrations of money and power, with fewer and fewer competitors. Wall Street capitalism has fostered a 21st Century brand of mercantilism (the very thing Adam Smith abhorred), where businesses buy political favors to insulate themselves from competition. Today's elitist and exclusionary economic system contradicts and undermines America's populist values and democratic institutions.

In the not-too-distant future, when most of the Baby Boom generation have entered their retirement years, the very foundations of America's economy will be tested. Our policy decisions today will shape the quality of life enjoyed, or suffered, by those retirees, as well as by the rest of society.

At some point, even the most financially secure, starry-eyed optimist will face the inevitable questions: Can Social Security really deliver on its promises? Can our present economic system generate sufficient rates of growth and broad-based prosperity to meet those promises? Will the system bring social harmony, or will it lead to class warfare and generational strife?

What we need for the long-term is an economic system based both on sound moral and sound market principles. What we need *now* is a plan for sustainable growth in which every citizen from birth can gain a viable ownership stake in the new capital frontier.

I.
THE PROPOSAL
IN BRIEF

How do we fix Social Security before it collapses? A comprehensive national strategy called "Capital Homesteading" would address this challenge through a radically new policy thrust — the *democratization of capital credit*. As will be presented in this book, the critical reform needed to democratize capital credit involves reactivating Section 13 of the Federal Reserve Act of 1913.

Specifically, this book proposes that the rarely employed "discount window" of the Federal Reserve be "reopened," with appropriate modifications and safeguards, to allow qualified banks and financial institutions to discount "eligible" industrial, commercial, and agricultural paper representing loans for productive purposes. Qualified lenders could then provide low-cost capital credit to businesses and farms through mechanisms that systematically broaden capital ownership of new private sector growth among workers and farmers, area residents, and citizens generally who own little or no productive assets.

Expanding the role of the Federal Reserve's discount window in national monetary policy is a proposition that policymakers are beginning to give serious consideration. As part of its strategy to manage interest rates more effectively, the Federal Reserve recently began overhauling its procedures for making loans to commercial banks via its discount mechanism.[19]

Big problems require big solutions. We realize that the scope of our proposal may appear grandiose to some. However, we believe that the crisis facing Social Security requires comprehensive "systems" re-engineering. Rethinking the fundamentals of a system often requires new terminology, or specifically nuanced usages of traditional terms. For the reader's convenience and for clarity of argumentation, we have included a glossary defining our terms.

Before examining each of the basic components of a national Capital Homesteading strategy in detail, we will briefly outline the proposal as it can be applied to address the fundamental problems underlying the Social Security System.

A Capital Homesteading Solution For Social Security

First, under the proposed Capital Homesteading reforms, *Congress would keep all benefit promises previously made to citizens under the Social Security and Medicare programs.* As will be described in greater detail below, Capital Homesteading reforms would increase the sources of taxes to cover the benefit promises.

The overall strategy would also offer an asset-backed supplement for retirement incomes not dependent on redistributive taxation or the somewhat speculative results of publicly traded securities. It would stabilize at present levels any future commitments under Social Security and Medicare. This would tend to "flatten out" the rate of increases in benefit levels, while increasing funding for current promises.

Second, to meet Social Security and Medicare commitments, *revenue sources would be shifted from the regressive 12.4% payroll tax (a combined tax paid by employers and employees on all wages below $87,000[20]) to general tax revenues paid from all sources of consumption income over a poverty level.* (This would eliminate one of the most harmful taxes imposed on the working poor. At the same time it would radically reduce production costs of American industry, improving America's competitive position in world trade.)

Incomes below $10,000 for each adult and $5,000 per child would be exempt from any taxes. Property incomes from dividends, rent, interest, and inflation-indexed capital gains would be fully taxed at the same rate as wage and salary incomes. Those above the poverty level would pay taxes at a single rate on all income above the exemptions, from whatever source their income was derived. The single tax rate would be calculated to balance the budget and retire the national debt over 20 to 30 years.

Under Capital Homesteading *all* income of individuals, not just wages and salaries, would be considered "earned." Thus, property incomes would be included in the definition of "earned income," and the income cap (currently at $87,000 of wage income) would be removed on earned income subject to supporting Social Security and Medicare benefits. *This change alone would help increase revenues to prevent bankruptcy of the social security system.*

Dividends on Capital Homesteading shares would be tax-deductible to the corporation, encouraging higher dividend payouts (which as mentioned above, would increase individuals' taxable incomes). This would give corporations a socially beneficial way to escape double and triple taxation on corporate profits, and would induce new share issuances for financing new capital assets.

Third, the Federal Reserve System would employ its discount powers under Section 13 of the Federal Reserve Act of 1913 [*see* Appendix 2, "Extract from Section 13 of the Federal Reserve Act of 1913"] so that member banks could make lower-cost, asset-backed, "non-recourse" Capital Homestead (CH) loans to enable every US citizen to invest in newly issued, full dividend payout, full voting shares voluntarily issued by "eligible" private sector corporations. Such shares would finance a growing portion of the nation's annual growth needs for new technologies, new plant and equipment, new rentable space and new infrastructure.

Democratized capital credit would also free economic growth from both government subsidies and the "slavery of past savings." It would offer all Americans a means of accumulating individual capital estates through "future savings" of the earnings from their own capital assets. [*See* Appendix 4, "A New Look at Prices and Money: The Kelsonian Binary Model for Achieving Rapid Growth Without Inflation."]

Re-Envisioning the Future of Social Security

According to the January 2001 *Economic Report of the President,* a growth increment of about $2 trillion dollars of new productive assets was added to the U.S. "capital tree" in the year 2001[21] — or about $6,755 for every man, woman and child in America. Let's see what would happen if the Federal Reserve System "monetized" a portion of that growth through privately insured Capital Homestead (CH) loans backed dollar-for-dollar by the newly formed productive assets.

Assume that every year each citizen could borrow $3,000 from local banks and financial institutions to invest in private sector shares representing about one-half of the real productive growth of the economy at present capital growth rates.[22] Under this national strategy, a child born today could retire at age 65 with a tax-sheltered Capital Homestead

(CH) stake of about $200,000, yielding a yearly "second income" of $30,000. Furthermore, over that period he would have received dividends totaling over $750,000. [*See* Appendix 3, "What Capital Homesteading Would Mean to the Average American: Projected Wealth and Income Accumulations Under Capital Homesteading."]

This scenario assumes (1) no increase in America's capital growth rate, (2) $3,000 for purchasing the newly issued CH "growth" shares, borrowed annually from local banks at an unsubsidized "pure credit" borrowing rate (interest-free with a service charge to cover administrative costs, risk and capital insurance premiums, and normal bank profit margins), (3) no increase in share values, and (4) a 15% annual pre-tax, pre-dividend return on investment[23] as the sole source for repaying the stock purchase loans.

When the dividend returns from this almost trillion dollar capital "growth pie" are spread among all citizens, consumer buying power would increase, fueling higher rates of investment. As consumption incomes expanded, growth rates could increase to the full productive capacity of the economy. This would lift the American economy from the inherently inflationary and feudalistic "wage system" to a more inclusive and more participative market economy, with much less pressure for redistributive taxation.

How Would Capital Homesteading Work?

The preferred method for democratizing access to CH loans is to allocate to each citizen and every member of his family an equal amount of CH loans periodically (*e.g.*, quarterly) based on periodic estimates of the total capital credit needed by private enterprises (*i.e.*, capital demand).[24] The citizen would then go to his or her local bank, where the citizen would receive investment advice. The bank would set up a "Capital Homestead Account" (a "CHA," similar to an IRA, but with differences noted below). The CHA would receive on the citizen's behalf periodic loans from the bank for the purchase of "eligible" full voting, full dividend-payout shares issued by "qualified" private sector enterprises in need of capital for expansion, modernization or for purchasing outstanding shares from present shareowners.

The citizen would have the choice to invest his allotment of credit among shares of (1) the company for which a member of the family works, (2) a company, like a utility, mass transit system, or comprehensive health care delivery system, in which he is a regular customer with a regular billing account, (3) a for-profit Community Investment Corporation for developing land and infrastructure in his local community or region, or (4) a diversified blend of mature companies with proven records of profitability and sound management.

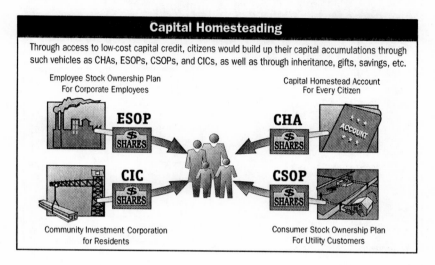

Capital Homesteading

Through access to low-cost capital credit, citizens would build up their capital accumulations through such vehicles as CHAs, ESOPs, CSOPs, and CICs, as well as through inheritance, gifts, savings, etc.

Employee Stock Ownership Plan
For Corporate Employees

ESOP

Capital Homestead Account
For Every Citizen

CHA

CIC

CSOP

Community Investment Corporation
for Residents

Consumer Stock Ownership Plan
For Utility Customers

Before taking the loan paper to the discount window of the regional Federal Reserve Bank for monetizing at a Fed service charge of 0.5%, the local bank would have the option of self-insuring the loan or insuring against loan default with a commercial insurer of CH loan paper. Loan default reinsurance, preferably offered by the private sector, would further spread the risk of default. Debt service, including risk premium charges, on each loan received by the citizen's CHA would be repaid from future pre-tax dividend distributions paid by each of the companies that issue the CH shares.

To further support Capital Homesteading, a Federal Capital Credit Corporation (FCCC) could be set up, similar to the Federal National Mortgage Association ("Fannie Mae") and the Federal Home Mortgage Corporation ("Freddie Mac"), to package and set national standards for insured, self-liquidating capital loans and then discount these loans at the discount window of one of the 12 regional Federal Reserve banks. The Federal Reserve would treat insured CH loan paper as backing for the U.S. currency, substituting for today's government debt paper.[25]

The following diagram illustrates the interrelationships between the different elements of the system and how money and credit can be created to bring about non-inflationary private sector growth linked to expanded capital ownership:

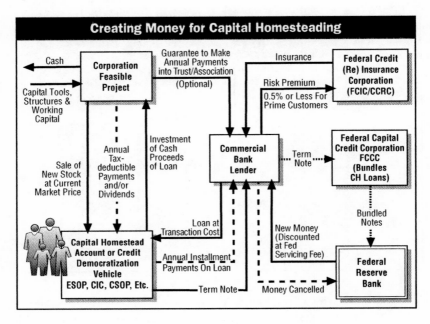

The projected annual yield from the proposed Capital Homestead program requires no reduction in take-home pay, savings, or consumption incomes to purchase "eligible" shares from "qualified" companies. No taxpayer subsidies would be required. All borrowings could be insured privately against the risk that an issuing company would not generate dividends to service the share acquisition loans. The "risk premium" included within each individual loan would generate the revenues to sustain the insurance pool.

Such insurance, structured like home mortgage insurance, represents a private sector solution for overcoming the collateralization barrier for the poor and middle-income borrowers who have no assets to pledge and who would otherwise have no access to capital credit on the same basis as the wealthiest 5% of Americans.

Insuring Minimum Social Security and Medicare Benefits

There is always the risk that some Capital Homestead Accounts will not generate enough capital incomes, after the shares are paid for, to meet the minimum benefit levels guaranteed under the Social Security and Medicare programs. Some of the investments will fail. Some capital homesteaders may squander their accumulations and have to start over again.

One way to address these risks is to establish what Milton Friedman once proposed as a "Negative Income Tax." An even better way is to establish a minimum income guarantee fund, supported by either general revenues or premiums charged each citizen having a CHA, or a combination of both. These funds could be used to purchase a blend of stock and bond index funds sufficient to cover guaranteed minimum Social Security and Medicare benefits in the event the yields from one's Capital Homestead Account drop below these minimum levels.

Capital Homestead Accounts (CHAs) vs.
Personal Savings Accounts (PSAs)

While there remains significant opposition by many Americans, support is growing for shifting at least a portion of Social Security to private investments by individuals, or allowing such personal investment as an "add-on" to Social Security income. An August 2002 Washington Post-Kaiser Family Foundation-Harvard poll indicated that 61 percent of young voters (30 and younger) favor individual investment accounts in Social Security, while 67 percent of the elderly are opposed.[26]

The Bush Administration has proposed the use of Private Savings Accounts (PSAs). Previously, a 1996 report by the Cato Institute's Project on Social Security Privatization recommended the use of PSAs in privatizing social security, characterizing such an approach as "A Big Boost for the Poor."[27] Michael Tanner, the director of the project and the report's author, asserted that in such a privatized system,

> [A]n individual's benefits would not be dependent on life expectancy [usually lower among the poor]. Individuals would have a property right in their benefits. Any benefits remaining at their deaths would become part of their estates, inherited by their heirs.... Privatization would increase national savings and provide a new pool of capital for investment that would be particularly beneficial to the poor."[28]

Functioning as a "mandatory savings plan," a privatized social security program would deposit into the PSA the portion of the payroll tax that comprises the employer and employee contributions to the Old-Age and Survivors Insurance (OASI) portion of the Social Security tax.

The PSA would operate like the current IRA, where individuals would be penalized for withdrawing funds before their retirement. PSAs would be managed by the private investment industry. Individuals could choose their own fund manager and change them whenever they wished. The government would establish regulations on portfolio risk to prevent speculation and protect consumers. In addition, the government could continue to provide a minimum safety net, through either a guaranteed minimum benefit or a floor benefit.

Citing Chile's success with its privatized pension system, Tanner highlighted another benefit of the proposed PSA approach:

> [I]t would give every American — including poor Americans — an opportunity to participate in the economy by owning it.... Through Social Security privatization, workers would become stockholders. The division between labor and capital would be broken down.[29]

For all its advantages over the present Social Security system, however, there are certain inherent problems with the Personal Savings Account approach.

First, PSAs as currently proposed are only meaningful to a person who (1) is employed and (2) has sufficient discretionary income to invest. Proposals to contribute welfare-type payments into PSAs or Individual Development Accounts (IDAs) of the poor (or as some have suggested, to every child upon birth[30]), are dependent on taxpayer dollars and thus remain politically vulnerable.

Second, the PSA approach is tied to Wall Street and the money managers and investment brokers who earn their living from a system that is based on speculation in secondary issuances, not real investment and growth. Rather than empowering workers and small investors, the financial system underlying such corporate debacles as Enron and WorldCom made it easy for corporate leaders and big accounting firms to dupe even the Wall Street gurus, and to betray investors and employee-shareholders. Does it make sense to entrust our retirement incomes to a top-down, non-accountable, power-concentrating system that undermines the property rights of individual shareholders?

Capital Homestead Accounts (CHAs) would overcome many of the weaknesses of the PSA/IDA proposals. Rather than requiring that people reduce their current consumption levels and personal savings, CHAs would provide access to nonrecourse, self-liquidating capital credit to every citizen from birth. In this way, every citizen could accumulate a growing tax-deferred capital accumulation, in the most equitable and direct fashion, from the bottom-up, and without depending on the taxpayer or the past savings of others.

Under the CHA approach, individuals could receive over the course of their lifetimes dividend incomes generated by their capital accumulations, once the loan for a particular capital acquisition has been repaid. (While the capital assets would accumulate tax-free up to a proposed $750,000 "Capital Homestead exemption" level, income taken out of the account for consumption purposes would be taxed at a regular income tax rate.) Thus the incomes generated by CHA holdings would be available to recipients much sooner, creating more effective consumer demand in the economy as well as demand for capital investment.

The CHA approach would put power and trust in individual Americans and their local bankers (who would have a long-term investor's interest in the feasibility of a capital project), rather than handing more dollars and power to Wall Street stockbrokers and asset speculators pushing the latest "hot stock."

Genuine Social Security: Sharing in a Growing Economy

It should be noted that the Capital Homesteading alternative for financing America's future investment assets would produce higher annual retirement incomes (conservatively estimated at $30,000) than most Social Security retirees receive today. Plus, as mentioned earlier, a person's Homesteading assets would have produced for him or her, *prior* to retirement, dividends totaling over $750,000.

Eventually, participation in the Social Security system (as a minimum income guarantee program) could be based entirely on need. This would protect those who have anticipated Social Security and Medicare benefits upon reaching retirement age, while reducing the burden on the system by not paying benefits to those who do not need them. Merging FICA and other payroll taxes into a single rate general tax system would both prevent the future bankruptcy of the system and dispel the myth that Social Security was ever intended as anything other than a redistributive, pay-as-you-go welfare system.

If properly implemented within economically feasible ventures, there would be no harmful inflationary effects to the economy. Future prices of U.S. goods and services would be more price competitive in global markets because the new equity entitlements offered to workers under Capital Homesteading would raise their incomes and accumulations without raising fixed labor costs. Rising consumption incomes would be tied directly to the rising productiveness of capital, linking people directly as owners to technological progress. In fact, these reforms would stabilize the value of the U.S. dollar since there would be real productive assets backing the U.S. currency, rather than nonproductive government debt paper as is the case today.

II.
THE CONCEPT OF
CAPITAL HOMESTEADING

The Historical Roots of Capital Homesteading

Widespread private ownership of the means of production is not a new idea. The connection between widespread distribution of property and political democracy was evident to America's founders. Following John Locke's triad of fundamental and inalienable rights, George Mason in the 1776 *Virginia Declaration of Rights* (the forerunner of America's *Declaration of Independence* and *Bill of Rights*) wrote that securing "Life, Liberty, *with the means of acquiring and possessing Property*" is the highest purpose for which any just government is formed.

In the 1860s, Abraham Lincoln's Homestead Act turned thousands of people into owners of land, the single most valuable productive asset at the time, by giving them the opportunity to earn ownership of one hundred and sixty acres. The land wasn't just given away. Each homesteader had to develop the land and work it for five years. He was then granted title.

In the early twentieth century, Hilaire Belloc and G. K. Chesterton advocated a program of expanded capital ownership they called "distributism." Widespread ownership of the means of production, they asserted, would raise the income level of the average worker as well as free him from his dependence on the government. In the nineteenth century, even *laissez faire* economists such as Charles Morrison[31] recommended that changes be introduced into the legal system to allow workers to become owners. These changes would allow such social advances as limited liability and, eventually, capital credit,[32] to be employed by ordinary workers to increase their incomes, even where the value of their labor was falling in competition with cheaper foreign labor or advancing technology.

Revisiting the Wisdom of George Mason and Abraham Lincoln

Today's vast corporate wealth in the United States was created mostly after the Homestead Act had turned many Americans into owners of productive property. Corporate ownership involved a kind of productive property not addressed by Lincoln's Act. When the U.S. economy shifted its focus from agriculture to industry, our policies failed to make the broad-based ownership connection. That most of the directly-held corporate wealth in the United States is appallingly concentrated is due largely to our methods of corporate finance, and tax and monetary systems that encourage that concentration of wealth.

But a land-based Homestead Act is not the only method that can be used by the average worker to accumulate income-producing wealth. Limiting everyone to ownership opportunities in the land would merely result in a growing population dividing up a static amount of wealth into ever-smaller pieces, ensuring poverty for themselves and their descendants. There are, however, social technologies that can be used to democratize future individual ownership of a type of wealth — new tools of production being added to the world's expanding technological frontier. This new man-made frontier has no effective limits, save human creativity and ingenuity.

In a July 1974 speech to the Young Americans for Freedom, then-Governor Ronald Reagan called for one of the most revolutionary policy reforms in the past century:

> "Over one hundred years ago, Abraham Lincoln signed the Homestead Act. There was a wide distribution of land and they didn't confiscate anyone's already owned land. They did not take from those who owned and give to others who did not own. *We need an Industrial Homestead Act. . . .*"[33]

> "[I]t is time to accelerate economic growth and production and at the same time broaden the ownership of productive capital. The American dream has always been to have a piece of the action."

In his February 1975 radio broadcast, Mr. Reagan hinted at the global implications of such an expanded ownership strategy when he commented:

> "Could there be a better answer to . . . Karl Marx than millions of workers individually sharing in the ownership of the means of production?"[34]

Just as Abraham Lincoln through his Homestead Act laid the foundations for America's industrial preeminence by opening up to all citizens ownership opportunities in the agricultural frontier of the 19th

Century, his counterpart today can extend that wisdom to a technological frontier of the 21st Century that has no known limits. It is worth noting that Lincoln's Homestead Act so increased the productiveness of America's farms, that many workers were released from working the land to build the technological frontier that lifted the American economy to the top of today's global economy.

Support for Capital Homesteading

Since 1973, Congress has passed over 20 laws encouraging employee stock ownership plans (ESOPs) and over 10,000 companies are gradually spreading equity ownership among their more than 11 million workers. In 1976 the Joint Economic Committee of Congress declared broadened ownership of new capital as a major new goal of national economic policy, a "twin pillar" alongside full employment.[35] Political support for the ESOP has come from both parties and from all across the ideological spectrum.

The first champion of the ESOP was the late Sen. Russell Long, for many years the powerful chairman of the Senate Finance Committee. Others who have spoken out in favor of the ESOP concept include such diverse personalities as Senators Richard Lugar and Christopher Dodd, former Senators Hubert Humphrey, Gary Hart, Paul Fannin and Paul Laxalt, Representatives Bennie Thompson, Charles Rangel, Phil Crane, and Dana Rohrabacher, and former Representatives Bill Frenzel, Jack Kemp, Mike Espy, Michael Barnes, and Parren Mitchell. Today there are more Congressional supporters of employee stock ownership plans, although none yet with the same power or level of commitment as Senator Long.

In recent years the White House has been friendly to the idea of expanding capital ownership to more Americans. Prior to his presidency, President Ronald Reagan had, as noted, praised ESOPs and called for an "Industrial Homestead Act." During Reagan's administration, Congress mandated the formation of a Presidential Task Force on Project Economic Justice (PEJ), chaired by former Ambassador to the Organization of American States J. William Middendorf II. The bipartisan PEJ Task Force, which delivered its report *High Road to Economic Justice* to President Reagan in a White House ceremony in 1987, called for expanded ownership reforms in U.S. policy in Central America and the Caribbean region. President Clinton reportedly expressed his support for the ESOP at a cabinet meeting. In a major address on Social Security during the Republican presidential primary campaign in 2000, then-Governor George W. Bush declared that:

> Ownership in our society should not be an exclusive club. Independence should not be a gated community. Everyone should be a part owner in the American dream.[36]

At a press conference with Russian President Vladimir Putin in Crawford, Texas in November 2001, President George W. Bush congratulated Russia for its efforts to reform its economy and create "an environment where there is a tax system that's fair," noting that "they've got a flat tax in Russia." President Bush went on to praise President Putin for reforms he is putting in place that are "making sense, where people can own something — own their own business, own their own land, own the opportunity if you work hard to be able to have a future that you dream about."[37]

Obstacles to Capital Homesteading

If expanded capital ownership is an idea whose time has finally arrived, what's holding it back?

One answer is, it still lacks a comprehensive strategy to lift remaining institutional barriers to ownership of free enterprise growth. Such impediments have been erected over the last century because we neglected to link private sector growth with a more just distribution of future ownership opportunities. This is especially true in our capital credit policies.

The second answer is that when our economic decision-makers reform our laws to encourage supply-side growth, they fail, unfortunately, to link these new incentives for growth to broadened ownership and profit sharing opportunities for more people.

And perhaps a third answer lies in the difficulty of changing any paradigm.[38] The theories and assumptions that underpin a prevailing paradigm are accepted as a given. Even when they no longer adequately explain reality or offer effective solutions, outmoded paradigms can continue to be transmitted to new generations of leaders and policymakers by our academic institutions.

For example, many policies today reflect "labor-centric" economic ideas taught in our universities and reinforced by standard economic textbooks. These ideas reflect blindly the pre-industrial assumption that, for distributive purposes, all wealth is produced by human labor. By ignoring the rising productiveness of technology in the modern world, this erroneous assumption treats ownership of capital assets as irrelevant as a moral means for distributing mass purchasing power in a market economy.

Whether coming from the left or the right, the reigning Keynesian and monetarist schools accept as a norm that only a small percentage of people will derive most of their income from ownership of productive assets. The rest of the population, these schools assume, will work for the owners of capital, or for their ownership interests in business corporations. Because our current economic paradigm views the maldistribution of ownership as irrelevant, our basic institutions end up perpetuating this moral omission.

Consequently, our tax and credit systems become structured to keep ownership patterns basically fixed and to finance future growth based on past savings. Under these structures for financing growth, most of the *direct* ownership of new wealth and technologies will continue to stay in the top 1%. Meanwhile, the concentrations of real economic power are masked by indirect ownership by the masses through their pension and mutual funds, a disconnection from property rights that Peter Drucker has called "pension plan socialism."

Syracuse University law professor Robert Ashford and Rodney Shakespeare, a former barrister from the United Kingdom, observe that "despite its promise of growth and efficiency and its claimed expertise, conventional economics (as reflected in the national economic policies of the unfree market societies) rests on a number of seriously faulty premises that stifle growth and prevent distributive justice." These premises include the following:

- labor is producing most of the wealth;
- growth is fundamentally a function of human productivity;
- technology creates more jobs than it destroys;
- the economic problems of the poor and middle classes can be solved primarily with capital for the well-capitalized, and jobs and welfare for everyone else; and
- capital has no distributive relationship with growth that is independent of human productivity.[39]

As Ashford and Shakespeare elaborate, there is an emerging worldview, or paradigm, that rests on a fundamentally different set of premises that will facilitate growth *and* distributive justice. In contrast to conventional economics, this new paradigm, resting on a fundamentally different perspective on how the world works, sees that:

- *capital* is producing most of the wealth;
- growth is fundamentally a function of capital productiveness;
- technology does *not* create more good jobs than it destroys;
- the economic problems of the poor and middle classes *cannot* be solved without effective, and efficient, capital acquisition rights for all people; and
- capital *has* a positive distributive relationship with growth that is independent of human productivity.

What the new paradigm recognizes, uniquely, is that "in the post-industrial world, *affluence is the product of capital* whereas labor alone increasingly produces mere subsistence.[40] This new paradigm reclaims the wisdom of George Mason by institutionalizing access to private property rights in productive assets as a fundamental human *right*. It is this essential principle that underpins Capital Homesteading.

A Free Market Way to Generate Mass Purchasing Power

Capital Homesteading reflects the new economic paradigm called "binary economics,"[41] developed by lawyer-economist Louis Kelso in the 1950s. Kelso proposed his revolutionary economic theory and financing technologies as a systemic solution to the paradox embodied in the Depression — massive productive capacity and surpluses coupled with poverty and insufficient purchasing power among the mass of the population to buy those goods. Kelso asserted that the reason people lack sufficient incomes to purchase the surplus produced is because they themselves lack sufficient means to produce either through their labor, their capital, or both.

Kelso, like Belloc, Chesterton and Morrison before him, observed that capital in its myriad forms was becoming increasingly more productive in comparison to human labor. Indeed, the whole point of technology and its development, Kelso asserted, is not so much to amplify human labor as it is to decrease or eliminate the need for human labor in the production process.[42]

The robot that replaces the worker, Kelso pointed out, could be a boon, rather a threat, to the worker being replaced. But for advancing technology to be a source of liberation and not impoverishment for the worker, Kelso concluded, property-less workers, indeed all citizens, must gain access to the means of acquiring and possessing the technology that could generate an independent income for them. This would allow them to supplement or replace entirely their dependency on wage incomes. Assuming they owned it, technology could in fact free people to develop their human capacities and to engage in what Aristotle called "leisure work," the unlimited creative work of civilization.

Distinct from conventional schools of economics, Kelso's "binary economics" weds market principles with clearly defined "natural law" principles of economic justice. In *The Capitalist Manifesto*, Louis Kelso's classic yet misleadingly titled bestseller co-authored with philosopher Mortimer Adler, the authors outline a system of economic morality based on (1) the input principle of "participation," (2) the outtake principle of "distribution," and 3) an "anti-monopoly" feedback and corrective principle of limitation (later renamed by some advocates as the principle of harmony or social justice).[43]

From the standpoint of "participative justice," binary economics recognizes that wealth must be produced before it can be distributed, and that, as "endowed by our Creator," every human being should have an equal opportunity to contribute to the economic process through his capital as well as his labor inputs.

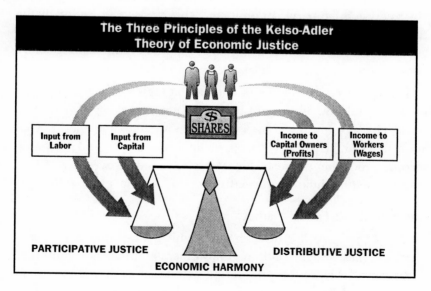

The Three Principles of the Kelso-Adler Theory of Economic Justice

SHARES

Input from Labor | Input from Capital | Income to Capital Owners (Profits) | Income to Workers (Wages)

PARTICIPATIVE JUSTICE   DISTRIBUTIVE JUSTICE

ECONOMIC HARMONY

The principle of "distributive justice" underlying binary economics dictates that incomes generated from labor and capital inputs should flow to their respective owners, according to the private property notion "to each according to his contribution." (As discussed in greater detail below, binary economics employs the free and open market as the most democratic and objective means for determining the value of each person's capital and labor contributions, and thus what are just wages, just prices and just profits.)

Finally, the restorative principle of harmony (or social justice) guides people in restructuring institutions and laws when either the participative or the distributive principle has been violated or when the economic system blocks equal opportunity and access of every individual "to the means of acquiring and possessing property," particularly to such social goods as money and credit.

Binary economics recognizes the distributive principle of "distribution according to need" as valid for *charity,* including organized charity through private or public sector programs, but it is not valid for justice. Charity should never be a substitute for justice, which properly applied, may lift many out of poverty.

In contrast to such Marxist notions as "surplus" or "windfall profits" or "unearned income" (now embedded in redistributive features of the U.S. tax system), binary economics recognizes as *equally* legitimate the contributions of both labor and capital to the production of marketable goods and services. Under a system of Capital Homesteading, every person wears "two hats," as a labor owner and as a capital owner.

The full earnings from labor and capital inputs, binary economics holds, should flow to their respective owners based on their relative contributions to production, as valued in a free and open market. That all citizens should have an equal opportunity of acquiring and possessing income-producing property, binary economics asserts, is also critical from the standpoint of market efficiency and sustainable growth.

Restoring Say's Law of Markets[44]

"Say's Law" is a law of economics which states that whatever is produced (*i.e.,* "supply") automatically generates sufficient income (*i.e.,* "demand") to clear the production at market prices. However, as John Maynard Keynes observed, as capital becomes more productive, excess production builds up that cannot be cleared at market prices. This is the phenomenon of "market gluts."

The essential problem, which Keynes also identified, is not "over-production," but "under-consumption." The wealthiest families, who own the vast majority of productive assets, can only spend a portion of the income that their capital generates for them, having reached the limits of what economists call their "propensity to consume."

Louis Kelso noted that the excess of income over expenditures is invested at an ever-increasing rate in new capital formation instead of being spent to clear the excess production. Thus, the operation of "Say's Law of Markets" is disrupted.

Most of those who want to restore Say's Law of Markets merely focus on the supply side, rather than the demand side of the economic equation, which is where Keynes and Marx centered their theories.[45] The problem with "demand-side " and "supply-side" solutions, Kelso pointed out, is that supply will generate its own demand and demand its own supply if, and only if, all economic participants can produce wealth and generate their consumption incomes from both their labor and capital, not just from their labor alone.

Kelso posited that Say's Law *would* function and avoid the problem of market gluts, as long as all new capital was financed in ways that systematically created new owners, so that capital incomes would flow legitimately and without redistribution into the hands of more and more people who would spend it on consumption.

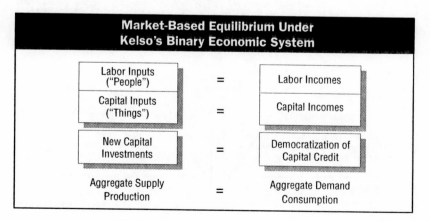

The Systems Logic for Spreading Ownership Incomes[46]

The model binary economy stands in sharp contrast to economies structured to distribute mass purchasing power exclusively through jobs and welfare redistribution. It would distribute an ever-increasing portion of consumer incomes through capital ownership and ownership profits spread directly among all households. Increases in aggregate demand would reflect increases in aggregate supply ("productivity" increases) belonging to new owners by virtue of their equity holdings in new, expanded, or transferred capital.

Existing owners with already large accumulations would no longer be allowed to monopolize access to the equity growth in the economy, but in return would be safeguarded against deprivation or erosion of their property rights in present capital assets. Thus, future ownership opportunities would be truly opened to all, by universalizing the right of access to private property and the means of acquiring productive assets needed in the future.

An economy built upon a binary income distribution system would enable free market dynamics to move toward a natural equilibrium, automatically linking future changes in productive inputs to future changes in labor and capital outtakes (incomes). It would create directly the expanded market power for sustaining and justifying vastly accelerated, non-inflationary peacetime growth rates. Potentially, a binary U.S. economy could grow as fast as that of today's China, and perhaps

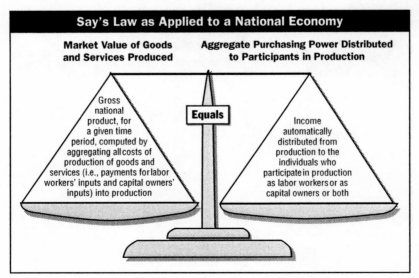

Say's Law as Applied to a National Economy

Market Value of Goods and Services Produced — Aggregate Purchasing Power Distributed to Participants in Production

Gross national product, for a given time period, computed by aggregating all costs of production of goods and services (i.e., payments for labor workers' inputs and capital owners' inputs) into production

Equals

Income automatically distributed from production to the individuals who participate in production as labor workers or as capital owners or both equal our own World War II growth rates of up to 13% annually. Even sustained non-inflationary growth of only 5% in the U.S. GDP within a binary economy would reverse the widening gap between poor and middle-income Americans and the richest 1%.

Instead of *artificially* stimulating aggregate demand and mass purchasing power through easy consumer credit and government tax, spending, and monetary policies (as Keynes believed necessary to clear the markets in periods of over-production), Kelso's binary economic system would build an expanding productive sector that spreads market-based job incomes and widespread profit distributions to new as well as current owners. This would allow the law of supply and demand to create directly the private purchasing power needed to clear the market of future capital goods and consumer goods.

Under a Kelsonian growth strategy, the source of mass production in society — the corporate sector — would become the means of distributing mass purchasing power among all consumers in society. Redistribution of income and governmental interferences with the price mechanism in determining wages, prices, and profit levels would become increasingly unnecessary.

The Four Pillars of a More Free and Just Market System: A New Policy Framework

Ironically, capitalism and socialism share certain characteristics that hinder the development of a truly free and just global marketplace.

For example, virtually all economies are arranged today as wage systems, an approach that is inherently conflict-ridden and counter-productive. If the owners are the better wage system bargainers, wages will be low. If the workers can out-argue the owners or force them to implement minimum wages supported by the monopoly power of the state, wages will be high. Since capital is more mobile than labor in the global marketplace, being able to relocate to take advantage of lower wages in other areas, wage system workers remain at a permanent disadvantage.

Neither capitalism nor socialism, with or without a "human face," provides a sufficiently moral economic system. The first institutionalizes greed, concentrated economic power and exploitation of the many by the few. The second institutionalizes envy and hatred of those who accumulate wealth, and creates even greater concentration of economic power through State ownership or control. What is needed to bring about a truly free and just market system is a truly moral or "Just Third Way,"[47] which transcends and transforms both capitalism and socialism, providing mechanisms to accomplish what the two discredited systems have only promised.

All wage system "solutions" ignore one or more of what can be called the "Four Pillars," or the minimum essential principles, for building a more free and just economy. As can be seen, for example, during the dangerous transition period in Russia following the collapse of the Soviet Union, leaving out any one of these pillars weakens the entire fabric of the economy and leads to societal conflict, mounting levels of non-performing debt, and increased levels of poverty and corruption. The four pillars of a "Just Third Way" consist of:

- Universal Access to Capital Ownership
- Limited Economic Power of the State
- Free And Open Markets
- The Restoration of Private Property

Universal Access to Capital Ownership: The Moral Omission

One of the most crucial problems that Marx addressed in his economic theories was that ownership of productive assets — "capital" — was limited to the very few. In a global high technology market system, working people would have only their labor to sell in direct competition with labor-displacing technology and a growing world population of workers willing to work for lower wages. Denying the validity of Say's law, Marx asserted that the capitalist system had the seeds of its own destruction.

Unfortunately, Marx's solution to this mismatch between the rising productiveness of technology and market-based consumption incomes was to concentrate even more control over productive wealth and power by mandating state ownership of all productive assets. This resulted in enormous concentrations of wealth and power in the hands of a new political elite.

The real problem that Marx faced in confronting capitalism, however, was not private ownership of productive property, but *concentrated* private ownership. Making every citizen an owner of a growing *direct* stake of income-producing property would, in effect, "turn Marx upside-down." It would achieve economic justice for all, while sustaining quality growth within the disciplines of a free and market-based economy.

The pillar of expanded capital ownership — the moral omission in traditional free market theory — balances the demands of participative and distributive justice by lifting institutional barriers that have historically separated owners from non-owners.[48] This involves removing the institutional roadblocks that prevent people from owning their own capital, as well as owning their own labor, in order to participate fully in the economic process.

The emphasis in Capital Homesteading as a policy framework is not on redistribution of income (or achieving equality of results), but on providing people with equal opportunity and access to the means for them to acquire and create their own new wealth and property incomes.

Limited Economic Power of the State

It is the nature of the state to be a monopoly — a monopoly over society's instruments of coercion, wielded ultimately by the police at the local level and the armed forces at the national level. This monopoly makes government at any level an inherently dangerous social institution. Since the state is arguably the only legitimate monopoly, its power should be made subject to checks-and-balances and democratic accountability when it rules "in the name of the people."

In a democratic social order, real sovereignty is vested in the people. The state, as the servant of the people, acquires its powers only as a grant from the people. The ultimate sovereignty of every citizen, however, can be maintained only if economic power and responsibility (*i.e.*, economic self-reliance) is kept directly in the hands of the people, both as an inherent right and as a safeguard and protection against the potential abuses of politicians and bureaucrats.

Limiting the economic power of the state ultimately involves the goal of shifting ownership and control over production and income distribution, from the public to the private sector, from the state to the people. In order to shift primary power over the economy from the state to the citizens generally, the economic power of the state should be specifically constrained to:

- Encouraging sustainable and life-enhancing growth and policing abuses within the private sector;

- Ending economic monopolies and special privileges;

- Lifting barriers to equal ownership opportunities, especially by reforming the money-creating powers of the central bank to provide widespread access to low-cost capital credit as the key to spreading ownership and economic empowerment for workers;

- Preventing inflation and providing a stable currency for sustainable development;

- Protecting property, enforcing contracts and settling disputes;

- Promoting democratic unions or voluntary associations of workers to bargain over worker and ownership rights;

- Protecting the environment; and

- Providing social safety nets for human emergencies.

Within these limits the state would promote economic justice for all citizens. Coincident with this economic objective would be the goals of (1) reducing human conflict and waste and (2) erecting an institutional environment that will encourage people to increase economic efficiency and create new wealth for themselves and the global marketplace. Increased production would also increase total revenues for legitimate public sector purposes, reducing the need for income redistribution through confiscatory income taxes and social welfare payments.

Restoration of Free and Open Markets

Artificial or coercive determination of prices, wages and profits leads to inefficiencies in the use of resources and scarcity for all but those who control the system. Those in power either have too little information or wisdom to know what is right, or will set wages and prices to suit their own advantage. Just prices, just wages, and just profits are best set in a free, open and democratic marketplace, where consumer sovereignty ultimately reigns. Assuming economic democratization in the future ownership of the means of production, everyone's economic choices or "votes" on prices and wages influence the setting of economic values in the marketplace.

Establishing a free and open market would be accomplished by gradually eliminating all special privileges and monopolies created by the state, reducing all subsidies except for the most needy members of society, lifting barriers to free trade and free labor, and ending all non-voluntary, artificial methods of determining prices, wages and profits.

This would result in *decentralizing economic choice* and *empowering each person* as a consumer, a worker and an owner.

Wealth distribution assumes wealth creation, and technological and systems advances, according to recent studies, account for almost 90% of productivity growth in the modern world.[49] Thus, balanced growth in a market economy depends on incomes distributed through widespread individual ownership of the means of production. The technological sources of production growth would then be automatically linked with the ownership-based consumption incomes needed to purchase new wealth from the market. Thus, Say's Law of Markets — which both Marx and Keynes attempted to refute — would become a practical reality for the first time since the Industrial Revolution began.

Restoration of Private Property

Owners' rights in private property are fundamental to any just economic order. Property secures personal choice, and, as John Locke observed, it is the key safeguard of all other human rights. By destroying private property, justice is denied.

Private property, contrary to Marx, is the individual's link to the economic process in the same way that the secret ballot is his link to the political process. When either is absent, the individual is disconnected or "alienated" from the process. Without private property there is no institutionalized means to empower the individual economically.

"Property," it should be noted, is not the thing that is owned, but the bundle of rights and powers that owners have in their relationships to the things owned. One of the fundamental rights of private property is that an owner is entitled to receive the full fruits produced by the assets he owns. When all or some of the fruits (profits) are taken away coercively before they flow into the owner's hands — whether by theft, by an arbitrary decision of a co-owner, a board of directors, or corporate management, or by unjust government action — the private property rights of the owner are automatically violated.[50]

The laws in the United States have systematically whittled down the property rights of shareholders in their corporate equity. We can trace this deterioration to the case of *Dodge v. Ford Motor Company* where the court ruled, unjustly in our opinion, in favor of management to withhold the payment of dividends to shareholders in order to finance corporate growth.[51] The discriminatory double- and triple-tax on corporate profits also, in our view, represents an unjust and direct attack on private property in corporate equity.[52]

Restoring private property rights, particularly in corporate equity, would involve the reform of laws that prohibit or inhibit acquisition, possession and exercise of private property. This would include ensuring that all owners, including shareholders, are vested with their right to control their own equity, to hold management accountable through their elected shareholder representatives on the corporate board of directors, and to receive profits commensurate with their ownership stakes.

Restoring owners' full rights in private property, and making property rights accessible to today's non-owners, results in securing personal choices and economic self-determination for every citizen. This would link income distribution to economic participation — not only by present owners of existing assets, but also by new owners of future wealth. And it would lay a foundation for an effective economic democracy within a competitive free enterprise system.

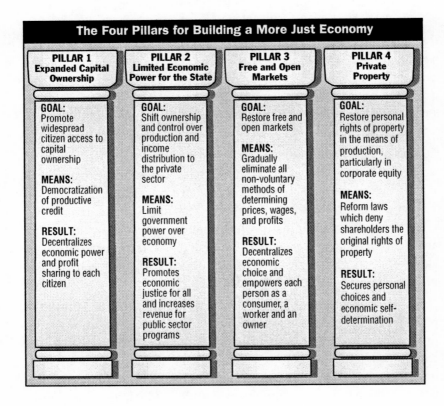

The Four Pillars for Building a More Just Economy

PILLAR 1 Expanded Capital Ownership	PILLAR 2 Limited Economic Power for the State	PILLAR 3 Free and Open Markets	PILLAR 4 Private Property
GOAL: Promote widespread citizen access to capital ownership **MEANS:** Democratization of productive credit **RESULT:** Decentralizes economic power and profit sharing to each citizen	**GOAL:** Shift ownership and control over production and income distribution to the private sector **MEANS:** Limit government power over economy **RESULT:** Promotes economic justice for all and increases revenue for public sector programs	**GOAL:** Restore free and open markets **MEANS:** Gradually eliminate all non-voluntary methods of determining prices, wages, and profits **RESULT:** Decentralizes economic choice and empowers each person as a consumer, a worker and an owner	**GOAL:** Restore personal rights of property in the means of production, particularly in corporate equity **MEANS:** Reform laws which deny shareholders the original rights of property **RESULT:** Secures personal choices and economic self-determination

III.
AN OVERVIEW OF
CAPITAL HOMESTEADING

Moving from principles of economic justice and binary economic theory to the structuring of national economic policy to lift the American economy to its fullest productive capacity, Capital Homesteading requires fundamental infrastructural reform on a systematic and comprehensive basis. The basic interdependent components of the Capital Homestead strategy are like the legs of a three-legged stool:

(1)   Democratization of productive credit

(2)   Simplification of tax systems

**(3)   Linkage of all tax and monetary reforms
        to the goal of expanded capital ownership**

(1) **Democratization of productive credit**, by reforming monetary policy to conform to the goal of sustainable, market-oriented, noninflationary growth. The new policies would aim at an immediate reduction in prime credit charges to an actual transaction service fee for broadly owned private-sector investment, through a two-tiered credit policy. Central banks would:

(a) Be restrained from further monetization of deficits and from encouraging other forms of nonproductive uses of credit (*i.e.*, demand-side credit), which would then be forced to seek out already accumulated savings at market interest rates; and

(b) Use the Fed discount mechanism exclusively for discounting "eligible" industrial, agricultural and commercial paper financed through its member commercial banks, which would be subject to a 100% reserve requirement. At a "zero" interest rate (plus a Fed service charge, lender transaction fees, and risk premium charges, applied to the funds borrowed), Fed-discounted credit would result in "prime rates" (the rates charged to a bank's best customers) of roughly 2.5%-3%. This reform would synchronize the supply of real money with broadly owned, environmentally sound, sustainable growth of the productive economy. It would provide an asset-backed currency reflected in more efficient instruments of production and keep basic economic decisions in local hands.

(2) **Simplification of tax systems,** centered around taxing incomes from all sources at a single rate (offering a universal yardstick for political hopefuls to compete against), as a direct means for:

  (a) Balancing national budgets and restraining overall spending, including Social Security and Medicare programs;

  (b) Ending the use of the tax system to circumvent the appropriations process; and

  (c) Eliminating double taxation of profits in ways that maximize greater savings and investments in new plant and equipment, plus removing other features that discourage expanded capital ownership and rising property incomes among the poor and middle-income citizens.

(3) **Linkage of all tax and monetary reforms to the goal of expanded capital ownership.** This would encourage all citizens to share directly in the equity growth and profits from our ever-expanding high-technology frontier and to insure the broadest possible base of direct beneficiaries (and thus political supporters) of all future tax and monetary reforms.

In contrast to today's pay-as-you-go social security program, the Capital Homesteading approach would create for every voter a "Capital Homestead Exemption" for accumulating over his or her working lifetime a personal estate that would be exempt from income, capital gains, gift, estate and other taxes, a modern equivalent of the 160 acres of land that government made accessible to American pioneers.

Citizens would accumulate their Capital Homestead shares in many ways, including through such "credit democratization" vehicles as: individualized Capital Homestead Accounts (CHAs), Employee Stock Ownership Plans (ESOPs); Community Investment Corporations (CICs); and Customer Stock Ownership Plans (CSOPs). These high-powered financing vehicles would link the new monetary and tax incentives for productivity growth under the Capital Homestead program, with an ever-expanding base of citizen-shareholders.

IV.
POLICY OBJECTIVES OF
CAPITAL HOMESTEADING

To save Social Security and provide for its eventual phasing out as the mainstay of retirement income for most Americans, and to shift the Federal Government's role from today's income redistribution policies to the more limited and healthy role of encouraging economic justice through free enterprise growth, a Capital Homestead program would:

- **Promote Private Sector Growth Linked to Broadened Ownership.** Recreate in the 21st Century the conditions that resulted from the first Homestead Act of 1862, including full employment, declining prices, and widespread, individual and effective ownership of income generating assets. Set a realistic long-term target, based on the nation's industrial growth potential, to achieve a minimum Capital Homestead stake for every American family. As an initial measure, this could be geared conservatively toward an equity accumulation of, for example, $100,000 over the next 20 years.

- **Save the Social Security System.** Keep existing promises and reduce the growing burden on the Social Security System, by enabling every American to accumulate (through inheritances, gifts, CHAs, ESOPs, IRAs, community investment corporations and other expanded ownership vehicles sheltered from taxes under the "Capital Homestead Exemption") sufficient wealth-producing assets to provide each person with an adequate and secure taxable income from property, independent of Social Security benefits and incomes from other sources. [*See* Section 1, "The Proposal in Brief."]

- **Stimulate Maximum Growth, with a Balanced Budget and Zero Inflation Rate.** Remove barriers to maximum rates of sustainable and environmentally sound private sector growth to achieve a balanced Federal budget and a zero inflation rate under the Capital Homestead program.

- **Stop Federal Reserve Monetization of Government Debt.** Terminate use of the Federal Reserve's money-creating powers to support foreign currencies or to buy and sell primary or secondary Treasury securities. This would force the government to borrow directly from savers in the open markets.

- **Stabilize the Value of the Currency.** Create a stable currency backed by productive private sector assets rather than non-productive public sector debt.

- **Reduce Dependency on Past Savings for Financing Growth.** Create money to expand bank credit to enable every American to become an owner of a viable accumulation of new income-producing assets, thus reducing America's dependency on past savings, corporate retained earnings, or foreign investors advantaged by America's growing trade imbalances, while increasing consumption incomes. Require the Federal Reserve System to supply sufficient money and credit through local banks to meet the liquidity and broadened ownership needs of an expanding economy. Such "Fed monetized" loans would be subject to appropriate feasibility standards administered by the banks and limited only by the goal of maintaining a stable value for the dollar.

- **Establish a Tax System That is More Accountable to Taxpayers.** Radically simplify the existing Federal tax system in ways that automatically balance the budget and make Congress more directly accountable and responsive to all taxpayers. Eliminate tax provisions that unjustly discriminate against or discourage property accumulations and investment incomes, especially for poor and non-rich families.

- **Discourage Monopolies and Monopolistic Ownership.** Link all economic reforms to methods that discourage privileged access to or monopolistic accumulations of private property ownership of the means of production. Enforce anti-trust laws by providing access to capital credit to broadly owned new competitors to enhance and sustain market-oriented growth.

- **Introduce a Market-Driven Wage and Price System.** Gradually eliminate rigid, artificially-protected wage and price levels and other restrictions on free trade, which afford special privileges to some industries, businesses and workers at the expense of American and foreign customers of US products. Replace subsidies with credit incentives to farmers who wish to associate voluntarily in cooperatives and in enterprises jointly owned by farmers and workers, including integrated agribusinesses. The income generated by the resulting enterprises would supplement farm incomes and reduce the need for subsidies.

- **Restore Property Rights in Corporate Equity.** Restore the original rights of "private property" to all owners of corporate equity, particularly with respect to the right to profits and in the sharing of control over corporate policies, while still safeguarding the traditional functions of professional managers.

- **Offer a More Just Social Contract for Workers.** A top priority during the next decade would be developing a more just "social contract" for persons employed in the private sector. This would be geared toward establishing maximum ownership incentives. Instead of inflationary "wage system" increases, employees can begin to earn future increases in income through production bonuses, equity accumulations, and profit earnings. These increases would be linked to their personal efforts and to the productivity and success of their work team and the enterprise for which they work.

- **Encourage More Harmonious Worker-Management Relations.** Promote the right of non-management workers to form democratic trade unions and other voluntary associations. Instead of promoting the traditional "conflict model" of industrial relations, however, the labor union would be encouraged to transform itself into society's primary institution for promoting a free market version of economic justice, while continuing to negotiate and advance workers' economic interests, including their ownership rights, *vis-à-vis* management. Under Capital Homesteading, unions could expand their role in a free market system by organizing and educating other shareholder groups and helping to protect and expand their ownership rights.

- **Downsize the Public Sector.** Reduce taxpayer costs, by providing America's military, policemen and firemen, teachers, and other public-sector workers with a growing and more direct equity stake in the free enterprise system, both as a supplement to their costly pension plans and so that they will better understand and defend the institution of private property. Whenever feasible, transform government-owned enterprises and services into competitive private sector companies, by offering their workers (and customers and other stakeholders in capital-intensive operations like TVA) opportunities to participate in ownership, governance and profits.

- **Promote a Life-Enhancing Environment.** Encourage special ownership incentives for those engaged in research and development, especially in the search for new and sustainable sources of energy, ecological restoration and labor-saving technologies. Provide sufficient low-cost credit and royalty-free licensing for enterprises capable of commercializing life-enhancing technologies developed for the military and space programs. Subsidize the development of new methods of conserving and recycling non-replenishable and limited natural resources that are vital to civilization's long-term survival, at least until suitable substitutes can be discovered and developed. Promote the teaching at all levels of education of universal principles of personal morality and social morality, that are based on the inherent dignity and sovereignty of every human person under the higher sovereignty of the Creator.

- **Initiate New Challenges for Multinationals.** Provide special encouragement to US-based multinational corporations and global financial institutions to become instruments of peace and a more just world economic order, by broadening access to their ownership base to all citizens of the world community. Encourage businesses to open up future ownership opportunities as they begin harnessing the resources of the sea and other planets.

- **Establish Workable Demonstrations of Capital Homesteading at the Community, State, Regional and Global Levels.** Launch several Capital Homesteading demonstrations. These would be most effective in areas of high unemployment, such as the Super Empowerment Zone proposed in 1996 for the District of Columbia, and for the New Millennium Project now being developed in East St. Louis, Illinois. Similar projects could be developed on Native American reservations. The goal would be to evaluate ownership-broadening Federal Reserve reforms, innovative broadened ownership mechanisms and advanced concepts of worker participation in decision-making and self-management. Encourage State and local governments and other countries to promote widespread capital ownership as a basic pillar for building a sound market economy.

- **Promote a New Global Monetary System.** Encourage the convening of a second "Bretton Woods Conference" to consider the implications of the Kelsonian binary economic model on global currency standards and foreign exchange rates. The new policy should seek to reform global financial markets to address the challenge of global poverty and sustainable development, as well as leveling the playing field among nations for global free and open trade.

V.
BASIC VEHICLES FOR DEMOCRATIZING CAPITAL CREDIT

The Employee Stock Ownership Plan (ESOP)

The Employee Stock Ownership Plan ("ESOP") is one of several Kelsonian applications for democratizing access to money and credit. The ESOP, the first Kelsonian credit mechanism to be recognized in U.S. law, is significant mainly because it contains a new logic for overcoming barriers in the current corporate finance system that block most people from capital ownership.

The ESOP provides widespread access to capital credit to each employee in a company on a systematic basis. Technically, the ESOP uses a legal trust that is "qualified" under specific U.S. tax laws encouraging employee ownership. (In Egypt, a Worker Shareholders Association was developed at the Alexandria Tire Company as an advance over the U.S. ESOP.) Thus, while it is closely policed by the Internal Revenue Service and the Department of Labor to insure that the ownership plan operates in ways beneficial to employee-owners, the ESOP provides special tax privileges and incentives for the company, existing owners, and the employees.

Fortunately, the laws are extremely flexible, so that each plan can be tailored to fit the circumstances and needs of each enterprise, and deficiencies in the design of an ESOP can easily be corrected.

An ESOP may be designed to combine many elements into a single package. It is an employee benefit program. It is a tax-deferred means for workers to accumulate equity. It can be an incentive and productivity program for all employees. It can be a retirement program. It can be a new reward system, working best when a modest base salary is supplemented with cash bonuses and equity shares, linked to the proceeds of the operation. It can be a two-way accountability and communications system between management and non-management employees. It can be a means for workers to participate both as workers and as stockholders in corporate direction. It can be an in-house tax-exempt stock exchange, for both new equity issuances and repurchase of outstanding shares. It can offer workers a source of current dividend incomes. An ESOP can be all of these and more; but one of its most unique features is that *it is a basic innovation in corporate finance.*

An ESOP is the only tool in the world of investment finance that can create new owners and generate new sources of capital credit for corporate growth or transfers of ownership, while insulating these new owners from direct personal risk in the event of default and allowing repayment of the entire debt with pre-tax corporate dollars.

The leveraged ESOP operates in this way: it channels capital credit through a trust representing employees, from the *same sources* and subject to the *same feasibility standards* and corporate guarantees as direct loans to the corporation. The loan funds are used to buy stock for the workers, either from present owners or for financing expansion or modernization of the corporation. The loan to the trust is wholly secured by and repaid with future corporate earnings.

Normally, the workers make no cash outlay from payroll deductions or their savings, and none of their present savings is at risk. Shares of stock are allocated to the individual accounts of workers only as blocks of shares are "earned;" *i.e.,* the company contributes cash out of future pre-tax profits to the trust. The cash, which is treated as a tax-deductible employee benefit or a tax-deductible dividend, is used to repay the stock acquisition loan.

Whereas traditional uses of leveraged corporate credit work only for present owners, the ESOP uses corporate credit to convert its workers into stockholders. Thus, the magic of self-liquidating capital credit can be used to lift more individuals into an expanding ownership system.

A well-designed ESOP clarifies subtle distinctions between "ownership," "management," and "worker participation." Operationally under an ESOP, day-to-day control remains in the hands of professional managers who, under a carefully designed system of checks-and-balances, simply become accountable to a broader shareholder base, including other workers, and a more broadly representative board of directors.

Employee stock ownership, therefore, involves a delicate balancing of the goal of efficiency with that of justice, and the goal of continuity of the firm with accountability of management to its new owners. It simply applies the genius of the republican form of government to the business world.

These charts show how the ESOP is used to enable workers to buy new shares:

Employee Stock Ownership Plan (ESOP)

Stage 1
Stock Corporation Forms ESOP

① Board approves ESOP

② Appoints ESOP trustees

③ Company approves sale of new shares to finance expansion of plant and equipment

Stage 2
New Stock Purchased with Loan to ESOP

① Bank loans money to ESOP

② ESOP trustees signs ESOP note to bank

③ Corporation guarantees to make contribution and dividends to ESOP to repay loan

④ ESOP pays corporation for new shares

⑤ Corporation transfers new shares to ESOP

⑥ Shares pledged as collateral or held in suspense account

⑦ ESOP accounts set up for each employee

⑧ Credit purchase requires no cash or guaranty by employees

⑨ New plant and equipment installed

⑩ Corporation pays contractors and suppliers

Stage 3
Company Pays Out Profits for Repaying Buyout Loan, Bonuses, and Dividends as New Employee Benefits

① Company makes annual contribution and dividends to ESOP for loan repayment (tax deductible)

② ESOP pays annual principal and interest due on loan

③ Shares released for annual allocations

④ Released shares allocated and held in ESOP accounts of participants (non-taxable)

⑤ Distribution of monthly and annual cash bonuses and dividends, if available

Stage 4
Distribution of Vested Shares Upon Retirement or Termination

① Distribution of cash and ESOP shares (taxable)

② Sale of distributed shares at appraised fair market value

The Capital Homesteading Account (CHA)

The CHA would be designed as a special kind of Individual Retirement Account (IRA) to be established at any bank or approved financial institution, for financing new stock issuances by any enterprise that can convince a commercial bank that it has a viable (*i.e.*, self-liquidating) capital project. Like the ESOP, this stock acquisition credit would be secured and repayable wholly with pre-tax corporate earnings, assuming that higher dividend payouts were encouraged by making them deductible as proposed above.

Through their Capital Homesteading Accounts, if given the same tax treatment as ESOPs, citizens could purchase on non-recourse credit a diversified portfolio of new "qualified" equity issuances, as an alternative method for financing the growth of American industry. Upon retirement, the accumulated assets in the CHA could generate a significant stream of retirement income.

With such credit available to the nation's CHA market, active and retired public sector workers, for example, could acquire a growing diversified portfolio of full dividend payout shares in new and expanding enterprises or mutual funds holding such shares. This would provide annually significant retirement benefits for public sector employees. This new source for funding retirement benefits would also help radically reduce future pension obligations of the government, generally one of the most costly items in a government's budget. And it could also be used to meet unfunded pension obligations.

The Community Investment Corporation (CIC)[53]

The Community Investment Corporation (CIC) has been designed to serve as a for-profit land planner and private sector real estate developer geared to rational innovation and change at the community level. The CIC, with appropriate tax and credit features, would plan land use and develop the land within designated urban and rural enterprise zones for industrial, commercial, agricultural, residential and public purposes. It would sell and lease the land and structures for public and private uses and impose charges for improvement and maintenance. To avoid restraints on competition the CIC would normally not own other businesses that choose to locate on CIC-developed land.

The Community Investment Corporation (CIC) was inspired by a legal mechanism known as the "General Stock Ownership Corporation" (GSOC), which was added as Subchapter U of the Internal Revenue Code by the Revenue Act of 1978. As enacted, all citizens of a State could become stockholders of such massive projects as the Alaskan gas pipeline. Subchapter U proved so unwieldy that no State adopted a GSOC despite its many attractive ownership incentives

This mechanism, however, is extremely feasible if applied at a local community level, particularly if used as a real estate planning and development corporation, financed so that all present and future residents could become stockholders, as proposed above in connection with "free enterprise zones" initiatives. (*See #17 in Section VIII*, "Detailed Tax Reforms for Implementing Capital Homesteading.")

The Customer Stock Ownership Plan (CSOP)

Similarly, a Customer Stock Ownership Plan (CSOP), with appropriate tax features, could be structured for regular customers of such capital-intensive regulated enterprises as electric utilities, mass transit systems, cablevision systems, and other natural monopolies. Again, using low-cost capital credit, these companies would have new sources for financing their equity growth, while turning their customers into new stockholders.

CSOPs could also be combined with ESOPs for establishing for-profit comprehensive health care delivery systems whose ownership and control would be shared by all doctors, other healthcare providers and employees, and subscribers, supplemented by health care vouchers for subscribers with incomes below the poverty line. For-profit educational systems owned by teachers, other school employees, and parent-subscribers, could be similarly financed and organized.

The stock acquisition credit for CSOP participants would be repayable with their share of future profits, in the form of tax-deductible patronage bonuses and/or dividend payouts. After paying for the stock, dividends and patronage bonuses earned by the customers would help to offset their utility bills.

VI.
SUPPORTING VEHICLES FOR FACILITATING CAPITAL HOMESTEAD LOANS

The FCCC: A New Type of "Fannie Mae" for Bundling Capital Homesteading Loans

Two institutions created to promote home ownership among Americans — Fannie Mae and Freddie Mac — offer a model that could be used for Capital Homesteading. While differing slightly in their business strategies, both Fannie Mae and Freddie Mac operate by purchasing certain qualified home mortgages from lenders, allowing mortgage brokers to replenish their cash available for loans to potential homeowners. They then pool those loans together and sell shares in the form of mortgage-backed securities. Neither company offers loans itself. Fannie Mae and Freddie Mac have been credited with significantly lowering the cost of mortgage rates for home borrowers and establishing a stable and accessible real estate market, helping to create a nation of many homeowners.[54]

A house lived in by the owner is not, however, an income-producing asset. On the contrary, it is a substantial financial drain on the owner/occupant. There is, paradoxically, no lender of last resort and no liquidity backup for income-producing capital assets.

Dr. Norman A. Bailey has proposed the creation of a "Federal Capital Credit Corporation" (or FCCC) to provide a Fannie-May type "bundling" facility that could operate in conjunction with Federal Reserve's discount window, to assist Americans in building capital estates.[55] The FCCC, which could be owned and controlled by CHA lenders and citizens, would package insured CHA loans, create software for helping lenders to scrutinize the feasibility of CHA loans, and set uniform standards for CHA insurers, reinsurers, and lenders. The FCCC and competitors qualified by the Federal Reserve would then bundle and take these securitized CHA loans to the discount window of the regional Federal Reserve Bank.

The Federal Reserve would treat these insured dividend-backed securities (DBSs) as it currently treats government debt paper, using them as substitute backing for the currency. Then as the Federal Government pays down the national debt, the productive assets of the economy — the real economy — would stand behind the nation's currency. Productive capital owned and controlled broadly among the people and linked to the money supply would replace gold as a measure of value and as a safeguard against inflation and irresponsible or non-democratic policies by the nation's central bankers. Under Capital Homesteading, money will again be a servant of the people, not their master, and will become an instrument to promote humanity's creative potential and quest for a just market economy.

The FCIC and CCRC: Managing Risk
Through Capital Credit Insurance and Re-Insurance

If lack of collateral is one of the major barriers to closing the wealth gap between the rich and the poor through the democratization of capital credit, how can this collateralization barrier be overcome? A substitute is needed for the collateral generally required by lenders to cover the risk of default. That substitute would be a system of credit insurance and reinsurance.

Lenders making "qualified" loans could either self-insure or pool the "risk premium" portion of debt service payments by insuring with commercial capital credit insurers against the risk of default, perhaps 80% to 90% of the unpaid balance. To spread further the risk of loan default, these commercial insurers could come together to establish a Capital Credit Reinsurance Corporation ("CCRC") as an "insurer of last resort." Some of the CCRC's reserves could be provided in the form of investments by the already wealthy. Or a portion of the reserves could be provided by the Federal, state or local governments, but only if the CCRC is structured to avoid the unlimited liability that taxpayers were exposed to by making the Federal Government "the insurer of last resort" of failing savings and loan banks in the 1980s.

Since loans already include a "risk premium" in debt servicing charges, it would be conceptually easy to turn the risk premium into a real insurance premium. This would allow the feasibility of business loans to be determined on the basis of the feasibility of the actual project, instead of a borrower's existing collateral.

Capital Portfolio Insurance

Predictably, the Enron debacle evoked a knee-jerk reaction among many financial advisors who parroted the conventional wisdom that employees should never invest more than 10% of their 401(k) investments in their company's shares. ESOPs became a natural target for many in the financial community, but fortunately not in Congress, which exempted ESOPs in privately held companies from legal requirements designed to protect employees contributing to their 401(k) plans. Aside from demonstrating widespread ignorance of how ESOPs really work and ignoring the fact that there are extremely successful companies that are, and want to remain, majority employee-owned, the misplaced response to Enron does highlight a risk certain investors may face.

It also suggests the need to develop another insurance product to handle such risk, where there may be insufficient diversification in a person's CHA. Capital portfolio insurance could provide a safeguard against a person's entire retirement equity stake being wiped out, and may even be useful for participants in ESOP companies under today's system. It should also be noted that by enabling people to invest, not only in their own companies, but in their utility company, local community investment corporation, and the primary issuances of blue chip stocks, the CHA approach by its nature builds a diversified approach to building an income-producing equity stake for one's retirement.

VII.
REFORMING
THE MONEY AND CREDIT SYSTEM

Capital Credit: A Better Way to Finance Private Sector Growth

In *The Formation of Capital* written in 1935,[56] Harold G. Moulton, former president of The Brookings Institution, laid the theoretical foundation for the monetary reforms advocated under Capital Homesteading. Moulton pointed out that economic growth did not depend exclusively on past accumulated savings, that there need not be a tradeoff between expanded consumption and expanded investment.

In fact, Moulton pointed out that demand for capital goods is a derived demand. In other words, demand for capital is derived from the demand for consumer goods, and the latter depends on consumption incomes.

Moulton's insight, interestingly enough, is supported by Paul Samuelson in a footnote in his leading textbook on Keynesian economics:

> We shall later see that, *sometimes* in our modern monetary economy, the more people try to save, the less capital goods are produced; and paradoxically, that the more people spend on consumption, the greater the incentive for businessmen to build new factories and equipment.[57] [*emphasis in original*]

Moulton concluded that forcing people to reduce their consumption to purchase new capital assets is counter-productive. It reduces the viability of that investment and other investments, which ultimately depend on consumer demand. He then posed the question, "Where could funds be procured for capital purposes if consumption was expanding and savings declining?"

Moulton answered his own question:

> From commercial bank credit expansion. Such expansion relieves the possibility of shortage in the "money market" and enables business enterprises to assemble the labor and materials necessary for the construction of additional plant and equipment.[58]

Most economists assert there can be no growth without savings, unless we cut back on consumption. Moulton argued, however, that the real limits to expanded bank credit were physical ones: unexploited technology, unused capital resources and raw materials, an unemployed or underemployed work force, unused plant capacity, and ready markets for new capital goods and new consumer goods.

Moulton's study of one of the fastest growth periods of U.S. economic history, 1865 to 1895, revealed that, while bank reserve requirements remained relatively constant, the volume of outstanding commercial bank credit rose substantially. At the same time, price levels declined for the period by about 65%.[59]

Moulton also demonstrated that even in periods of great business activity, our productive energies are normally under-used; there is always some slack in the system. He proved that we can have rapid growth without inflation.

On the other hand, we can also have rising prices alongside recession, as we experienced for the first time in the "stagflation" of 1974. Moulton's conclusion is worth noting:

> [T]he expansion of capital occurs only when the output of consumption goods is also expanding; and ... this is made possible by the [simultaneous] expansion of credit for production purposes.[60]

Unfortunately, in drawing the connection between expanded bank credit and expanded capital creation, Moulton failed to make the next logical connection. He failed to recognize that expanding the base of capital ownership and capital income distributions could serve as a new, more direct, and more efficient source of mass buying power to absorb future outputs of final consumption goods,

Fortunately, Kelso picked up where Moulton left off.[61]

"Pure Credit":
Society's Key for Freeing Economic Growth from Past Savings

"Where will the money come from?" is a common reaction to those encountering the Kelsonian model for the first time. In answering this question, it is important to understand why we need "money" in the first place.

According to the 2001 Economic Report of the President, the U.S. economy adds an annual "growth ring" of about $2 trillion in new technology, plant and equipment, new rentable structures, and new infrastructure in both the private sector and in the public sector. This amounts to about $6,755 annually per man, woman, and child in America.[62]

As things stand, these growth assets will be financed in ways that create no new owners. This constitutes an exclusionary approach to financing capital and private sector growth.

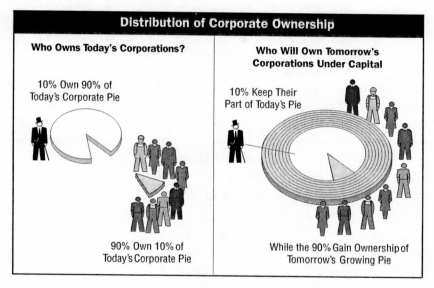

Distribution of Corporate Ownership

Who Owns Today's Corporations?

10% Own 90% of Today's Corporate Pie

90% Own 10% of Today's Corporate Pie

Who Will Own Tomorrow's Corporations Under Capital

10% Keep Their Part of Today's Pie

While the 90% Gain Ownership of Tomorrow's Growing Pie

The question then becomes: How can we begin to finance America's future capital needs in an *inclusionary* manner? Is there a way to expand the role of the private sector and enable excluded Americans to accumulate enough savings to purchase that growth capital and gain the right to share in profits as owners?

The answer is "pure credit." "Pure credit" is a modern society's mechanism for easing disparities in wealth. The power already exists in the hands of the Federal Reserve Board of Governors, waiting to be used for meeting our projected capital needs and for democratizing the ownership base of the U.S. economy in the process.[63]

"Pure credit" is based upon the legal concept of "promise" and the enforceability of contracts, two main ingredients of a free and orderly economy. Pure credit is nothing more than the power of people (including legal associations of people, such as corporations) to contract freely with one another under a system of law that enables everyone affected by the contract to enforce their rights and claims over property under the contract. It thus involves elements of volition as well as control.

Pure credit is limited only by the willingness and ability of people, their associations, and government itself to keep the promises they make. Since promise is the "glue" that holds any society together and determines how confidently people view the future, the making and breaking of promises determines whether that society is strong or weak, orderly or disorderly, growing or disintegrating.

Credit by its very nature is a social phenomenon. Control over money and capital credit will determine in large measure the nature and quality of America's future technological frontier as well as its future ownership distribution patterns. Because the ownership of productive capital is so crucial to freedom and human happiness, discriminating among citizens as to who has access to capital credit constitutes as gross a violation of equal protection of the laws as discrimination in access to the ballot. Americans are beginning to discover that such a violation of our fundamental constitutional rights is taking place daily on a systematic basis.

This violation of equal opportunity is institutionalized in the present system of corporate finance, and is inadvertently exacerbated by our own Federal Reserve System. Today's financial system channels capital credit to the already rich and ever-more burdensome consumer credit to property-less workers. It is not surprising that many people who misunderstand the workings of the central bank advocate the abolition of the Federal Reserve, rather than its reform.

The way credit is used, the persons to whom it is made available, and the purposes for which it is used, are proper subjects of governmental policy. When the "full faith and credit" of government stands behind the nation's currency and the demand deposits in our commercial banking system, this involves "pure credit" in the ultimate sense. Government, by controlling the total volume of currency and commercial bank credit needed to facilitate economic transactions, controls the direction of private enterprise. Government also has the power to be "lender of last resort" under our Constitution, if that becomes necessary.

When the government misuses its money-creating powers, we have inflation and a breach of one of government's most important "promises" to its citizens — that the value of currency will remain constant. When government does not keep this basic promise to its people, all debts are jeopardized, property is arbitrarily redistributed among debtors and creditors, and the trust that holds society together begins to deteriorate. As one nineteenth century economist observed:

> Confidence and credit are only moral elements in society; they may be said to be, to a great extent, mere matters of opinion; yet their importance in the production and distribution of wealth is so great, that the whole machinery of material production is kept at work, disordered, or paralyzed, according as these principles act in a healthy manner, irregularly, or not at all.... [I]f credit and confidence should be from any cause destroyed, all these resources seem to have lost their virtue, and general distress prevails. Let confidence and credit be restored, and the whole system is immediately set in motion again, and in a very short time general prosperity returns.[64]

Creating Money: The Role of the Federal Reserve System

To understand the money and credit creation process, we must first ask the question, "What is money?" Economists have traditionally answered that it is: 1) a medium of exchange, 2) a store of value, 3) a standard of value and 4) a common measure of value.[65]

As a lawyer-economist concerned with the impact of contracts and property on the economic system, Louis Kelso delved even further into the nature of money.

> Money is not a part of the visible sector of the economy; people do not consume money. Money is not a physical factor of production, but rather a yardstick for measuring economic input, economic outtake and the relative values of the real goods and services of the economic world. Money provides a method of measuring obligations, rights, powers and privileges. It provides a means whereby certain individuals can accumulate claims against others, or against the economy as a whole, or against many economies. It is a system of symbols that many economists substitute for the visible sector and its productive enterprises, goods and services, thereby losing sight of the fact that a monetary system is a part only of the invisible sector of the economy, and that its adequacy can *only* be measured by its effect upon the visible sector.[66]

The process of money creation using a central bank (such as our Federal Reserve System) is neither mysterious nor occult. The system was designed to allow the creation or destruction of money as needed by the economy, so that there would never be too little (resulting in deflation) or too much (causing inflation).

The House Banking and Currency Committee, in its widely circulated publication, *A Primer on Money* (August 5, 1964), noted:

> When the Federal Reserve Act was passed, Congress intended [the purchase of "eligible paper"] to be the main way that the Federal Reserve System would create bank reserves....When this practice was followed, the banks in a particular area could obtain loanable funds in direct proportion to the community's needs for money. But in recent years, the Federal Reserve has purchased almost no eligible paper....(p. 42).

> When the Federal Reserve System was set up in 1914, ... the money supply was expected to grow with the needs of the economy.... It was hoped that by monetizing "eligible" short-term commercial paper, by providing liquidity to sound banks in periods of stress, and by restraining excessive credit expansion, the banking system could be guided automatically toward the provision of an adequate and stable money supply to meet the needs of industry and commerce.... To safeguard their liquidity and provide a base for expansion, the member banks... could obtain credit from the nearest Federal Reserve bank, usually by rediscounting their "eligible paper" at the bank — *i.e.*,... selling to the Reserve Bank certain loan paper representing loans which the member bank had made to its own customers (the requirements for eligibility being defined by law). If necessary, the member banks might also obtain reserves by getting "advances" from the Federal Reserve bank.... (p. 69).

In other words, under a standard central banking system, businesses or other productive enterprises would obtain loans at their local commercial bank. The commercial bank, in a process known as "discounting," would then sell the qualified loan paper of the business enterprises to the central bank. In the case of the United States, the commercial bank would sell its paper to one of the twelve regional Federal Reserve Banks. To be able to purchase the "qualified paper," the Federal Reserve would either print new currency or simply create new demand deposits.

As originally intended when the Federal Reserve System was established, this process would create an asset-backed currency that increased as the need for money increased, preventing deflation. As the loans were repaid, the currency would be taken out of circulation, or the demand deposits "erased" from the books. This would remove money from the economy that was not linked directly to hard assets, and would thus prevent inflation.

Contrary to the original intent for founding the Federal Reserve System,[67] today new money is created by the central bank to purchase Treasury paper and destroyed when the central bank sells its accumulation of government debt. Thus, rather than a having a currency backed by productive assets, America today has a currency backed by government debt.

Although no actual teller's window exists where commercial banks stand in line to sell loan paper to the Federal Reserve, the transaction is described as taking place at "the discount window." When the "discount window" is "open," commercial banks can sell their "qualified industrial, commercial and agricultural paper" to the central bank. When the "discount window" is "closed," commercial banks must go elsewhere to obtain excess reserves to lend, or cease making loans.

Despite the fact that the discounting mechanism was intended under the Federal Reserve Act of 1913 to be the main means for controlling the American money supply, it has long been abandoned as an integral part of the United States financial system. The discount window has been used instead to help bail out a few companies or countries considered "too big" or too important to fail.[68]

Overall, however, the money creation powers of the Federal Reserve have been used to monetize government debt. Since this was not how the system was designed to operate, a number of problems have resulted.

Our economic problems are usually blamed on decisions by Congress or the President, particularly those decisions which result in non-productive or counter-productive spending and tax policies. Little is said about decisions by the Federal Reserve, many of which, as Louis Kelso and others have pointed out for over forty years, have been equally counter-productive.

Fed policies have added to the problem of government deficits, fueling the growth of the national debt to today's level of $6.3 trillion[69] (making the United States the highest government debtor in the world). This has artificially and unnecessarily slowed the growth rate of the private sector.

As a result, what Kelso and other expanded ownership pioneers predicted is becoming increasingly evident:

- Continuing economic disenfranchisement of the American people.
- Low rates of peacetime economic growth.
- Rates of private sector investment far below U.S. potential.

- Excessive use of non-productive credit in the public and private sectors.

- Downsizing of U.S. companies in competition with foreign companies with lower labor costs.

- Mounting trade deficits in the global marketplace.

- A growing gap in consumption incomes between the wealthiest Americans and ordinary workers and the poor.

- Under-use of human talent and advanced technologies developed by the military and in our space and energy programs that could be employed to improve America's competitiveness in the global marketplace.

An Untapped Source for Private Sector Growth

Supplying funds to the money market and controlling the cost of these funds through the discount rate has long been recognized as the orthodox instrument of monetary policy. In *Lombard Street*,[70] Walter Bagehot outlined the principles of central banking, arguing that the main function of the Bank of England was to serve as the lender of last resort, mainly by supplying liquidity to a capital-deficient economy through the flexible use of its discount powers.

The Federal Reserve currently makes little use of its power to discount "eligible paper" held by commercial banks or to make direct loans to banks to meet their liquidity needs in fostering commercial and industrial development. Instead, the Federal Reserve controls the money supply and interest rates through its other main money-creating powers:

- By its open market purchases and sales of Treasury securities,

- By altering reserve requirement ratios, and

- By controlling the "federal funds rate" (the rate at which one bank charges another for overnight borrowed funds).

The Federal Reserve allocates 100% of the money it creates to support public sector growth, none to support private sector growth.

An important staff study released in December 1976 by the House Subcommittee on Domestic Monetary Policy, entitled "The Impact of the Federal Reserve System's Monetary Policy on the Nation's Economy," recommended a 4% to 6% growth in the M-1 money supply (currency plus demand deposits), "as a foundation for sustained economic growth." This is about the same as the Federal Reserve's growth targets back in the summer of 1977 of 4.5% to 6.5%. Note that in 1995 the Federal Reserve lowered its "cap" on U.S. growth rates to 2.5% of GDP.[71]

The House Subcommittee's report — which reflects the heavy influence of Milton Friedman on U.S. monetary policy — shares one thing in common with those who advocate expanding the money supply for "welfare state" purposes. The new money supply, under either conservative or liberal game plans, would be pumped indiscriminately into the economy through the economy's existing "credit irrigation" system. Part of our present credit system channels funds into expanding market-oriented production, but a significant part of the system channels money into non-productive, resource-wasting, and non-market-oriented purposes. Thus quality control (in terms of sharply distinguishing between the "productive" versus "non-productive" uses of credit) has not been factored into the strategies of either side of the debate on monetary policy.

Conservatives, of course, would favor closing the non-market-oriented "leaks" in the present irrigation system. Unfortunately, they also ignore the fact that this would channel even more credit into ownership-concentrating modes of capital creation, thereby increasing the political pressure for redistribution that caused the "leaks" in the first place. While favoring private property, monetarists like Friedman offer no solutions to the dangers inherent in a society where the majority of voters own no capital.

Under a comprehensive, long-range national Capital Homesteading strategy, the key to growth without inflation is the highly selective use of the Federal Reserve's discount powers and control over credit costs. Ideally, the Federal Reserve, in controlling and channeling monetary growth, would differentiate sharply between interest rates on already accumulated savings (*i.e.*, "other people's money") and credit costs on newly created central bank credit for stimulating private sector investment growth among new owners ("pure credit").

What is missing is a refinement in the present irrigation system — a two-tiered credit policy that would permit increases in the money supply to be channeled more selectively into new private sector plants, equipment, and advanced technology, but through routes that gradually and systematically create new capital owners, thus reducing the pressures for forceful redistribution.

Moving from a Debt-Backed to an Asset-Backed Currency

One of the major monetary reforms proposed under Capital Homesteading is to shift the backing of U.S. currency from government debt to newly created private sector assets.

Why is such a reform necessary from the standpoint of economic growth and expanded capital ownership? As pointed out by Dr. Norman A. Bailey, former Special Assistant to President Reagan for International Economic Affairs:

> The huge disparities in the ownership of productive capital lead inexorably to derivative imbalances in the international sphere, which in turn result in serial over-indebtedness and misallocation of capital investment to areas where the return is often nil or negative or at best below that level which would enable countries involved to service their debt burden. The result of this is recurring debt/financial/economic crises that are both endemic and resistant to treatment. The measures taken to respond to these crises have often exacerbated the disparities which led to them in the first place, thus completing the vicious circle.[72]

Dr. Bailey explains the inherent weaknesses of a debt-backed currency:

> [A] central bank can purchase any asset with the currency and credit it issues. Over the history of central banking, starting in the late seventeenth century, central banks have issued currency and credit on the basis of purchases of precious metals, other currencies, commercial paper (industrial, commercial, agricultural or export) and other asset. The fact that at present most central banks, including the Federal Reserve System in the United States, fund their currency and credit issues primarily through the purchase of government securities (their own or other governments') is simply part of the vicious circle ... the monetary system is based on the government debt, a logical absurdity made necessary by the requirements of the welfare state. The total bankruptcy of this system was amusingly demonstrated when at the end of 1999, terrified by the specter of hordes of depositors demanding their money at banks paralyzed by the (as it turned out non-existent) Y2K computer problem, the Federal Reserve greatly increased the money supply, and since it had run out of government obligations to buy it bought huge quantities of Fannie Mae and Freddie Mac paper instead. Perhaps a better metaphor for this operation than that of a vicious circle might be that of a dog chasing its own tail.[73]

To prevent the current monetization of government deficits, the U.S. Treasury Department under a Capital Homesteading policy would be forbidden from selling the government's debt paper to the Fed. The Federal Reserve would be forbidden to deal in both primary *and* *secondary* government securities. The need to manipulate reserve requirements of commercial banks, the justification for the current provision allowing the Federal Reserve to deal in secondary government securities, would be obviated by the implementation of a 100% reserve requirement and discounting of all eligible paper. This is similar to "the Chicago Plan," proposed in the 1930s as a solution to the banking problems of the day.[74]

The Federal Reserve would be required to supply sufficient money and credit through local banks to meet the liquidity and broadened ownership needs of an expanding economy, thus responding automatically to the demands of a more democratic private sector. Such "Fed monetized" loans would be subject to appropriate feasibility standards administered by the banks and limited only by the goal of maintaining a stable value for the dollar.

Capital Homesteading also requires the promotion of the availability of private sector capital credit insurance. This insurance would serve as a substitute for collateral to cover the risk of default on "eligible" Capital Homesteading loans. This would open up ownership opportunities by expanding share ownership among workers and other capital-deficient citizens. This would be similar to the role played by home mortgage insurance for broadening home ownership in America.

Capital Homesteading would create a more stable currency than we have today. The Federal Reserve's current ability to use its money-creating powers to support foreign currencies or to buy and sell primary or secondary Treasury securities would be terminated. This would force the government to borrow directly from savers in the open markets. This is possibly the most sensitive aspect of Capital Homesteading, and raises a number of questions as to how to deal with it.

Why Focus on the Federal Reserve?

Some have accused the Federal Reserve of being the source of many economic ills; it can also be the source of the cure. The central bank is government's main instrumentality for controlling the costs and volume of new credit and money extended through the commercial banking system. The Federal Reserve can play a pivotal role in restructuring the future ownership patterns of the economy and stimulating noninflationary private sector growth, while leaving the actual allocation of credit in the hands of commercial bankers.

No other institution has the control over money, credit, and interest rates as that exercised by the Federal Reserve, particularly in the person of Alan Greenspan, Chairman of the Federal Reserve Board of Governors.[75] The Fed Chairman's enormous influence over the economy is a fact reported in many studies of the Federal Reserve, most graphically in the best-selling book by William Greider, *Secrets of the Temple: How the Federal Reserve Runs the Country.*[76]

Greider confirmed what Louis Kelso and others have observed for years: The Federal Reserve uses its money-creation powers in ways that favor Wall Street over Main Street. This is not due to evil motivations as much as the paradigm from which economists like Greenspan view the world and shape their policies. The processes of creating money and credit and controlling interest rates are little understood by the American people, and hardly more by the Congressional committees to which the Federal Reserve reports. Hence, the activities of the Federal Reserve remain a mystery and its money-making powers remain an untapped source for creating more rapid, non-inflationary growth and much more widespread capital incomes for more Americans.

The monetary proposals contained in this report are fully consistent with the original intent of the Federal Reserve Act: to provide an adequate and stable currency and foster private sector growth. These proposals would allow our country to take full advantage of the immense potential of a properly designed central banking system. They would restore a more healthy balance between Main Street and Wall Street, and between the non-rich and the already rich. The proposed reforms would shift the focus of the Federal Reserve from support of public sector growth and from indifference to non-productive uses of credit, to support of more vigorous private sector growth, the favoring of productive uses of credit, and broadened citizen access to capital credit.

Most important, the proposed new boost to expanded capital ownership for private sector workers and other citizens would not be constrained by Congressional balanced budget restrictions. It would involve no new "tax expenditures" or subsidies. Nor would it rely on existing pools of domestic or foreign wealth accumulations. It would be "A Proposal to Free Economic Growth From the Slavery of [Past] Savings"[77] — a shift to what Kelso called "pure credit."

Half the battle is already won. The Fed has shown a new interest in encouraging the use of the discount window by its member banks.[78] Furthermore, the current Chairman of the Federal Reserve, Alan Greenspan, supports the goal of "broader ownership of capital" and the capacity of well-structured ESOPs to improve productivity. In a letter dated April 7, 1995 to Congressman Bennie Thompson (a Mississippi Democrat representing one of America's most poverty-stricken areas), Chairman Greenspan agreed that "a broader ownership of capital" was a "worthwhile goal," and added that "ESOPs have a number of attractive features in addition to a wider ownership of capital."[79]

Unfortunately, Mr. Greenspan does not yet see the constructive role the Federal Reserve could play to support the worthy objectives of a comprehensive Capital Homestead program. We hope, however, that this report will help persuade policy-makers like Mr. Greenspan that our proposal can be implemented without abandoning the Federal Reserve's mandate to stabilize the dollar or work toward maximum, sustainable rates of growth.

Detailed Monetary Reforms for Implementing Capital Homesteading

Capital Homesteading would conform monetary policy to the goal of sustainable, market-oriented, non-inflationary growth.[80] The following describes in greater detail the specific monetary and credit features proposed under Capital Homesteading:

- **Special Discount Rate.** The "discount rate" is the interest rate charged by the Federal Reserve on the loans it makes to its member banks. It is the rate used to calculate the amount "held back" by the Federal Reserve when a commercial bank "sells" loans to the central bank in exchange for new currency or demand deposits. For example, if a bank selling a bundle of loans with a face value of $1 million at the term of one year had its loans "discounted" by the Federal Reserve at 0.5%, the bank would receive $995,000 in new currency or demand deposits. It would thus be paying to the central bank an effective "service fee" of $5,000.

  The special discount rate for expanded ownership credit extended by qualified financial institutions would be set at 0.5% or less, whatever is calculated to be the cost of creating and administering new money and credit. This "service fee" would return to the original idea of central bank discounting, where the rate "charged" by the central bank would cover only the administrative costs of the Federal Reserve and other government banking agencies that regulate commercial banks and other institutions controlling the flow of money and productive credit. It would not allow the Federal Reserve any profits for its role in monetizing expanded citizen access to capital credit. Qualifying lenders would be free to add their own markup above their cost of money to cover their administrative costs, risk premiums and profit, with overall transaction charges set by the market.

- **No Central Bank Allocations of Credit.** The fear most often expressed when the reactivation of the discount window is discussed is that the Federal Reserve will begin allocating productive credit to businesses based solely on political considerations. This can be guarded against by implementing a private-sector checks-and-balances mechanism. All credit allocations would be handled exclusively by participating banks and financial institutions, subject to market competition, with special safeguards to prevent government allocations of credit or the use of such funds for speculative purposes, consumer loans, or public sector projects. The Federal Reserve properly opposes political allocations of credit, which this proposal is designed to avoid. Local lenders, not the Fed, would determine the technical financial feasibility of each loan and the demand for new credit.

- **Asset-Backed Currency and Collateralization.** In conformance with sound central banking practice, all newly created money and bank credit would be asset-backed. Assets would be in the form of pledged shares acquired with the loans discounted at the Federal Reserve, plus guarantees and collateralized assets of the enterprise needing capital. The new capital owners would also be insulated against having their personal assets seized, just as corporate shareholders are today, if future profits do not cover the cost of capital credit.

As a substitute for traditional collateral requirements (a major barrier to expanded ownership among the poor and middle-class), Congress and the Federal Reserve would encourage the establishment of commercial loan default insurance and reinsurance pools (like FHA mortgage insurance), funded by the risk premium portion of debt service charges. In contrast to the handling of the savings and loan crisis, the full faith and credit of the Federal Government *should not* stand behind these bank loans or insurers of capital credit in the event of default by companies issuing expanded ownership shares. (In order to encourage responsible lending practices by member banks, capital credit insurance might cover only 80-90% of the unpaid balance of a defaulted loan.)

- **100% Reserves.** Under today's "fractional reserve" banking, commercial banks can "multiply" the amount of money supplied to them by the central bank. Banks are required to hold as mandatory reserves only a fraction of the cash they take in as deposits. (For example, under a 10% fractional reserve requirement, a bank with $1 million in reserves, could lend out $900,000, which will be spent and deposited with other banks. As the "excess reserves" (*i.e.*, cash in excess of the amount the banks are required to have on hand or on deposit at the Federal Reserve Bank) are lent and re-lent through the banking system (decreasing each time as each bank withholds part of its new deposit to meet its increased reserve requirements), the ultimate effect of a 10% reserve requirement is to increase 10-fold the amount of new money available for loans throughout the system.

To avoid the potentially inflationary effect of fractional reserve banking, expanded ownership loans could be made subject to a 100% reserve requirement. This would empower the Federal Reserve with more direct regulatory control over the amount of money in circulation, enabling the central bank to pursue its anti-inflation mandate more effectively. For every dollar of new money created to finance eligible capital loans, the lender would have collateralized or commercially insured loan paper as an equivalent asset on its balance sheets. As the loan is repaid and the new money retired from circulation, the outstanding principal on the lender's asset would be correspondingly reduced.

- **Termination of Monetization of Public Sector Deficits.** A great deal of new, inflationary money enters the economy because the Federal Reserve purchases government securities in its open market operations. As described above, this effectively "monetizes" government deficits, rather than private sector production. In restoring the original discount powers of the Federal Reserve, Congress may wish to consider eliminating control of the money supply through the Federal Reserve's Open Market Committee. This would discourage future monetization of Federal budgetary deficits and would require that the Treasury sell securities directly in the capital markets to finance government debt.

- **Eligible Shares.** Under Kelsonian monetary reforms, ESOP and other expanded ownership shares that should be eligible for Federal Reserve discounting privileges should be "full dividend payout, full voting shares," with dividends tax-deductible to the corporation and fully taxable as any other source of consumption income to shareholders. The shares should provide workers and other new capital owners with first-class shareholder rights, including the right to vote the shares on all matters subject to a shareholder vote. This reform would broaden and democratize the accountability system of the corporate sector, a goal impossible to achieve through public and private retirement systems or traditional institutional investors. It would also overcome the "closed system" of corporate finance by shrinking retained earnings while offering corporations a cheaper way (*i.e.*, new stock issuances) to combine growth assets with new shareholders. And finally, by adding transparency and greater management accountability to worker-owners and other shareholders, most ESOP abuses can be minimized.

- **Two-Tiered Credit System.** To shift the economy toward faster growth rates and broader participation in capital ownership, the floor price on the cost of money would be determined by (1) the nature of the assets behind the money, (2) the impact of the money on ownership diffusion or concentration, and (3) the money's source (*i.e.*, "pure credit" or "past savings).

    — *Tier One: New Money ("Pure Credit" or "Future Savings").* Credit and "new money" for Capital Homesteading, *i.e.*, feasible business projects linked to broadened ownership, would be generated "interest-free" through the discount mechanism of the central bank, at a service charge based on the cost to the central bank of creating new money and regulating the lending institutions (0.5% or less).

    The newly developed "pure credit reservoir" would gradually supplant conventional sources of the economy's expansion capital, becoming the main source for financing the trillions of new equity issuances representing the growth capital required by the economy in the coming decade. The replacement of existing ca-

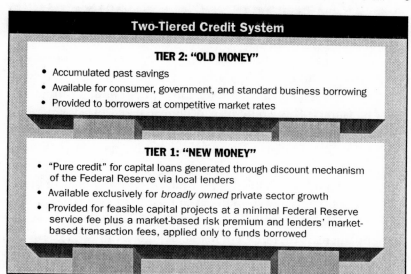

Two-Tiered Credit System

TIER 2: "OLD MONEY"

- Accumulated past savings
- Available for consumer, government, and standard business borrowing
- Provided to borrowers at competitive market rates

TIER 1: "NEW MONEY"

- "Pure credit" for capital loans generated through discount mechanism of the Federal Reserve via local lenders
- Available exclusively for *broadly owned* private sector growth
- Provided for feasible capital projects at a minimal Federal Reserve service fee plus a market-based risk premium and lenders' market-based transaction fees, applied only to funds borrowed

pacity (*i.e.*, plant, equipment and infrastructure) would continue to be addressed through depreciation accounting, so that the financing of growth would not deprive present owners of any property rights in their existing assets.

As explained above, pure credit is based wholly on promise secured by the future profits anticipated from the new investments. Because pure credit would be limited to self-liquidating capital formation and would be cut off by the Federal Reserve whenever the economy operated at 100% of its capacity, "pure credit" is not inflationary. In fact, because low-cost capital credit is geared to increasing production levels without artificially raising labor costs and entitlements, it should bring about lowered overall costs, and thus be counter-inflationary. "Pure credit" should never be permitted for consumer financing, government deficits or for speculating in previously issued securities or derivatives from the open market. These would be financed through the "past savings reservoir."

— *Tier Two: Old Money ("Other People's Money" or "Past Savings").* Credit and money for nonproductive, ownership-concentrating uses would come from past savings ("old money"). Yields on already existing investments ("past savings") should be permitted to rise to whatever levels the money market will permit. Interest rates on "Tier Two" would, therefore, level off at yields on alternative investment opportunities.

Existing savings (to the extent present owners do not convert them into funds for their own consumption) would be freed up and channeled into reserves for capital credit insurers and reinsurers. This would provide an expanded funding pool for consumer loans, housing loans, highly speculative ventures, loans for speculating in securities on the open market, small business loans, Treasury bonds, and other risky or inflation-prone purposes. "Old money" would also be available for building museums and monuments, or for funding charity, education, and other noble causes. Since this separate reservoir would not increase the output of marketable goods and services to any appreciable degree, its interest rate might contain an "inflation premium" to offset inflationary pressures arising from the use of these funds for stimulating consumer demand or for wasteful and speculative purposes.

Steps for Introducing CHA Monetary Reforms

The steps for implementing Capital Homesteading monetary reforms to accelerate private sector growth linked to expanded capital ownership would be as follows:

1. Declare a moratorium on any future purchases by the Open Market Committee of the Federal Reserve System of U.S. Treasury bills and other public debt paper, including foreign currencies, thus forcing the U.S. Treasury to sell directly its paper on the open market, and putting an end to further monetization of government deficits.

2. Simultaneously, the Fed should announce a *two-tiered credit policy* under which Fed-monetized credit for Capital Homesteading (broadly owned private sector growth) would be set at a service fee of 0.5% or less. The Fed's discount window would be exclusively available to member banks and members of the Farm Credit system for discounting "eligible" paper for feasible industrial, commercial, and agricultural projects.

3. Legislators would then structure citizen accessibility to the lower-cost, Fed-monetized capital credit, ideally from the bottom up. For example, like the one-time $10,000 home loans to World War II veterans, allotments of Capital Homestead credit (*e.g.*, $3,000 *per*

capita annually) could be extended directly to eligible individuals through individual Capital Homestead Accounts (CHAs) for investments of their choice, as long as local banks (subject to Federal feasibility criteria) determine the venture to be feasible and the loan repayable with future pre-tax earnings.

With the *"bottom-up" approach to Capital Homesteading*, loans from local banks to IRS-approved, tax-exempt Capital Homestead Accounts (CHAs), would provide every citizen and all members of his family access to capital credit to invest in full dividend payout, voting shares of new and expanding enterprises or SEC-approved private offerings of existing shares. Pre-tax profits would secure and repay the loans, which ideally would be insured by private sector capital credit insurance and re-insurance.

Citizens through CHAs would have the choice of investing that credit in companies in which the individual or his family has a stakeholder interest, such as (1) a company for which a member of the family works, (2) a community investment corporation that aggregates local land for large-scale development, (3) a utility or other natural monopoly servicing his community, (4) a company in which he is a regular customer or supplier, or (5) a diversified portfolio of SEC-approved mature companies with a solid track record of profitability.

This option would place enormous economic power (the power over money and capital credit) in the hands of the American people, where it belongs. Local banks and financial institutions would still guide the process, backed up by capital credit insurers and ultimately by Federal and State banking and tax authorities. To discourage bad investments, high-risk ventures would be automatically subject to high premium rates for capital credit insurance, thereby creating a protective shield against the use of bank credit for blatantly non-feasible projects.

An *alternative, more top-down, management-controlled approach* to credit diffusion would be to channel capital credit through existing or new enterprises that adopt ownership-expanding legal entities like ESOPs, Community Investment Corporations, and Consumer Stock Ownership Plans. In this way, entrepreneurs, farmers, professionals — those who conceive and launch enterprises — could start their own new ventures. Corporations and farms needing expansion capital would then have new lower-cost sources for meeting their funding requirements.

All lower-tier credit, except for credit to purchase one's primary residence, would have to be supported by a bank-approved business feasibility study reflecting the self-liquidating nature of the transaction. In the case of the top-down approach, the loan paper would also be:

(a) guaranteed and secured by the general credit of the enterprise as a going concern;

(b) collateralized by equity instruments, accounts receivable, land and other hard assets involved in the transaction, plus the shares of stock acquired with the loan;

(c) insured to cover the risk of default by commercially available credit insurance, through premiums paid by borrowers or lending banks;

(d) designed to be repayable principally from the future pre-tax earnings of the enterprise guaranteeing the loan's repayment;

(e) endorsed for negotiability by the commercial banks making the loans; and

(f) endorsed and guaranteed by every collective bargaining unit or voluntary association representing workers of the enterprise, adding further security to the loans to its members.

4. Banks negotiating loan paper that is eligible for discount with the Fed would be free to allow market forces to determine the bank's mark-up for money, above the Fed's 0.5% Capital Homesteading service fee. Thus, commercial bank lenders could cover their normal administrative costs and profits, plus a premium to cover the anticipated risk of default on the specific investment being financed. Lending rates for prime customers should drop to 3% or less under the two-tiered credit system, without any taxpayer subsidies.

5. All new currency issued by the Fed to meet the discount needs of its member banks under the Capital Homestead program should be subject to a special 100% reserve requirement, thus creating a 100% asset-backed currency. (This new money would be supported by promissory notes collateralized by the new equity issuances and new business assets financed under the program; and reinforced by

highly-motivated borrowers disciplined by ownership incentives.) This added level of accountability to shareholders would simplify the policing role of the Fed and help guard against misuse or abuse of their discount privileges by the member banks.

6. The Fed should be specifically prohibited from purchasing or discounting paper representing any non-productive uses of credit (such as U.S. Treasury Notes, consumer loans, loans for speculating in commodities or securities, unfriendly leveraged acquisitions, local and State government debt, etc.) or other uses of credit that do not encourage broadened capital ownership and competitive markets. However, as already stated, existing savings (*i.e.*, "old money") freed up by the lower tier of the new credit system would remain available at market rates for high-risk ventures, capital credit insurance reserves, consumer finance, speculation, and other non-productive uses of credit, as well as future public sector borrowings.

7. A "Federal Capital Insurance Corporation" or FCIC could be established, on a self-financing basis, similar to MGIC or FHA home mortgage insurance, to offer commercial insurance to bank lenders against the risk of default on Capital Homestead credit and to offer, for a premium paid by the new owners, some "down-side risk" portfolio insurance. These risks could be spread even further through a reinsurance facility established either by the private sector or by the public sector.

8. The amount of annual credit to be discounted each year by the Fed under the Capital Homestead program should meet at least 50% of the $2 trillion[81] added each year in new plant and equipment, new infrastructure, and new rentable space by the U.S. private and public sectors. Spreading access to ownership stakes in only $858 billion, or less than one-half of America's capital growth pie, equally among America's 286 million Americans, each person could be allotted around $3,000 annually in Fed-discounted capital credit to invest in the capital growth of the U.S. economy. A family of four could borrow $12,000 annually for Capital Homesteading investments without reducing their household budgets. A child born today and his or her future spouse would be able to retire on independent combined dividend incomes of $60,000, while receiving combined dividends during the accumulation process of $1.5 million. [*See calculations in* Appendix 3.]

Each year the credit allotted to each voter could be adjusted to the nation's projected capital requirements for that year. Higher allotments of low-cost production credit might have to be provided to farmers, in order to keep America's agricultural lands in private hands, particularly younger farmers, and to maintain present high levels of productivity in food production.

VIII.
REFORMING
THE TAX SYSTEM

Few Americans today would label the U.S. tax system as either simple or fair. Many Americans believe that tax breaks are mainly benefiting the extremely wealthy. While the top 5% of Americans account for more than half of all personal income tax revenues, through advantageous arrangements wealthy taxpayers frequently are able to avoid paying anything but a token amount of taxes on their capital incomes. The payroll tax and sales and excise taxes take a much bigger share of disposable income from middle and low income Americans than from wealthy Americans, according to the Institute on Taxation and Economic Policy.[82]

Meanwhile, our current approach to taxation continues to be justified under the erroneous assumption that there is no other way than through supply-side tax incentives to stimulate new investments and create jobs.[83]

When business corporations, voluntary associations, or any other specialized social inventions become socially dysfunctional and create, rather than solve, problems for society, government is the instrument through which we overcome the problem, directly or through a restructuring of our institutions and laws. It is not in the nature of government to leave social vacuums unfilled.

Today, as a result of the maldistribution of ownership and income, we have reached a point where government itself is suffering from an acute case of functional overload. Public redistribution and efforts to control the economy have placed responsibilities on government that go far beyond its originally conceived and more normal functions of enforcing contracts, protecting property, suppressing violence and otherwise maintaining a just and peaceful society.

The mere shifting of centralized governmental activities to state and local levels totally ignores the underlying defects within our economic system that have engendered and exacerbated the growing wealth, income and power gap. Reorganization of the federal bureaucracy is a similarly futile palliative.

Capital Homesteading offers a solution, not an excuse for perpetuating or ignoring structural flaws in our major economic institutions. Behind Capital Homesteading is a philosophy of taxation[84] and a carefully conceived strategy to remove gradually the tax system's present bias against property and property accumulations, on the one hand, and, at some point, to reduce the government's use of the tax system as an income redistribution mechanism, on the other.

The Purpose of Taxation

Any rebuilding of today's overly complex, inherently unjust tax system must start with the simple question, "Why do we have a tax system?" From the standpoint of Capital Homesteading, the answer is simple: to yield the revenue to pay the costs of a limited government, without damaging the incentives for maximum production of wealth and the broadest distribution of capital ownership. From this point, a whole new set of conclusions follow:

The bias in the present tax laws against property accumulations and property incomes should be removed. The bias in favor of redistribution, as a practical matter, must be more gradually phased out, as redistribution of income is supplanted with an effective program of redistributing future ownership opportunities. The tax system and federal laws generally should be restructured to encourage the creation, accumulation and the maintenance of property, its widespread distribution among all households, and the maximum generation of new wealth and improved technology within the free enterprise system.

Government should announce a target goal for the economy of *a minimum floor of capital self-sufficiency* for every household to achieve within the next thirty years. A national ownership plan, including new tax laws, would be launched to reach that goal, similar to the manner in which government assisted Americans in the building of our agricultural base through the Homestead Act of 1862.

The 160-acre ceiling made sense in distributing shares of our necessarily finite land frontier. The amounts that could be accumulated under the proposed Capital Homestead program, however, are limited only by our talent, our knowhow, our technological potential, and our ability to mobilize all our resources in building a new and more productive industrial frontier during the next several decades. Hence, in today's world, a target floor is more appropriate than a ceiling as the focus of government initiatives under a national ownership program.

An effective tax system would offer incentives for the enterprise system itself, as the principal source of wealth production, to become a more direct and efficient distributor of mass purchasing power for all consumers in the economy.

As the need for income redistribution and governmental intervention within the private sector lessens to an irreducible minimum, the functions and costs of government should drop progressively, eventually to the tolerable levels projected by the founding fathers. Instead of constricting private initiatives and production, as under today's tax laws, government under a soundly conceived national ownership strategy, would become the catalyst for stimulating expanded production of a more competitive free enterprise system.

Since the wealth necessary to cover the costs of government are products of private labor and private capital, *taxes should be viewed as charges to consumers for essential services not available through the private sector.* Unlike other services, however, the buyer of public services is compelled to buy and the government will remain the sole seller, at least until these same services can be satisfactorily provided through the competitive enterprise system. This seemingly minor change in emphasis could open up some new ideas for privatizing (democratizing) government services and new opportunities for creative businessmen.

Direct or Indirect Taxation

Any tax blunts incentives, but a direct income tax on individuals is the least damaging, and, at the same time, places before the electorate the cost of government. User fees for government services, like camping fees and grazing fees, are also legitimate direct taxes. But sales taxes, value added taxes, payroll taxes, most excise taxes, and other indirect taxes are not just or economically sound methods for covering government spending, since they mask the spending patterns of public servants and elected officials from close taxpayer scrutiny and direct accountability.

Indirect taxes (including Social Security and unemployment taxes) also add to the costs of goods, thus shifting taxes to the consumer, reducing the competitiveness of U. S. enterprises and also our growth within the global marketplace. Taxes on property discourage new construction, improvements, and maintenance. But taxes on corporations are the most counterproductive of all forms of indirect taxes. The corporation income tax damages the corporation, an invention of man that is indispensable to the maximum production of wealth. To the extent return on investment is reduced, growth is stifled and the investment will go elsewhere.

But there is a more serious adverse and unjust effect of present corporation income tax laws flowing from the wide array of incentives the tax system now offers to the financing of industrial growth without the issuance of new equity instruments. The nondeductibility of dividends encourage the use of retained earnings or conventional borrowings for financial growth. (This is reinforced by tax subsidies, investment tax credits, tax exclusions and other loopholes to encourage investments in ways which make the rich richer.) By perpetuating exclusionary patterns of corporate finance, the corporation tax minimizes opportunities for all households to share in the growth opportunities of the economy.

Rates of Taxation

A growing number of tax scholars have argued that the case for progressive or graduated rates of taxation is uneasy at best.[85] If redistribution of income (in contrast to redistribution of future ownership opportunities) is a form of direct discrimination against property, a progressive income tax is inherently an unjust tax, assuming one accepts the Kelso-Adler, rather than the Marx-Engels, version of economic justice.

But what about the poor? No more effective aid can be provided the poor than allowing them to share in the new job and ownership opportunities within a healthy and growing private economy. The problem of those still too poor to share in the cost of government can be handled through tax exemptions or direct vouchers, or perhaps even the kind of negative income tax advocated by Nobel prize winner Milton Friedman.

Yet responsible citizenship is best served when everyone pays some direct tax. In an economy productive enough to provide a high standard of living for all households, which would be the long-range goal of economic decision makers, the cost of government would be minimal. Since government benefits should be equally accessible to each member of society, absolute justice would demand an equal per capita charge on all individuals, without regard to their income levels. But this, of course, is impractical at this stage of our economic history.

A more realistic and just tax today would be *a flat or proportionate rate* imposed on all directly earned and so-called "unearned" incomes above a poverty-level income for all taxpayers. A single tax rate would be administratively more efficient than a progressive or graduated tax. Ideally, the flat tax on individuals would cover all government expenditures each year, including welfare, defense, interest on the Federal debt, social security obligations, unemployment and all other current spending not covered by user fees. It could also cover the cost of health insurance premiums under universal minimum health care coverage, including health vouchers for the poor.

This will allow for the gradual or immediate elimination of regressive payroll taxes on workers and companies, making the economy more competitive. And it would help make government vastly more accountable and transparent to the electorate. If tied into a vigorous national growth and expanded ownership strategy, one could easily imagine future candidates for public office actually competing for votes on the basis of who could offer the best government services at the lowest flat rate. *Each year's single direct tax rate could be adjusted up or down to provide sufficient revenues to avoid budget deficits and pay off government debt over time.*

Under a progressive or graduated tax, on the other hand, political irresponsibility and waste is more easily tolerated. Many voters believe that the cost of increased government spending can be shifted to a tiny fraction of high-income individuals or fat cat corporations, and overlook the dangers of "printing press money" where there are sizable budget deficits. A flat tax would help raise the levels of economic sophistication of the taxpayers.

Another shortcoming of a progressive or graduated tax is that tax evasion and the search for tax loopholes by wealthy taxpayers increase as tax rates increase. And when inflation forces workers into higher tax brackets, pressures for additional pay increases add more fuel to the inflationary fires.

Resources tend to be misallocated under a progressive or graduated tax. Economic decisions become increasingly made, not on their economic merit, but on tax considerations. Thus, high tax brackets stifle growth and incentives to innovate and increase production, making all of society the poorer and less competitive.

Earned or Unearned Income

Under the Kelso-Adler theory of economic justice, the earnings from one's property in the means of production are morally indistinguishable from the earnings produced by one's skill or brainpower. Since they are both rewards directly related to their contributions to production, they should be taxed alike. And discrimination against property discourages investment and reduces society's overall productive capacity.

Karl Marx considered profits as income stolen from labor. Our tax laws that discriminate against property incomes reflect the same bias. But if capital is recognized as a producer of wealth, then capital incomes (whether distributed or undistributed) are legitimately earned by those who share property rights in that capital, the same as those paid for their skills and ingenuity.

The most serious problem with laws that discriminate against property incomes is that they hurt the poor more than they do the rich. Access to the full, undiluted stream of earnings from capital is a prerequisite for the financing on credit of broadened ownership opportunities and for more widespread distribution of profits as second incomes among today's nonowning citizens, including civil servants, many professionals, teachers, the military and the unemployable.

The only form of income that can properly be classified as unearned is that which is truly gratuitous and wholly unrelated to the production of marketable goods and services. Examples of unearned income, which should be included for direct taxation (once poverty-level incomes are exceeded) at the same rate as earned incomes, are: welfare checks, unemployment checks, social security checks, food stamps, gifts and bequests, gambling gains, and other gains not immediately converted into tax-free or tax-deferred individual capital accumulations, as described below.

Individual Capital Accumulations

As discussed previously, building capital self-sufficiency into every American household will not take place overnight. But once we establish a specific minimal level or floor for individual asset accumulations as a ten- or twenty-year goal to strive toward, it allows everyone to focus on the importance of property and the need to remove all institutional barriers to the broader distribution of ownership opportunities as expeditiously as possible. *The floor of capital accumulations per household should represent the industrial equivalent of the 160 acres of frontier land that the federal government made available to its propertyless citizens under the Homestead Act of 1862.* Thus the tax laws should be reconstructed to encourage the tax-free (or at least tax-deferred) accumulation of a "Capital Homestead" for all Americans over their working careers, consisting of a growing number of equity shares in the economy's expanding industrial frontier.

A tax-qualified CHA could be set up in the name of each individual, from birth, at a local bank to serve as his or her tax-free accumulator of capital. Shares acquired through ESOPs, CSOPs and CICs could be rolled over into one's CHA account tax-free,[86] as well as income-producing property acquired through tax-free gifts and bequests. Each individual's total acquisitions would continue to accumulate in a tax-free manner until the federally established capital self-sufficiency floor was reached. Thereafter, future accumulations would lose these tax privileges and become taxed at the current flat rate, thus discouraging grossly excessive, monopolistic accumulations of capital in the future. Upon death or when all or part of the assets are sold to increase consumption incomes, such tax-deferred assets would be taxed at the flat rate then prevailing. Fairness in the distribution of future ownership opportunities would mainly be controlled through the traditional IRS tax-qualification controls over discriminatory allocations and, more importantly, through the Federal Reserve Board's control over credit extended by commercial bank lenders to ESOPs, CSOPs, CICs and CHAs to foster growth of the private sector economy.

Under H.R. 462, the proposed Accelerated Capital Formation Act introduced in 1975 by Ways and Means Committee member Rep. Bill Frenzel (R-MN), this tax-free floor was set at $500,000. Whatever the target amount, it should be set at a level that both fosters initiative and a desire for income independence for its owner, and it could be adjusted to rise with cost-of-living increases. To encourage the continued accumulation and retention of income-producing investments, and to discourage squandering, all tax-qualified accumulation trusts would be required to pay out all property incomes on a regular basis as second incomes to the owners, subject to direct personal income taxes.

The rationale behind permitting tax-free accumulations below excessively large wealth concentrations follows the principle that new capital formation and widespread capital accumulations should be encouraged, both for promoting economic democracy and for raising the standard of living for all citizens. Taxes on property slows down the capital
creation and accumulation process. On the other hand, a direct tax on
the *incomes* from already accumulated capital assets is simpler to understand, less harmful to investment and the care of property, and easier
for tax authorities to administer.

Government Debt and Government Deficits

Since tax policy affects the size of the government's debt and government deficits in general, a few comments on the wisdom of debt and
deficit spending policies are in order.

Under the influence of Keynesian economic concepts, the objective
of many tax decisions since the early part of the 20th Century has been
to cure inflation and unemployment. Keynes assumed the continuance
of historic patterns of extreme maldistribution of capital ownership,
and sought merely to fine-tune that malstructured economy through
the bureaucratic manipulation of government tax, spending, interest,
and money-creation machinery. Structural reforms to our corporate
ownership patterns were not part of Keynes' approach to the problems
of unemployment and inflation.

In the Capital Homesteading strategy, however, the structural void
left by Keynes is met head-on. Capital Homesteading would attack inflation and unemployment at the roots. The main thrust of this approach
is to super-stimulate expanded rates of private sector capital investment,
financed so as to broaden the base of equity owners in society.

The credit financing of corporate expansion must meet rigid standards of feasibility and must be repaid as a self-liquidating investment.
New dollars flow directly into new productive capacity. In sharp contrast, government debt seldom, if ever, finances any production increases.
Rather, it goes into nonproductive spending, war, and even into waste
of human talent and natural resources. Government debt is therefore
inherently inflationary. Even worse, when government spending is not
matched with current tax revenues, the inflationary impact worsens.
Funds must either be borrowed (thus diverting those same funds from

productive investment in the private sector) or simply issued as printing press money.

From a standpoint of economic justice, government deficits make no sense at all. They cause inflation and are therefore a pernicious form of hidden tax on the public, most painful to the poorest members of society. A just tax system would work toward the elimination of future inflationary budget deficits and to curb further increases in the already bloated government debt. Better yet, a concerted effort should be made to begin to repay this debt.

Inheritance Policy

Under a national ownership strategy, inheritance policy should be restructured to discourage excessive concentrations of wealth and, in order to promote individual initiative and capital self-sufficiency, to encourage the broadest possible distribution of income-producing assets. Gift and estate taxes therefore should not be imposed on the donor or his estate (including assets accumulated within proposed Capital Homestead vehicles). Rather, taxation should be based on the size of the recipient's total accumulations after receiving the gift or bequest. If the value of the recipient's asset accumulations remain below the floor of capital self-sufficiency described above, no tax would be imposed on the newly acquired assets. Above that floor, a reasonable generational asset transfer tax (or a flat rate tax on "excess" Capital Homestead accumulations) would be paid.

Avoidance of Generational Asset Transfer Taxes

Above the targeted homestead accumulation floor, a generational asset transfer tax or the flat rate tax would be imposed on each new owner to discourage future excess concentrations of wealth and economic power when assets transfer from one generation to the next. This would replace the existing estate and gift tax systems. The generational asset transfer tax and flat rate tax could be avoided by distributing excess accumulations to others, including family members, friends, and employees, as long as their personal accumulations remain below the floor.

Integration of Personal and Corporate Income Taxes

The double tax penalty now imposed on corporate profits is becoming widely accepted as an unjust form of tax discrimination that should be eliminated. Some reformers are proposing to mitigate this problem through a highly complicated and arbitrary compromise that not only avoids the problem but worsens it. Instead of eliminating the double tax directly at the corporate level, they would permit a partial deduction for dividend payouts to the corporation and a redistribution oriented partial tax credit for shareholders. Hence, it neither restores private property in corporate equity nor does it promote expanded distribution of equity issuances. It merely makes the top 1% who own the majority of directly-owned outstanding corporate shares even richer.

Tax reform under Capital Homesteading would attack this problem directly with elegant simplicity. It would recognize that property and profits are inseparable and therefore *all corporate net earnings, whether distributed or retained by the corporation, would be treated as earned by its owners and therefore should be taxable at the personal level, on the same basis as any other direct income.* Under this alternative, *the corporation would be treated for tax purposes like a partnership*, with its business expenses (including depreciation and research and development) attributed and deductible at the enterprise level and all capital incomes attributed individually according to each owner's proprietary stake in the business. To encourage more equity financing of corporate growth, higher dividend payouts must be encouraged and alternative low-cost credit sources for financing must be made available to expanding and viable new enterprises.

Capital Gains Taxation

How to tax capital gains is a continuing source of much of the complexity and confusion that now plague our tax laws. How would a property-oriented Capital Homestead policy handle this problem?

First, it would restructure the tax laws to encourage investment and discourage speculation. At least for non-wealthy individuals it would add disincentives to gambling in high-risk securities and the commodities market. Tax laws would be designed to facilitate the acquisition, accumulation and retention by today's capital-deficient Americans of long-term investments, held mainly for their potential of yielding high, steady, and relatively secure second incomes to supplement their paychecks and retirement checks in the future.

As under present law, to the extent capital gains income results from short-term purchases and sales of commodities and securities, realized capital gains should be treated like any other kind of direct personal income. Such capital gains are no different than the purchase and sale of any other goods for a profit, or for that matter, gambling gains.

Capital gains from long-term holdings deserve different treatment, however, under a national strategy to broaden the base of capital ownership. As recommended above, to the extent that investments are accumulated within a tax-qualified vehicle, the gains should be permitted to increase tax-free or tax-deferred, until the individual affected reaches a targeted floor of capital self-sufficiency. Above that level capital gains would be subject to normal taxation after indexing for inflation.

If all of the proposals recommended here were adopted, the capital gains problem would gradually disappear. Much of the appreciation in the values of corporate common stock can be traced to the retention by management of earnings for meeting their capital requirements. As dividend payouts increase (encouraged by tax-deductibility of dividends at the corporate level) and as new sources of equity financing become readily available through the discount mechanism of the Federal Reserve System, the value of individual shares would tend to stabilize over time and be based on current and projected dividend yields per share. Hence, long-term capital gains would be less a source of future government revenues.

To some extent, long-term capital gains result, not from the increased productive value of the underling assets, but from a gradual debasement of the American currency. Inflation-inducing government economic policies can be blamed for these artificial increases in profits and capital values. Except where prices increase from natural shortages, government should assume total responsibility for inflationary increases in the value of investments. Therefore *capital gains taxation should always be inflation indexed to see if any gains in value actually exist.*

State and Local Tax Systems

Today, a heavy portion of local revenues come from the taxation of property, thus discouraging investment and improvement of industry and residential property in their areas. Sales taxes also increase price levels, encourage tax evasion by local merchants, discourage trade, and generally can cause one area to become less attractive than another. Since high production, high incomes, and a higher quality of life rests on the quality of the structures, industrial equipment and facilities, and technology available to the residents of an area, it should be obvious that *taxes on local property are counter productive and should be gradually sup-*

*planted with a universal system of state and local taxation based upon the
direct incomes of its residents from whatever sources.*

Thus federal tax policy should create additional incentives for state
and local taxing authorities to gradually shift to direct flat rate income
taxes at the individual level, for the same reasons outlined above. To
simplify tax collections, the state and local rates could be set at a
percentage of the federal taxable incomes of residents of the area. Another
advantage of this approach is that all areas of the country would become
tax-neutral for investment purposes, thus increasing the nation's overall
efficiency in the allocation of our manpower and other resources.

Tax Simplification

Although corporate income tax returns would still be important for
disclosure purposes and for corporations unwilling to pay out their earnings fully to their stockholders, most of the tax revenues would flow
from the expanded personal tax base. The personal income tax return
and the tax system itself would, as result, be enormously simplified and
easier to understand. A simple one-page personal income tax return
would be well-received by the American taxpayer.

Most personal deductions and tax credits could be eliminated under a
flat-rate tax system, restoring the neutrality of the tax system over people's
consumption choices. Personal exemptions, however, could be raised to
the poverty level, so that the poorest families only would pay no taxes,
including payroll taxes. But by filling-in a simple annual income tax return, a poor family could qualify for a negative or reverse income tax (or
refund) as proposed by the conservative economist Milton Friedman.

Detailed Tax Reforms for Implementing Capital Homesteading

Sound tax policy recognizes that government does not produce wealth,
and that every subsidy originates with those whose productive labor
and capital actually produce marketable goods and services. It also recognizes that wealth is produced most efficiently within competing privately owned enterprises vying to satisfy private consumer demand, with
every buyer voting with his or her own money to reflect a choice among
available goods and services.

How then could the tax system be restructured to achieve responsible,
sustainable and fair fiscal policy, while encouraging the objectives of
Capital Homesteading?

1. Replace the graduated tax on personal income above the poverty level with a *single flat rate* on income from all sources, whether "earned" or "unearned," including employment and property incomes, interest, dividends, inflation-indexed gains from sales and exchanges of property, unemployment compensation and welfare, social security and pension incomes, winnings from gambling, gifts and bequests [that are not reinvested or exempted by the "Capital Homestead Exemption" described below], etc.[87]

2. Exempt all household incomes of the genuinely poor by excluding from the flat rate tax all incomes below $10,000 per adult household member and $5,000 per dependent child.

3. Eliminate all existing deductions and tax credits to businesses and individuals, except:

   (a) Ordinary and necessary business expenses, including full and immediate deductions for current expenditures or full debt service payments to replace existing productive assets and otherwise to protect the property rights of current owners;

   (b) All incomes channeled by businesses or individuals into dividend and patronage distributions or into the financing of business growth or transfers of equity ownership through employee stock ownership plans (ESOPs), Capital Homestead Accounts (CHAs), community investment corporations (CICs), pension plans, Keogh plans, or other IRS-"qualified" expanded ownership investment vehicles, but in no case where such amounts cause the accumulations of individual beneficiaries to exceed the "Capital Homestead Exemption" described in paragraph (13) below. These "savings" could be treated as tax deductible by either the businesses or individuals that make them; and

   (c) charitable contributions, with appropriate limitations to encourage expanded capital ownership and discourage monopolistic accumulations and control over productive assets;

4. Eliminate:

   (a) the tax penalty on married couples;

   (b) tax credits;

   (c) tax-free interest on public-sector financing;

     (d) tariffs on imported goods (except when used selectively to encourage just market competition);

     (e) tax shelters for speculative and non-productive investment;

     (f) all forms of indirect taxes not based on consumption incomes.

5. Allow the full deduction of the purchase price or the current mortgage payment (principal as well as interest) for the purchase of a taxpayer's principal home. However, to provide tax neutrality between renters and homeowners, add the "imputed rent" of each dwelling of a taxpayer to his annual taxable earnings.

6. Convert Individual Retirement Accounts (IRAs) into Capital Homestead Accounts (CHAs) as a mechanism for enabling all individuals to accumulate income-producing assets on a tax-deferred and/or exempt basis and permit CHAs, like employee stock ownership plans, to be used for acquiring corporate shares on credit secured and repaid with dividends deductible at the corporate level. Gifts or bequests to CHAs, ESOPs, and other ownership-expanding vehicles could be made tax-deductible for income and estate tax purposes, as they are today for tax-freefoundations.

7. Tax all dividends and interest income at the personal level without exclusions to the extent the taxpayer's total income from all sources exceeds the exemption levels for the poor.

8. *Only* allow exemption of capital gains from taxable personal income, to the extent that:

     (a) The taxpayer's spendable gains are equal to or less than the inflation-adjusted value of the assets during the period over which the assets were held before being sold; and

     (b) The taxpayer's gains are reinvested within 60 days (or 18 months for a home) into income-generating investments held within an IRS-qualified capital accumulation mechanism (*e.g.* CHA, ESOP, etc.) but not exceeding the "Capital Homestead Exemption" listed in paragraph (12) below.

9. Avoid double and triple taxation by maintaining a tax on corporate net earnings but allowing corporations to avoid taxes on earnings they (a) pay out as dividends, cash productivity bonuses, ESOP and profit sharing contributions, purchases or debt service payments

on replacement assets, patronage refunds, etc.; or (b) retain for research and development or (c) use for working capital.

10. Allow ordinary business expenses, like wages, to remain deductible at the corporate level as under present laws, while encouraging ownership expansion by allowing:

    (a) Full debt service deductions on credit to acquire replacement assets.

    (b) Full dividend deductibility on all corporate shares, thus permitting stockholders to purchase newly issued corporate shares with profits deductible both from corporate as well as personal earnings. In the alternative, employees through ESOPs, and other shareholders through CHAs, CSOPs, CICs, etc., could use these tax-deductible dividends to repay loans for the acquisition of larger blocks of stock on a leveraged basis.[88]

    (c) Increasing the ceiling on tax-deductible contributions to a leveraged ESOP for financing new equity issuances representing growth capital of the company. This would effectively allow the current expensing of annual debt service payments for financing growth through the company's ESOP.

11. Liberalize depreciation rules by allowing full first-year deductions on all purchases of replacement assets (to maintain existing levels of capital productiveness, profits and property rights of existing owners).

12. Allow the tax advantages of a leveraged ESOP to be extended to all taxpayers through IRS-qualified Capital Homestead Accounts (CHAs), to utility customers under consumer stock ownership plans (CSOPs), and to citizen-shareholders of State and local Community Investment Corporations (CICs) for developing local land and natural resources.

13. Integrate with the Social Security System a tax-deferred "Capital Homestead Exemption" to encourage every man, woman, and child to accumulate through Capital Homestead Accounts, ESOP rollovers, Keogh Plans, IRAs, gifts, bequests, savings, etc., a personal life-time estate of wealth-producing assets, tax-sheltered up to $750,000, including up to $250,000 for one's equity in his primary residence. This reform would be targeted to provide all Americans with growing property incomes and direct ownership participation in the

competitive free enterprise system. Such an estate would provide the same degree of income self-sufficiency and economic security for a family as the 160 acres of productive farmland granted under the original Homestead Acts.

14. Eliminate all contribution limits on "savings" through CHAs, ESOPs, IRAs, Keogh Plans, etc., until individual accumulations exceed the proposed Capital Homestead Exemption.

15. Provide an existing owner with a tax-deferred rollover of the proceeds from the sale to an ESOP of shares or assets of any enterprise, including shares trading in the open market, as long as the proceeds are reinvested by the seller in other productive assets within 18 months. This would encourage employee participation in ownership as well as provide a new source of equity financing for new and growing businesses. (This expands the present rollover provision for sale of shares to an ESOP to shareholders of publicly traded companies.)

16. Permit an ESOP, CHA, CIC, or other ownership-expanding mechanism to be treated as a charitable organization for income, gift, and estate tax purposes provided the donated stock is not allocated to the donor, family members of the donor or 25 percent shareholders.

17. Amend the Internal Revenue Code (following the precedent in the former Subchapter U for General Stock Ownership Corporations) to allow the use of Community Investment Corporations (CICs) for land planning, acquisition and development of "super empowerment zones" so as to encourage comprehensive, large-scale development of designated urban and rural areas combined with widespread participation among residents in the ownership, profits, and appreciated real estate values that would otherwise flow exclusively to outside land speculators.

18. Absorb the annual cost of the Social Security System entirely within the single flat rate income tax imposed on all incomes above the poverty level. As expanded growth and expanded ownership provide noninflationary property incomes for retiring Americans, social security benefits can become stabilized and perhaps eventually reduced as they are replaced by Capital Homesteading incomes.

IX.
OTHER POLICY
REFORMS

Fiscal Policy Reforms

By restructuring the Federal monetary and tax system to promote accelerated rates of private sector investment linked to expanded ownership, unemployed people and resources would be put back into full production. This would not only reduce Federal spending for welfare and unemployment and increase the earnings base for Federal tax revenues, but it would also begin to transform today's inherently inflationary "wage system" by linking labor's increased gains to rising productivity and profits.

Thus, many inflation-indexed costs would be eliminated, including the interest costs on the Federal debt. The proposed flat rate tax would also serve as a brake on runaway Federal spending by making taxpayers more directly aware of the government's "bite" out of what each taxpayer earns.

Public and Private Employee Retirement System Reforms

Instead of gaining a direct private property stake in our free enterprise system, civil servants at the State and local levels today acquire through their pension plans an extremely remote and indirect ownership stake in the Nation's productive capital. The same holds for private pensions, which Peter Drucker has aptly described as "pension plan socialism." Such collective ownership of the means of production is hardly distinguishable from the way it was for the workers in the former Soviet Union.

As they now stand, these pension plans distort stock values, place enormous power in the hands of money managers, large institutional investors, and stockbrokers, but do little to meet directly the financing needs of capital-starved industries. In fact, many vulnerable companies are threatened with bankruptcy because of their large and growing pension liabilities, a burden that becomes exacerbated when stock market values drop radically, as occurred in 2000-2002. Furthermore, pension trustees have become willing allies for corporate raiders and hostile takeovers of major U.S. corporations, causing losses of millions of jobs in the process.

At the Federal level, whatever assets are held to pay for rising military and civilian pension benefits are mainly in Treasury paper, not in the productive assets the economy needs to generate taxable incomes. The Capital Homestead program would create a piece of the action in America's growth frontier for all public and private employees covered by today's defective retirement systems.

Privatizing Government Enterprises and Services

The Postal Service and the Air Traffic Control System are but two examples of enterprises that could probably be run more efficiently and more profitably if they were run as employee-owned operations. Waste, absenteeism, featherbedding, and resistance to automation are less tolerated by employee-owners than by those with no ownership stake in bottom-line profits.

The TVA could also be re-organized as a stock corporation owned by its employees and customers. So could mass transit systems if they had access to low-cost credit from local banks under the monetary reforms proposed under the Capital Homestead program. In fact, even new local schools could be organized by parents and frustrated teachers as for-profit corporations if sufficient low-cost capital credit were available (reinforced by a voucher system) to enable them to enter into effective competition with the public school systems. The Scottsdale, Arizona Fire Department and San Francisco's garbage collectors work very well as employee-owned operations.

Anti-Monopoly Reforms

A pro-competition approach to anti-monopoly challenges involves a two-pronged approach: (1) where courts have ordered that a violator divest itself of a subsidiary or a division, the Federal Government should advocate leveraged divestitures to stakeholders as a remedy, so that the divested operation could operate independently as an employee- and stakeholder-owned company, with the violator taking back paper to provide some or all of the buyout credit; and (2) to prevent excessive concentration from occurring in the first place, potential competitors should be provided with access to sufficient low-cost capital credit, as proposed in the Capital

Homestead program, to enable them to meet economies of scale. In general, however, private monopolies never occur without some special privilege or power conferred on them by government.

Super Empowerment Zones

So-called "free enterprise zones" offer a laboratory for converting economically depressed urban and rural areas into prototypes for free market policies linked to expanded ownership. So far, however, the ownership thrust has been muted to the point of virtual silence, offering critics another example to deride as "trickle-down" economics. By adding the ownership strategy outlined in paragraphs 2 and 3 above in "Steps for Introducing CHA Monetary Reforms" and paragraph 16 in "Detailed Tax Reforms for Implementing Capital Homesteading," an enterprise zone would become a microcosm of a socially just market economy (a "*Super* Empowerment Zone") rebuilt from the bottom-up.[89]

Environmental Protection Reforms

Another way of describing pollution is "resources out of place." Recapturing those resources and keeping them from harming innocent victims and other living things generally require expensive technology. Customers must be able to afford the additional costs involved, and the technology required to preserve the environment must be financed in the least expensive way. The Capital Homestead program provides that financing and also enables the ultimate customers of corporate products to gain rising property incomes so that they can better afford the extra costs of a healthier environment.

A "special burden" tax on industrial polluters might also be considered to cover damages to victims and the environment and as an incentive to minimize pollution. This would pass on to customers the unavoidable costs of technological development, which inevitably is an imperfect process.

Multinationals and Foreign Assistance

American assistance to the developing countries could be vastly expanded, with reduced taxpayer support, if U.S.-based multinational corporations could be encouraged to link their investments overseas with the expanded ownership objectives called for under the Capital Homestead program. American programs of foreign economic development assistance should also provide technical help in implementing the Capital Homesteading model, especially in "nation-building" initiatives in world trouble spots like the West Bank, postwar Iraq, Afghanistan, the Balkans, Kashmir, etc.

For example, through use of ESOP financing the multinationals would not only convert their foreign employees into capital owners, but in so doing would automatically be creating a broadened political constituency for a global common market based on free enterprise principles.

No troops or foreign aid could offer a more effective safeguard against future expropriations and nationalizations of U.S.-based companies around the world. This would also facilitate the transfer of U.S. know-how and technology in ways that would further peaceful growth and expanded U.S. markets.

Law of the Seas Treaty

Through employee-owned subsidiaries of multinational corporations, the ocean beds could begin to be mined in ways that would simultaneously offer training, job and ownership opportunities to individuals from all parts of the world, thus enabling them to return home after 5-year tours of service as affluent individuals. The more efficient the operation, the faster affluence could be produced from the sea and injected into the developing economies. No international income redistribution scheme could conceivably do better.

Capital Homestead Planning Commission

To refine the Capital Homestead program and chart its future, the President should convene a task force of action-intellectuals and prime movers from the business, labor and political world. It could outline targets and priorities to guide the program and help in communicating it to the media and the general public. Some of its members could be appointed to a Capital Homestead Planning Commission to oversee and give continuing policy direction to the program.

U.S. Office of Expanded Capital Ownership

A Capital Homestead program should provide for a small permanent staff to administer and evaluate the progress of the President's expanded ownership programs. It should be given equal status with the Office of Management and Budget, whose tasks should be greatly simplified as the Capital Homesteading initiatives prove successful.

X.
A NEW
SOCIAL CONTRACT

A top priority during the next decade should be developing a more just "social contract" for persons employed in the private sector. To encourage this development, the laws affecting employee ownership should favor employee stock *ownership* plans (ESOPs) over employee stock *accumulation* plans (ESAPs). More favorable credit and tax incentives should be given to plans that create genuine ownership cultures and give all workers the same rights and dignity extended to its most favored shareholders, including the same voting rights as traditional shareholders.

Capital Homestead policies would encourage corporations to establish maximum ownership incentives for creating worker- and other new shareholders. Instead of inflationary "wage system" increases, workers would be educated to understand that, in the long-term, as owners they are better off gaining future increases in income through production bonuses, equity accumulations, and profit earnings, rather than through ratcheting up *fixed* labor costs. These variable increases coming from the bottom-line would be linked to their personal creative efforts as workers and as owners, and to the productivity and success of their work team and the enterprise for which they work.

As new leadership philosophies and management systems based on the principles and values of broadened capital ownership are introduced into our graduate business schools and corporations, encouraged by a new policy environment of Capital Homesteading, a new corporate culture of shared ownership rights, shared responsibilities, shared risks and shared rewards, will begin to emerge.

What Can We Learn From ESOP Failures?

It cannot be emphasized too strongly that such a cultural shift from wage-system thinking and behaviors to an ownership ethic is essential for Capital Homesteading to succeed. This is particularly true inside the enterprises that will be producing for our economy. Merely setting up an ESOP or any other worker ownership program will not guarantee a company's success or even that workers will begin thinking and acting like owners. This same cautionary point will hold true as we begin to introduce other Capital Homesteading vehicles to build ownership into other stakeholders.

Much attention has been focused on the recent bankruptcy of United Airlines, the world's second largest airline with one of the largest ESOPs established to date. Many critics in the media and on Wall Street have labeled United's downfall as clear evidence of the unworkability of employee ownership, especially majority ownership by employees. Aside, however, from the elitist undertone of such conclusions, there are some important lessons to be learned from the United experience, as one of the more thoughtful commentators pointed out:

> For employee ownership to work, employees have to act like owners, not employees. At United that didn't happen. Employees wanted their money up front, cash in the paycheck, not down the road in the form of appreciating stock or a growing company.
>
> Perhaps more importantly, employees thought the company should be run for employees, not customers....[90]

Closer examination of the United Airlines ESOP reveals other critical gaps. From the outset, there was disunity among the major bargaining groups, with the flight attendants' union choosing not to join the employee ownership program. Corporate leadership, which changed several times after the buyout, soon dropped its commitment to United's future as an employee-owned company that could out-compete other carriers by providing superior service and value to the customers. There was never a coherent plan for building and sustaining a true ownership culture where all members of the United team would think and act like owners, not just workers-for-hire.

While there were significant resources spent on "ownership education" at the beginning of the employee buyout, such efforts (which eventually dwindled away) never helped workers move out of the old style labor deal. Consequently it came as no surprise when the unions, management and employees began bargaining away any semblance of real ownership sharing, reverting back to confrontational and non-competitive wage system patterns. The employee-elected board representatives (two union, one non-union), ended up reflecting the interests of employee-owners as *employees and union members,* not as owners of the company. And finally, the unions never developed their own stake in the ownership system, where at least a portion of their dues would have been based on ownership increases and a share of bottom-line profits that they bargained for their members (in exchange for higher fixed wages and benefits).

The challenges of shifting from the "wage system" to the "ownership system" have not been limited to the U.S., birthplace of the ESOP. Recently the *Washington Post* published a front-page article citing the failure of worker-owned firms in China, where workers had been given the opportunity to purchase shares in their formerly state-owned companies, often in order to save their jobs.[91]

In one such failure, at the Jing Wine Factory in Daye, China, so-called worker-owners began skipping work, challenging their supervisors ("How can you tell [us] what to do? [We're] shareholders!"), running up costs through waste and theft, and demanding dividends even while the company was losing money. As the operation slid toward bankruptcy, the factory director (whose own performance he himself admitted to be "negligent") managed to get a loan from Communist Party officials and bought the company from the workers, becoming the sole owner of a now better-managed and profitable enterprise.

Unless one believes that working people are inherently incapable of becoming owners of their own company, it was evident from the article that the problem was not the *existence* of worker ownership. The problem was the *absence* of any ownership culture within the company. Many of the old attitudes from the former state-ownership system had merely transplanted themselves into the new context of worker ownership.[92] Furthermore, along with confusion between "ownership" and "management," what was clearly lacking were the *structures* for building an expanded ownership system within a profitable business. As the article pointed out:

> [T]he company's owners, the workers...didn't fully understand the factory's finances, nor did they believe they should get involved. Jing Wine had been privatized, but its new owners had no notion of corporate governance and lacked the mechanisms needed to keep an eye on managers. Accounting and disclosure requirements were weak, and there was no agreement even on the duties of the board of directors.[93]

As experience in U.S. ESOP companies has shown, successful worker ownership systems require ongoing financial and ownership education of the worker-shareholders, a balanced board of directors, pay and reward systems connected to the bottom-line, management accountability, and worker participation in operations and corporate governance with strict checks-and-balances of power to avoid running the company "by committee" or as if the company were a "village democracy." What was also missing from the beginning in the case of Jing Wine, were quality checks and access by workers to sufficient capital credit to buy the firm, hire competent management, and adequately capitalize the company.

A true and lasting ownership culture won't happen by magic. What is needed is a new model for business leadership and management that will introduce, develop and sustain the new culture. One such ownership-based model, called "Justice-Based Management[SM]" ("JBM[SM]"), is uniquely constructed upon free market principles of economic and social justice and private property.[94]

JBM[SM] stresses that there are certain fundamentals that are critical for establishing a successful ownership culture. You need leadership that promotes a compelling vision and the shared values of economic and social justice, along with sound practices of business. You need well-designed organizational structures and processes that teach, reward, develop and empower all team members as workers *and* owners. You need a human sense of proportion in pay scale between the highest and lowest paid worker.[95] You need a corporate commitment to building significant,[96] not token, amounts of ownership into every worker. You need something like the republican form of government, where company governance and management systems are designed to achieve a "structured diffusion of power" led by leaders willing to be transparent and accountable to all members of the "going concern." And, because changing people's thinking and patterns of behavior takes time and constant reinforcement, you need patience and long-term commitment by a critical mass of people within the culture.[97]

With a broadened base of empowered worker-owners and other shareholders, corporations will have to become more transparent and their boards of directors more accountable. The role of managers, rather than being eliminated, will become even more critical for creating healthy, profitable and broadly owned companies, as their teaching and long-term strategic functions increase. "Empowerment" and "delivering value to the customer", will become more than the mere buzzwords they often are today. Within a corporate system and economic environment of broadened ownership, empowerment and value will become key determinants of a company's ability to grow and compete in the global marketplace.

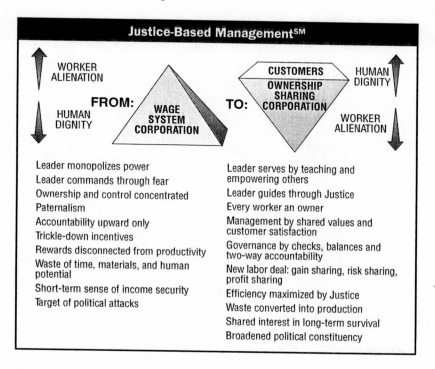

Justice-Based Management℠

FROM: WAGE SYSTEM CORPORATION	TO: OWNERSHIP SHARING CORPORATION
Leader monopolizes power	Leader serves by teaching and empowering others
Leader commands through fear	Leader guides through Justice
Ownership and control concentrated	Every worker an owner
Paternalism	Management by shared values and customer satisfaction
Accountability upward only	Governance by checks, balances and two-way accountability
Trickle-down incentives	New labor deal: gain sharing, risk sharing, profit sharing
Rewards disconnected from productivity	Efficiency maximized by Justice
Waste of time, materials, and human potential	Waste converted into production
Short-term sense of income security	Shared interest in long-term survival
Target of political attacks	Broadened political constituency

Capital Homesteading and the Labor Movement

Profound changes are taking place in the labor movement. From a peak of 35 percent of the American nonagricultural work force in 1954, union membership fell to 15.8 percent of employed wage and salaried workers in 1992. Evidencing an even more dramatic decline, just 9.8 percent of all U.S. private sector nonagricultural employees today are represented by a union, compared with 41.8 percent of federal, state and local government workers.[98]

Some within the labor movement are therefore questioning whether the old modes of thinking are sufficient or even viable. Irving Bluestone, former Vice President of the United Auto Workers, and his son and professor of political economy, Barry Bluestone, note in their book *Negotiating the Future: A Labor Perspective on American Business:*

> [I]n recognition of the requirements of the global marketplace, we believe that labor and management have more in common than in conflict. Finding a new structure for labor-management relations that rests on common interests and mutual concerns is, we argue, a *sine qua non* for economic prosperity if not outright survival.[99]

Justice-Based Management[SM] seeks to transform the corporation into a more inclusive and just mechanism for delivering value to the customer and generating broadly owned wealth for workers and shareholders. It is also designed to transform the labor union into a social institution for delivering economic justice for all members of society through expanded capital ownership.

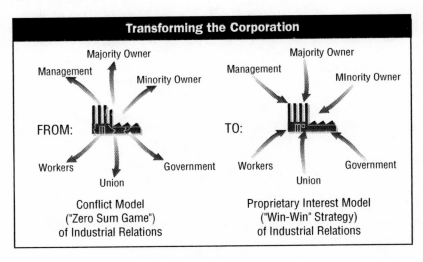

Transforming the Corporation

Majority Owner

Management

Minority Owner

FROM:

Workers

Union

Government

Conflict Model
("Zero Sum Game")
of Industrial Relations

Majority Owner

Management

MInority Owner

TO:

Workers

Union

Government

Proprietary Interest Model
("Win-Win" Strategy)
of Industrial Relations

The union was democratic society's original answer for addressing injustices at the workplace that attended the birth of the Industrial Revolution. In fact, unionism was born to bring social and economic justice for working people, particularly nonmanagement workers. This is, and will remain, a valid social need. The problem with the labor movement, from the standpoint of Justice-Based Management, is that it became transformed into an instrument for accommodating to the wage system and perpetuating conflict between workers and management, and thus not for achieving justice.[100] And in some cases, it can be fairly said, unions have empowered their leaders, not their members.

Rather than seeking direct ownership and empowerment for its members (which necessitates a thriving private sector and profitable companies), unions have sought to raise fixed labor wages and benefits. This strategy, in the long-run, is unrealistic, violates distributive justice,[101] and will make businesses noncompetitive. And it ultimately defeats the union's social purpose of protecting the rights and long-term welfare of workers, and promoting the common good of all members of society.

On the other hand, no matter how benevolent or participatory a company's management, there is always a human tendency at some point to withhold power from others. (This stems from the underlying fear of those who hold power that others may use their power unwisely or against them.) Whether the institution is a worker-shareholders' association formed voluntarily within the company (like the Solidarista associations that have been established in Central America) or whether it is a body organized by a union, nonmanagement worker-owners need some form of democratic organization that has the internal solidarity of the workers. This would give workers the status, access to information and power necessary to bargain effectively and settle grievances with management when they arise.

What would be the new role of the labor movement under Capital Homesteading? Simply, unions should become facilitators of Justice-Based Management[SM], cooperating with management on ways to increase productiveness and profitability, helping their members negotiate for larger ownership stakes, profit sharing and full shareholder rights, and for using their considerable political influence for promoting expanded capital ownership opportunities for all citizens. In sizeable enterprises, the union or similar body should also organize nonworker stockholders for asserting their ownership rights and prerogatives vis-à-vis management and the board of directors.

To realize its own stake in the growth pie of expanding ownership, the union should explore ways to expand its checkoff system to cover new capital formation, and the worker's growing stake in cash bonuses, dividends, and company stock. Potentially, a checkoff on ownership system benefits offers the union a much bigger revenue pie than the counterproductive checkoff on wage system benefits.[102] Under Justice-Based Management, and within an environment of Capital Homesteading, unions will recognize that by promoting the long-term good of the corporation, they can bring long-term good for working people.

The New Role of Wall Street Under Capital Homesteading

We are not proposing the elimination of the stock market and its trading of secondary issuances, or its traditional role in initial public offerings (IPOs). Under a Capital Homesteading program, Wall Street would continue to serve the speculative inclinations of the wealthy and other investors outside of the Capital Homesteading system.

As Fed Chairman Alan Greenspan recently stated, financial market innovations such as the creation of a secondary market for home mortgages and the widespread use of derivatives were instrumental in helping the U.S. economy weather the huge stock market decline and the aftereffects of the September 11th terrorist attacks. Greenspan noted that such financial innovations that allow the breaking down of various types of risks that can be sold to parties able to bear them, "significantly lowered the costs of, and expanded the opportunities for, hedging risks."[103]

Thus, an expanded role of Wall Street could be to offer a market for the trading of "derivatives" in order to hedge risks of new stock issuances under Capital Homesteading. This use of derivatives would provide not only an expanding role for those with strong gambling urges who can afford the high risks of derivative trading. It would also offer a market-based solution for assessing risks for new share issuances under Capital Homesteading, thus providing lenders and capital credit reinsurers a basis for determining premium rates for capital credit insurance (*see above*, "The FCIC and CCRC: Managing Risk Through Capital Credit Insurance and Re-Insurance.")

Under Capital Homesteading stockbrokers will continue doing what they're supposed to do, except that now they will have more customers with more disposable income to spend. However the difference is that Main Street, not Wall Street, will drive the economic fortunes of America and its citizens. Growth and not speculation will be the foundation of our retirement and income maintenance systems. A truly free, more just, and more efficient market system can then begin to operate.

XI.
RECOMMENDATIONS
FOR NEXT STEPS

Transforming a system is no small task. It means changing outdated paradigms and the mindsets that cling to them, which in turn requires effective and continuing communications of transformational concepts. The experience of ESOP pioneers working in the early 1970s to establish employee stock ownership plans within U.S. law[104] offers a "four-pronged" communications model for gaining acceptance and implementation of revolutionary ideas contained in the binary economic model. The four "prongs" (which can be moved on simultaneously or as opportunities arise) are: (1) Educate people about the concept (a slow, but necessary step); (2) Get the message to "prime movers" (such as the U.S. president) who can communicate it to a mass constituency; (3) Organize large numbers of people to push for the change; and (4) Show that the idea works.[105]

Of the four prongs, the last — "Show that it works" — communicates the message most quickly and perhaps, most convincingly, to most people. The efficacy of "ESOP financing" (using capital credit repayable with future profits to turn workers without collateral or available savings into shareholders of their companies) has been proven conclusively. A handful of companies, within the roughly 10,000 U.S. ESOP companies today, are exemplars of "Justice-Based Management[SM]," exhibiting in microcosm how business organizations can transform themselves into "ownership cultures."[106]

Before demonstrations can take place, it will be necessary for experienced professionals, policymakers, academics, and business, labor and community leaders to thoroughly critique and develop the criteria for implementing Capital Homesteading. The following are some practical steps that could help move ideas into successful applications.

First Steps for Promoting Capital Homesteading in U.S. Economic Policy

- *Convene a Blue-Ribbon Roundtable Discussion of the Capital Homesteading Model for Saving Social Security.*

  Bring together scholars from conservative and liberal think tanks to critique and discuss the merits of the Capital Homesteading proposal for saving Social Security.

- *Convene Leaders of Insurance Industry on Capital Homestead Insurance.*

  Have experts within the insurance industry assess the insurability of Capital Homesteading loans and recommend alternatives for establishing the Federal Capital Insurance Corporation and Capital Credit Reinsurance Corporation.

- *Convene a "Hometown, USA" Task Force to Plan and Promote a National Exemplar for 21ˢᵗ Century Communities.*

  An interdisciplinary task force would develop the socio-economic specifications for a model community based on Capital Homesteading principles, including the use of a citizen-owned community investment corporation for participatory land planning and development. The "Hometown, USA" task force would also determine the criteria and process for selecting the site for a major demonstration in the designated community. The "new community" model would be designed as a 21ˢᵗ Century prototype that could be replicated throughout the United States and exported to global markets. The task force would also structure and recommend funding for a national design competition, which would incorporate the most advanced Hydrogen Age energy, telecommunication, and construction technologies, offering a new wealth-producing base for all citizens of Hometown, USA.

- *Develop an Econometric Model Based on a National Capital Homestead Model.*

  We would strongly recommend the development of a new binary economic-based planning tool for policymakers. The problem with existing econometric models is that they are based on "one-factor" assumptions that presume that most people will earn the bulk of their life's earnings from labor, and can only acquire capital by using their accumulated savings and current consumption incomes.

Using binary assumptions, this new econometric model would help policymakers project rates of growth in the U.S. economy and the impact on distribution of wealth and income under Capital Homesteading scenarios. It would help track the inflationary impact and stability of the currency under Capital Homesteading conditions, as well as the capitalization needs of the private sector and the percentage of CHA financing to be made available through the money-creating mechanisms of the Federal Reserve System. It would also overcome the problem that most financing projections tend to assume after-tax, rather than pre-tax levels, thus distorting the time frame needed to repay capital loans as well as levels of capital incomes generated that could provide a second income for every American.

- *Develop a Model for Teaching Social Morality within Academia.*

  To begin shifting people's thinking from wage system to ownership system assumptions, it is critical that we begin educating academics, business and labor leaders, policymakers in economic theories, moral principles and practical applications of Capital Homesteading. CESJ is now working with leaders and faculty at Dayton University and the University of the District of Columbia to create an academic base for the ideas of Capital Homesteading, binary economics and Justice-Based Management. One idea under discussion is the establishment of an interdisciplinary School of Philosophy, Ethics and Leadership that would offer graduate degrees in Social Morality, Binary Economics, and Justice-Based Management. Initial seed funding should be raised for a series of lectures and seminars covering these subjects.

Demonstrating Capital Homesteading

The Center for Economic and Social Justice (CESJ) is helping to launch several projects that would demonstrate various aspects of Capital Homesteading, on the enterprise, local community, city and national level. The local community and model city demonstrations are perhaps most relevant for showing how Capital Homesteading would offer a viable alternative for saving the U.S. Social Security system. These demonstrations would draw attention to the Capital Homesteading concept and are designed to facilitate replication in similar situations.

- *Demonstration at the Enterprise Level —*
  Model Worker-Owned Garment Factory in Bangladesh.

  This model company is being launched in Bangladesh as a laboratory for demonstrating how access to sufficient capital credit can lift the poor out of poverty and enable them to compete in the global marketplace. The company, JBM Garments Ltd., which will be owned and managed by 300-400 women for producing quality garments for the US market, offers a model for eliminating sweatshops. It will create a new "social justice" standard for manufacturers, and a Justice-Based Management^{SM} label that could provide marketing advantages to the project.

  As part of a multi-phase development process, CESJ is working with the Marianist Social Justice Collaborative to organize (1) a blue-ribbon panel of business, labor, academic and religious leaders to formulate the JBM^{SM} certification criteria and process for licensing companies to use a "JBM^{SM} label" for marketing to customers seeking social justice alternatives to sweat shop-produced goods; (2) another independent group to certify and audit JBM^{SM}-certified companies, and (3) a for-profit JBM^{SM} marketing company made up of entrepreneurs committed to social and economic justice to market exclusively JBM^{SM}-labeled goods and services within the U.S., Europe and other major global markets. The JBM^{SM} marketing group could be launched initially as an entrepreneurial project by students, faculty and recent graduates under the auspices of a university committed to teaching Justice-Based Management^{SM}, binary economics and social and economic justice.

  CESJ is working with the Institute of Integrated Rural Development in Bangladesh, which has access to funding sources within the Marianist religious network. CESJ is also working with religious, business, union leaders, lawyers and academics in Bangladesh through the local chapter of CESJ in Dhaka. The proposed model would also offer a positive alternative to the emerging protectionist and anti-globalization agenda of many labor unions and mercantilist companies.

- *Demonstration at the Community and City Level —*
  "Old Man River City" Project in East St. Louis, Illinois.

  Legislation supporting "free enterprise zones" would offer a laboratory for converting economically depressed urban and rural areas into prototypes for free market policies linked to expanded ownership.

One such demonstration has been proposed for the citizens of East St. Louis — the creation of a new 21st Century city, called "Old Man River City." It weds the "post-scarcity/shared abundance" thinking of Buckminster Fuller, Louis Kelso, Martin Luther King, Jr., and William Ferree.[107] The project is being led by Illinois State Rep. Wyvetter Younge. It is designed to create a new industrial base, owned by worker- and citizen-shareholders. The new industries to be introduced involve the commercialization of advanced waste-to-energy systems developed within the U.S. space and energy programs and integrated by Equitech International LLC, which holds systems patents on these technologies.

The demonstration would be implemented in four phases: (1) saving St. Mary's Hospital and converting it into a national model for comprehensive health care; (2) the creation of a 50-apartment complex, which would integrate advanced waste-to-energy and telecommunications technologies; (3) establishment of a "Jubilee" satellite town, that would also incorporate those advanced technologies; and (4) the realization of the long-range vision of Old Man River City, a model city where control of and profits from the land and industrial base will be spread among all citizens as shareholders.

This project, which would ultimately be financed through the discount window of the St. Louis Fed, needs about $500,000 to perform all the necessary initial technical and feasibility studies, plus an additional $500,000 for community education, outreach, and organizing for social justice initiatives.

The JUBILEE Group (whose acronym stands for "Justice-Based Initiatives for Life, Equity and Equality") is working in East St. Louis to save financially struggling St. Mary's Hospital, the only trauma center in the local community. The group is organizing a buyout that would convert this hospital into a national exemplar of a comprehensive family health care system to be owned by all health providers, employees, and health plan subscribers, supplemented by health care vouchers for the poor. The objective is to create a model that can be replicated nationally as a private sector way to provide universal health care from cradle to grave.

- *Demonstration of Capital Homesteading at the National Level —
  The "Abraham Federation" for Citizens of the West Bank and Gaza.*

As described more fully in the paper, "The Abraham Federation: A
New Framework for Peace in the Middle East,"[108] this model has
been proposed to apply Capital Homesteading as the economic foundation for a new nation state, one founded on the sovereignty of
each person living in the "Holy Land." Based on the U.S. model of a
constitutional government and binary economics, it would be structured to achieve a religiously pluralistic "nation of owners."

Starting with the West Bank, Gaza and East Jerusalem, the Abraham
Federation concept could offer a fundamentally inclusionary, post-
scarcity model of nation-building that could be applied for bringing peace through justice in many conflict-torn areas of the world,
including postwar Iraq, Afghanistan, the Balkans, Kashmir, North-
ern Ireland and East Timor. Once the Abraham Federation has been
established from its initial base as an effective, inclusionary and more
synergistic model, other nations in the Middle East, including Israel, could become persuaded to join the Abraham Federation and
participate in its greater potential for peace through justice and
shared prosperity.

- *Demonstration for Rebuilding Post-War Iraq.*

One proposed application of the Abraham Federation that should
be given immediate consideration is to democratize the ownership
of Iraq's oil industry by converting the state-owned oil company
into a joint stock corporation and distributing its shares free of charge
to every Iraqi citizen and exile returning to Iraq. (*For more detail,
see* Appendix 9, "Executive Summary: A New Model of Nation-Building for Citizens of Iraq.") Combined with central banking and other
economic reforms, along with the technical assistance from the U.S.
and the international community, this would be an important first
step in helping Iraqis build a just market economy and a free, democratic society

Misguided and elitist "economic reconstruction" programs are about
to be foisted on Iraq's people. One such proposal calls for opening
up ownership of Iraq's oil and other industries to 100% foreign ownership, as well as to Iraqis who enriched themselves under Saddam
Hussein's regime. To Iraqis convinced that the War in Iraq was sim-

ply a ploy for U.S. companies to take over Iraq's wealth, such a short-sighted proposal would throw gasoline on an already explosive situation. The Abraham Federation framework, on the other hand, would offer more than just a job for the average Iraqi. It would offer every citizen the opportunity and means to acquire property, the economic foundation for true self-determination and sovereignty.

Potential Sources of Seed Funding for Capital Homesteading Demonstration Projects

The projects listed above need seed money to begin their initial phase, which would include:

- Education and community outreach on the principles and applications of Capital Homesteading, including Justice-Based Management as the ownership sharing leadership philosophy and management system for companies and communities.

- Developing each project's strategic plan and blueprint with people in the communities affected.

- Developing a local leadership core necessary for organizing and sustaining each project.

- Identifying additional sources of seed money needed for feasibility studies, technical assistance, educational programs, etc.

To fund the initial phase of these demonstration projects, foundations and economic development agencies could help establish a Capital Homesteading Technical Assistance Fund, by providing challenge grants to be matched by other foundations and other donor sources within the Christian, Jewish, Islamic and other religious communities, as well as by other funding organizations promoting broad-based economic empowerment.

XII.
CONCLUSION:
BUILDING A NATION OF OWNERS

In the 19th century Abraham Lincoln's Homestead Act enabled many Americans to own a piece of our land frontier. While the once abundant land frontier eventually closed, Lincoln's development strategy resulted in an agricultural success story that laid the foundation for America's rise to industrial prominence in the 20th century.

If we are to rebuild the free enterprise system — from the ground up — we must rediscover the profound wisdom that George Mason inscribed in one of America's founding documents as a fundamental human right, and what Abraham Lincoln sought to embed in America's economic policies. Today we must open up opportunities for more and more citizens to gain a viable private property stake in the virtually limitless technological frontier. We would argue that America needs a 21st Century counterpart to Lincoln's program of homesteading — today we need *Capital* Homesteading.

Expanding the number of people who derive a significant portion of their income from the ownership of productive assets would increase the tax base and decrease government expenditures for education, welfare and other social service entitlements. By relieving the growing burden on Social Security, Capital Homesteading would mend the growing generational rift between young workers forced to pay higher and higher social security taxes and retirees receiving social security benefits. And it would provide an investment pool for American business to use to grow and expand, becoming more competitive with low-cost foreign labor, without the need for protectionist trade barriers.

Capital Homesteading offers numerous advantages over conventional approaches to Social Security. This new policy framework:

- Provides the liquidity through the money-creating powers of the Federal Reserve to stimulate noninflationary private sector growth, rather than relying on manipulating the tax system.

- Is based on a more unifying expanded ownership paradigm, in contrast to the wage system paradigm which inevitably generates conflict — between those who have and those who don't; between management, unions and workers; between low-wage nations and high-wage nations.

- Closes the growing wealth gap between haves and have-nots without confiscating the property of existing owners.

- Promotes an ownership ethic that balances rights and responsibilities, risks and rewards, engendering an ownership culture throughout society.

- Builds a broadened political constituency for free markets, private property and limited economic power of the state.

- Shifts from speculation to real growth and production, from gambling in the Wall Street casino to investing prudently in business projects that must prove self-justifying and which are subject to the disciplines of loan repayment.

- Generates investment and ownership through "future savings" rather than past savings, allowing people to satisfy their demand by spending their incomes on consumption, purchasing the goods and services produced, which in turn helps producers pay off their capital loans, and creates additional consumer demand to justify new capital investment.

- Moves people from relying on the false promises of security offered under welfare state policies, to participating as owners in the growth of the private sector economy.

- Shifts people from a reliance on the tax system (and other workers' contributions) for their future retirement incomes to their own independent source of capital income.

- Promotes a healthier environment by providing expanded sources of financing for sustainable, green growth.[109]

Real change comes slowly. Transforming people's mindsets and behaviors — and moving from scarcity assumptions to shared abundance possibilities — is an evolutionary process. It starts by changing the opportunity environment, the technological environment and the institutional environment.

Capital Homesteading will not bear fruit overnight. It will not bring utopia. But, as a new direction for American economic policy, it will challenge us to educate and organize ourselves as a true democracy of empowered citizens. It will require the teaching and practice of a new philosophy of servant leadership, not only in politics, but also in business and other facets of human society. It will demand that we reassess our common values as a society, and equip our children with the moral principles, sense of rights and responsibilities, and global vision to live and prosper in an increasingly interdependent world community.

Capital Homesteading is designed to close the technology and knowledge gap between those at the top and those at the bottom. It can provide people the financial means to seek the best educational opportunities for themselves and their children. Even so, society will have to reorient its educational system, from training people for economic toil to teaching them to pursue leisure work and lifelong learning.

Some have raised a sociological and moral problem that could occur in a society where people "own the robots" that have eliminated the need for economic toil. They see a future population of "couch potatoes" who sit around all day watching television, wallowing in a world of excess and shallow consumerism.

Kelso, Adler and other binary economists, however, envision a different scenario where all citizens are economically liberated to pursue the "work of civilization," as well as volunteerism, lifelong education and self-improvement. The sorts of unpaid "leisure work" that could be opened up to more people would include: law, medicine, politics, teaching, religious vocations, counseling, senior care, day care, charity, philanthropy, art patronage, inventing, traveling, writing, art, music, exploration, scientific research, and any other form of creative work that people would do for the love and fulfillment of that work.[110]

A successful program of Capital Homesteading could have another positive impact on society. A two-income family (where today both parents are forced to work one or more jobs each) could now derive at least one of those incomes from capital ownership. This would allow parents to spend more time with their children and provide the critical moral education that takes place within the family.

How people adapt to the cultural shift in the nature of work, and how they use their "free time," will largely be shaped by the moral values of that society and the educational systems that nurture those values. The quality of our society will be determined by more than our standard of living. To what shall we aspire as a nation of the 21st Century? To become merely a society of accumulators? Or shall we strive toward the highest human ideals, toward a post-scarcity society, an "Athens without slaves?"

In the meantime, launching a national program of Capital Homesteading could help to level today's grossly uneven economic playing field. Every citizen could start to gain real economic independence through a direct ownership stake in America's future. By our example, America could bring new hope to those who thirst for economic and social justice, especially the poor and oppressed throughout the world.

What better place to start than turning today's Social Security crisis into an unparalleled opportunity for realizing more fully America's greatest promise — that of liberty and justice for all?

NOTES

Executive Summary

1 Originally named by Dr. Norman A. Bailey, the "Federal National Capital Credit Corporation" ("FNCCC"). See Norman A. Bailey, "A Nation of Owners: A Plan for Closing the Growing U.S. Knowledge and Capital Asset Gaps," *The International Economy*, September/October 2000.

2 Dr. Bailey called this the "Federal National Capital Insurance Corporation" ("FNCIC").

Introduction

3 Michael Grunwald, "Terror's Damage: Calculating the Devastation," *The Washington Post*, October 28, 2001, p.A12.

4 *Ibid.*

5 Social Security Board, "Security in Your Old Age" Washington, DC: Government Printing Office, 1935.

6 Michael Tanner, "Privatizing Social Security: A Big Boost for the Poor," report by the Cato Project on Social Security Privatization, July 26, 1996, SSP No. 4, p.8

7 Tim Penny, "Case for Return to Original Intent of Social Security," *The Wall Street Journal*, July 11, 1988.

8 Jagadeesh Gokhale and Kent Smetters, "How to Balance a $43 Trillion Checkbook," *The Wall Street Journal*, July 17, 2003, p. A16. This editorial page article in the *Wall Street Journal* examined the economic and demographic assumptions of the Bush administration's budget for fiscal year 2004. The authors calculated, in present value dollars, a shortfall of $7 trillion in the amount of money that Social Security will have to pay out for future benefits, compared to the money in its trust fund plus the money it is expected to collect in future taxes. Medicare, they calculated, would face a deficit of *$36 trillion*. Mr. Gokhale, a visiting scholar at the American Enterprise Institute, was a consultant to the U.S. Treasury. Mr. Smetters, a professor at Wharton and a member of the National Bureau of Economic Research, was Deputy Assistant Secretary for Economic policy at the Treasury. They are the authors of "Fiscal and Generational Imbalances: New Budget Measures for New Budget Priorities," published in July 2003 by the American Enterprise Institute.

9 Phillip Longman, "Justice Between Generations," *The Atlantic Monthly*, June 1985, pp. 73-81, quoting Paul Samuelson in a 1967 *Newsweek* editorial.

10 Edward D. Berkowitz, "The Insecurity of Privatization," *The Washington Post*, Outlook Section, December 8, 1996. p. C1.

11 Charles J. Zwick and Peter A. Lewis, "Apocalypse Not: Social Security Crisis is Overblown," *The Wall Street Journal*, April 11, 2001, p. A18.

12 Starting 2003, only wages and salaries below $87,000 are subject to Social Security's Old Age, Survivors and Disability Insurance (OASDI) tax rate of 12.4 percent. An addi-

tional payroll tax of 2.9 percent is imposed for Medicare's Hospital Insurance, without a taxable maximum. See Table, "OASDI Contribution and Benefit Base" October 18, 2002, *Social Security Administration* web site at www.ssa.gov.

13 Daniel Yergin, "Herd on the Street: A Quarterly Stampede," *The Washington Post,* June 6, 2002, p. B1

14 Yergin, *ibid.*

15 Yergin, *ibid.* As of December 17, 2002, the Dow is over 8600.

16 This is the idea that you buy a certain stock because you think other people will think that stock is worth more later than you think it's worth now. In other words you're counting on them being the greater fool. See endnote 15.

17 P.J. O'Rourke, *Eat the Rich: A Treatise on Economics,* Atlantic Monthly Press: New York, 1998, pp. 243-245.

18 Tate Hausman, "'Booming' Economy Benefits the Rich, Busts the Rest" AlterNet. URL: www.alternet.org/PublicArchive/Hausman924.html.

I. The Proposal in Brief

19 Greg Ip, "Fed is Overhauling Procedure for Discount-Window Loans," *The Wall Street Journal,* May 20, 2002, p. A2. The Fed is now trying to encourage direct loans to commercial banks through the discount window as a way of preventing volatility in the key Federal Funds Rate caused by temporary shortages in the required cash reserves of commercial member banks. The discount window had largely fallen into disuse, acquiring a "stigma" as the last resort for banks needing cash. But when the September 11 terrorist attacks disrupted banks' access to the money markets, the Fed announced to the public on September 12 that the discount window was available and that it intended to "get rid of" the "alleged stigma." The week following September 11, discount window loans topped a record $45 billion, where they normally fluctuate between $25 million and $300 million. While this step by the Fed may signal growing support for opening up the discount window for private sector growth, there is a danger. Without the Capital Homesteading requirement of linking new growth to new ownership opportunities for every citizen, the discount mechanism could accelerate the gross concentration of wealth and income.

20 The maximum taxed, indexed to wages, as of 2003. *Source: Strengthening Social Security and Creating Personal Wealth for All Americans,* President's Commission to Strengthen Social Security, December 11, 2001, p.3. Updated by "OASDI Contribution and Benefit Base," Social Security Administration web site at www.ssa.gov, October 18, 2002.

21 The annual new capital formation in all sectors of the American economy, as of the third quarter of 2001, consisted of (in $Billions):

New equipment and software, private	$1,019.4 B (Table B-19)
New equipment and software, public, state and local	63.6 B (Table B-21)
New equipment and software, Federal nondefense	36.4 B (Table B-21)
Structures, nonresidential, private, etc.	276.8 B (Table B-19)
Structures, public, state and local	145.7 B (Table B-21)
Structures, Federal nondefense	9.4 B (Table B-21)
Residential structures	380.5 B (Table B-19)
TOTAL Nondefense PRODUCTIVE ASSETS:	**$1,931.8 B**
PER CAPITA, AT 286 MILLION PEOPLE IN 2001:	**$6,755.00**

Sources:
Tables B-19 and B-21 from *Economic Report of the President,* February 2002.

Figures are for third quarter 2001; probably lower in 2002.

U.S. population figures are from the 2001 report of the Department of Commerce (Bureau of Economic Analysis and Bureau of the Census)

22 The percentage of real productive growth financed through Capital Homesteading is a political decision. Theoretically, all new growth could be financed in this way, but this would restrict the past savings of accumulators from being invested in high-risk ventures that would not meet the eligibility criteria for Capital Homesteading credit. We would recommend a Capital Homesteading target of at least "50%" of the nation's new capital formation. This is perhaps a question that could be examined within an econometric model, as included in the "Recommendations for Next Steps" section of this report.

23 According to a 1987 database by R. Buzzell and B. Gale, the average pre-tax return-on-investment (ROI) for businesses competing in unattractive markets was 13.4 percent, compared to 31.3 percent for those competing in attractive markets. See Stanley F. Slater and Eric M. Olson, "A Fresh Look at Industry and Market Analysis," *Business Horizons,* Indiana University Graduate School of Business, Jan.-Feb. 2002, v.45, p. 15.

24 A more top-down and paternalistic approach to Capital Homesteading would be to make the low-cost CH loans available to businesses so long as they channeled the Fed-monetized credit through expanded ownership vehicles such as ESOPs, CSOPs, CICs, producer cooperatives, etc., set up for the benefit of workers, customers, or local residents respectively, who would become the owners of the new capital. The problem with this approach, as evidenced by the experience of most ESOPs, is that the worker-share-holders are often treated by management as second-class shareholders with no effective control over their own property. Worker- and other shareholders could hold management much more accountable if management had to come to *them* for the money.

25 See Norman A. Bailey, "A Nation of Owners," *ibid.* Dr. Bailey points out the ultimate absurdity of having the U.S. currency backed by government debt, as represented by Treasury paper. At the time when the U.S. debt was "in danger" of being paid off, Dr. Bailey quipped that if that were ever to happen, we would suddenly have no backing for the dollar. Under our current monetary system, the government must stay in debt, saddling future generations of taxpayers with the interest costs.

26 Michael Barone, "The Deeper Currents," The National Interest column, *U.S. News and World Report,* November 11, 2002, p. 34

27 Michael Tanner, "Privatizing Social Security: A Big Boost for the Poor," report by the Cato Project on Social Security Privatization, July 26, 1996, SSP No. 4.

28 Tanner, *ibid.,* p. 1.

29 Tanner, *ibid.,* p. 8.

30 Ted Halstead and Michael Lind, *The Radical Center: The Future of American Politics,* New York: Doubleday, 2001, pp. 99-102.

II. The Concept of Capital Homesteading

31 Charles Morrison was the author of *An Essay on the Relations Between Labour and Capital,* London: Longman, Brown, Green, and Longmans, 1854.

32 Morrison was favorably inclined to the use of capital credit by associations of workers, but did not see how this could be achieved. As the workers lacked collateral, no capitalist would lend at low rates of interest, while high rates of interest would ensure that the business would fail through inability to meet the debt service payments. Conse-

quently, Morrison ruled out democratic access to capital credit not on principle, but on the grounds of practicality and expedience — a problem of defective institutions and outdated thinking. According to Morrison:

"A fourth course is, that the working man should become the sole proprietors and conductors of a business, supplying the requisite capital either from their own savings or by borrowing. The cooperative associations of workmen of different trades, established by the Provisional Government of France in 1848, were an attempt to prove by actual experiment, the advantages of this system. The capital of these was supplied by the Government as a loan from the Treasury: and it is hardly necessary to add that the result has been unsuccessful. It would not, however, be fair to judge of the principle by such an example. Supposing it to be tried under more favourable circumstances, and without the violation of principle involved in the advance of funds derived from taxation, it is not probably that the resource of borrowing could be made use of to any great extent. For, at the ordinary rate of interest, it cannot be expected that capitalists will risk their funds by lending them to a body of poor men, who would have little capital of their own to furnish a sufficient margin for security. If, on the other hand, the money were borrowed at a usurious rate of interest, the prospect of benefit to the borrowers would be small. The establishment of such cooperative associations to any considerable extent would therefore require the possession of a sufficient amount of savings by great numbers of the working classes to furnish the indispensable funds for their operations." (Morrison, *ibid.*, pp. 121 – 122)

33 Ronald Reagan, speech before the Young Americans for Freedom, San Francisco, CA, July 20, 1974.

34 Ronald Reagan, "Tax Plan No. 1," *Viewpoint with Ronald Reagan,* radio show (Ronald Reagan urges ESOP financing), February 1975.

35 Joint Economic Committee of Congress, *The 1976 Joint Economic Report,* March 10, 1976, pp. 98-100. See also "Broadening Capital Ownership," letter to the editor from Senator Hubert H. Humphrey, Chairman of the Joint Economic Committee, published in the *Washington Post,* July 20, 1976.

36 As quoted in *Strengthening Social Security and Creating Personal Wealth for All Americans,* report of the President's Commission, December 11, 2001, p. 6.

37 "Remarks by President Bush and President Putin to Russian Exchange Students and Students of Crawford High School," Crawford High School, Crawford, Texas, November 15, 2001, Office of the White House Press Secretary. (Complete text available from http://www.usembassy.it/file2001_11/alia/a1111504.htm)

38 Thomas S. Kuhn, *The Structure of Scientific Revolutions.* Second Edition, London, U.K.: The University of Chicago Press, 1970.

39 Robert Ashford and Rodney Shakespeare, *Binary Economics: The New Paradigm,* University Press of America: Lanham, Maryland, 1999, p. 70.

40 Ashford and Shakespeare, *ibid.*, p. 71.

41 The term "binary economics" refers to the two fundamental factors of production — labor and capital (in all their various forms). In a global, technologically advancing economy, it becomes increasingly important for every person to be able to produce both through his labor and vicariously through his capital in order to generate a viable income. Over time, in fact, income from one's capital could become the predominant source of one's purchasing power. If every person had access to both sources of income, supply and demand would be able to be synchronized, the need for government redis-

tribution would be virtually eliminated, and the economy could grow at faster rates, without inflation. An in-depth, scholarly discussion of Kelsonian economics appears in the book, *Binary Economics: The New Paradigm* by Robert Ashford and Rodney Shakespeare, University Press of America: Lanham, Maryland, 1999; *Two Factor Theory: The Economics of Reality* by Louis Kelso and Patricia Hetter Kelso, New York: Random House, 1967; and "A New Look at Prices and Money: The Kelsonian Binary Model for Achieving Growth Without Inflation," *Journal of Socio-Economics*, Vol. 30, 2001, 495-515, by Norman G. Kurland (*see* Appendix 4).

42 A recent article in the *Wall Street Journal* describes a growing trend called "lights-out manufacturing" — unattended operation with remote access." The fourth-generation head of Evans Findings, a 73-year-old, family-owned manufacturing company, states: "The future of manufacturing for me is doing it whenever possible with no labor at all." (See "Workers Not Included," Timothy Aeppel, *The Wall Street Journal*, 11/19/02, p. B1.) We are also witnessing the elimination of human labor in more than only blue-collar manufacturing areas. A forecast of future trends that appeared in a 1982 *Business Week* article ("Artificial Intelligence," March 8, 1982) has been gradually coming to pass:

"Experts agree that 'thinking' computers almost certainly will replace people in millions of jobs in many industries and offices. 'Currently, around 25 to 18 million people are employed in manufacturing in America. I expect it to go down to less than 3 million by the year 2010,' predicts Carnegie-Mellon's [Dr. Raj D.] Reddy. 'So we have only 30 years to decide what those millions of people are going to be doing.' He adds that society cannot expect the slack to be taken up by jobs in the service industries, leisure, research and white-collar work — 'because even there the same revolution is coming.' Reddy worries that 'no one (in power) understands what's happening or grasps the extent of what's coming.'"

43 Louis O. Kelso and Mortimer J. Adler, *The Capitalist Manifesto*, Random House: New York, 1958. See also "Economic Justice in the Age of the Robot," Norman G. Kurland, published in *Curing World Poverty: The Role of Property*, John H. Miller, ed., Social Justice Review, St. Louis Missouri, 1994, pp. 61-74.

44 For an in-depth discussion of how Kelso's binary economics would allow Say's Law of Markets to operate, *see* Appendix 4, "A New Look at Prices and Money," *ibid.*, pp. 505-507.)

45 Thomas Sowell, *Say's Law: An Historical Analysis*. Princeton, New Jersey: The Princeton University Press, 1972.

46 For one of the most scholarly presentations of Kelsonian economics, see Robert Ashford, "The Binary Economics of Louis Kelso: A Democratic Private Property System for Growth and Justice" in *Curing World Poverty: The New Role of Property* (St. Louis: Social Justice Review, 1994). Also see "Kelsonian Monetary Weapons for Fighting Inflation" (Proceedings of the Eastern Economics Association Conference, April 1977), and "Money and Prices: Rapid Growth Without Inflation Under Kelso Plan for Expanded Ownership" (December 5, 1972), two papers by Norman G. Kurland available from the Center for Economic and Social Justice, Arlington, Virginia.

47 The "Just Third Way" as described in this report should not be confused with the "Third Way" model advanced by Tony Blair and Bill Clinton that represents a Keynesian blend of political democracy and Wall Street capitalism where maldistribution of effective ownership and control is acceptable. See Norman Kurland's letter to the editor, "The Elusive Third Way," published in the Washington Post, September 22, 1998, p. A16.

48 The moral framework of the Third Way is discussed in greater detail in Chapter V of Louis Kelso and Mortimer Adler's profound book with the misleading title, *The Capitalist Manifesto* (New York: Random House, 1958). A further refinement of the specific principles can be found in *Curing World Poverty: The New Role of Property (1994)* Center for Economic and Social Justice, P.O. Box 40711, Washington, DC, 20016.

49 John W. Kendrick, "Productivity Trends and Recent Slowdown: Historical Perspective, Causal Factors, and Policy Options," *Contemporary Economic Problems*, 1979, American Enterprise Institute; also R. M. Solow, in K. J. Arrow, S. Karlin, and P. Suppes, eds., *Mathematical Methods in the Social Sciences, 1959*, pp. 89-104, Stanford University Press, 1960. Also: Edward Denison, "Accounting for United States Economic Growth: 1929-69," Washington, DC: Brookings Institution, 1974, and *Accounting for Slower Economic Growth: The United States in the 1970s*, Washington, DC: Brookings Institution, 1979.

50 See Louis O. Kelso, "Karl Marx: The Almost Capitalist," *American Bar Association Journal*, March 1957, Vol. 43, No. 3.

51 *Dodge v. Ford Motor Company*, 204 Mich. 459 (1919), 170 N.W. 668, 3 A.L.R. 413. See also 20 Columbia L. Rev. 93.

52 See Norman G. Kurland, "Beyond ESOP: Steps Toward Tax Justice," *The Tax Executive*, two-part article, April and July 1977, pp. 187-199, 386-402.

V. Basic Vehicles for Democratizing Capital Credit

53 For a detailed description of the Community Investment Corporation and a discussion of its application in Super Empowerment Zones and land development projects, see "The Community Investment Corporation: A Vehicle for Economic and Political Empowerment of Individual Citizens at the Community Level," by Norman G. Kurland, published as an occasional paper of the Center for Economic and Social Justice, 1992. Also see "The Community Investment Corporation: Linking People to Land and Technology Through Ownership," by Norman G. Kurland, published as an occasional paper published by the Center for Economic and Social Justice, 2000.

VI. Supporting Vehicles for Facilitating Capital Homestead Loans

54 "Two Firms Keep American Dream Alive," *Washington Times*, September 14, 2001, F1.

55 Norman A. Bailey, "A Nation of Owners," *op.cit.*

VII. Reforming the Money and Credit System

56 Harold G. Moulton, *The Formation of Capital*, Washington, D.C.: The Brookings Institution, 1935.

57 See footnote under the heading, "The Need to Forego Present Consumption," in *Economics: An Introductory Analysis*, by Paul A. Samuelson, Sixth Edition, New York: McGraw-Hill, 1964, p. 47.

58 Moulton, *op.cit.*, 107.

59 Moulton, *op.cit.*, 87, 116.

60 Moulton, *op.cit.*, 118.

61 A critical tenet of Kelso's binary economics is that the purpose of production is consumption. Within the logic of the Kelsonian economic system, all income (particularly income produced by capital), should be spent for consumption, instead of saving it for reinvestment and using it to increase capital gains (which traditionally have been ac-

corded more favorable tax treatment than dividends). The feasibility of investment, after all, depends on consumption sufficient to buy the goods and services produced by the investment. Hence, where there is a more effective way for financing new capital formation, it makes no sense to force people to reduce their consumption incomes to buy capital. It weakens the feasibility of private sector investments by draining off cash needed to repay the capital acquisition loans.

This means that corporate profits, after being used to pay off capital acquisition loans, should be paid out to owners as consumption incomes instead of being used for capital growth. The formation of new capital, under Kelso's system, should be financed with additional pure credit loans monetized by the central bank, while corporate profits could be used to sustain or even increase consumer demand, thus improving the market picture for the entire private sector.

62 See footnote 21.

63 The second book by Kelso and Adler, *The New Capitalists*, *op.cit.*, introduced this point with an appropriate subtitle, "Freeing Growth from the Slavery of Savings." By "savings", Kelso and Adler were referring here to "past" savings, as opposed to the use of "future" savings (or future profits generated by the newly added capital assets) as advocated under binary economics.

64 Charles Morrison, *An Essay on the Relations Between Labour and Capital* (London: Longman, Brown, Green, and Longmans, 1854), 200.

65 William Stanley Jevons, "The Functions of Money," *Money and the Mechanism of Exchange.* New York: D. Appleton and Company, 1898, pp. 13-18, see also Paul Samuelson, *Economics, op.cit.*, p. 277.

66 Louis O. Kelso and Patricia Hetter, *Two-Factor Theory: The Economics of Reality.* New York: Random House, 1967, p. 54.

67 U.S. Congressional House Committee on Banking and Currency, *Report of the Committee Appointed Pursuant to House Resolutions 429 and 504 to Investigate the Concentration of Control of Money and Credit.* Washington, DC: U.S. Government Printing Office, 1913.

68 In May 1984, the discount window created $3.5 billion in cash to support a 5-year loan to the troubled Continental Bank of Illinois. On a smaller scale the window was used to bail out the Franklin National Bank. When Freedom National Bank of Harlem was in similar trouble, it was refused similar access to newly created money. See *Washington Post*, February 20, 1985, D1.

69 "Daily Treasury Statement: Cash and debt operations of the United States Treasury, November 22, 2002, Table III-C. Available on the Financial Management Service (FMS) website www.fms.treas.gov.dts.

70 Walter Bagehot, *Lombard Street* (1873).

71 The 2.5% potential GDP growth target represents a combination of roughly 1.1% annual growth in the labor pool (including the unemployed, underemployed and dropouts), plus 1.4% annual growth rates in productivity (output per worker, including present capacity utilization rates). Federal Reserve economists suggest that growth levels above 2.5% would be inflationary. The Kelsonian analysis suggests that noninflationary growth considerably beyond 2.5% is possible. This conclusion is based on the fact that technological and systems changes account for almost 90% of all productivity growth (according to economists John Kendrick and Robert Solow). Kelsonian pure credit reforms could pro-

vide funds for financing faster rates of technological growth and draw more underutilized workers into the labor pool in a manner designed to stabilize fixed labor costs.

72 Norman A. Bailey, Ph.D., "Central Bank Funding of Economic Growth and Economic Justice Through Expanded Capital Ownership." Speech delivered at the 2002 Conference on Globalization, Capital Ownership Group, Washington, D.C., October 2002.

73 *Ibid.*

74 The "100% Reserve Requirement" of the Chicago Plan would effectively prevent the "multiplier effect," which allows creation of money by banks for either productive or nonproductive purposes, at will, thus fueling inflation when indiscriminate use of this power is made for nonproductive purposes. See Joseph A. Schumpeter, *The Theory of Economic Development.* New Brunswick: Transaction Publishers, 1993, pp. 72 - 74, for a discussion on the noninflationary (or minimally inflationary) impact of extending pure credit loans for productive purposes. The 100% reserve requirement states simply that a bank must have sufficient cash on hand to cover the total of its demand deposits. The idea has been around since at least the 1930s as a formal proposal, and the literature is extensive. A selection would include James W. Angell, "The 100 Per Cent Reserve Plan" *The Quarterly Journal of Economics.* November, 1935, pp. 1 - 35; G. L. Bach, *Federal Reserve Policy-Making: A Study in Government Economic Policy Formation.* New York: Knopf Printing, 1950, pp. 36 - 50; Board of Governors of the Federal Reserve System and the U.S. Treasury Department, *The Federal Reserve and the Treasury, Answers to Questions from the Commission on Money and Credit.* Englewood Cliffs, New Jersey: Prentice-Hall, 1963; Lauchlin Currie, *The Supply and Control of Money in the United States.* Cambridge, Massachusetts: Harvard University Press, 1934, pp. 151 - 157; John Davenport, "The Testament of Henry Simons" *Fortune* 34, 1946 1:116 - 119; James C. Dolley, "The Industrial Advance Program of the Federal Reserve System" *Quarterly Journal of Economics* (50), 1936, 2:229 - 274; Henry C. Simons, *Economic Policy for a Free Society.* Chicago, Illinois: University of Chicago Press, 1948, pp. 62 - 65, 160 - 183, 312 - 335.

75 Claudia Rossett, "Greenspan's Dilemma," *Wall Street Journal*, December 12, 1997, A18.

76 William Greider, *Secrets of the Temple: How the Federal Reserve Runs the Country* (New York: Simon & Schuster, 1988). See also "How the Fed Lets the Deficits Flourish," *Business Week,* May 20, 1985, by Thibaut de Saint Phalle, author of *The Federal Reserve: An Intentional Mystery* (1985), as well as Louis O. Kelso and Mortimer J. Adler, *The Capitalist Manifesto* (New York: Random House, 1958).

77 The subtitle of Kelso's second book with Mortimer Adler, *The New Capitalists* (1961).

78 John M. Berry, "Fed Proposal Would Remove 'Stigma' from Discount Windows," *The Washington Post,* May 18, 2002, p. E1. Under a proposal put out in May 2002, banks would be free to borrow, but they would pay a discount rate set at a percentage point higher than the federal funds rate, unlike the Capital Homesteading two-tiered discount rate proposal that would set the discount rate at about 1/2%, the administrative cost of creating and administering the money supply. The Fed's proposal would allow borrowing institutions to relend the money received through a discount window loan, something that is now prohibited. All borrowing institutions would still be required to put up collateral such as U.S. Treasury securities to secure the loan. In contrast, under Capital Homesteading, private sector loan paper would stand behind the Fed-monetized loan, with capital credit insurance serving in place of collateral.

79 Letter from Federal Reserve Chairman Alan Greenspan to the Honorable Bennie G. Thompson, April 7, 1995, 3 (available at the CESJ web site at www.cesj.org).

80 Norman G. Kurland, "The Capital Homestead Act: National Infrastructural Reforms to Make Every Citizen A Shareholder," Washington, D.C.: Center for Economic and Social Justice, 1996 (revised from 1982 paper originally entitled "The Industrial Homestead Act: National Infrastructural Reforms to Make Every Citizen A Shareholder").

81 See footnote 21.

VIII. Reforming the Tax System

82 E.J. Dionne, Jr., "Low-Income Taxpayers: New Meat for the Right," *The Washington Post,* November 26, 2002, p. A29.

83 Under the current United States tax code, capital gains are given favorable treatment under the assumption that past savings are required to form new capital. Absent the speculative influence of the stock exchanges, capital gains are, in large measure, generated by corporations retaining earnings to finance new investment. This, in theory, increases the value per share which, when the shares are sold, generates a short- or long-term capital gain. This gain can then be used to finance additional new capital. To encourage new capital formation, and presumably create jobs for nonowning workers, capital gains are traditionally given favorable tax treatment, either a lower tax or no tax. Since the rich, by definition, control the vast majority of directly held corporate equity and thus the source of capital gains, favorable tax treatment of this source of income generates substantial tax breaks for the wealthy, thus exacerbating the wealth gap and the rigid stratification of society into a small minority of capital owners and a large majority of capital-less workers.

84 The serious reader will find the justification and tax philosophy behind these Capital Homesteading reforms described in detail in the article, "Beyond ESOP: Steps Toward Tax Justice," by Norman G. Kurland, published in the April and July 1976 issues of *Tax Executive* and updated in chapter 8 of *Curing World Poverty: The New Role of Property,* John H. Miller, ed., Social Justice Review, St. Louis, 1994.

85 Walter Blum and Harry Kalven, *The Uneasy Case for Progressive Income Taxation,* University of Chicago, 1953.

86 In 1984, Congress allowed for an analogous tax-deferred rollover of ESOP assets into an Individual Retirement Account or other qualified deferred compensation plan which a participant received in one lump sum. This was liberalized in 1992 to include incremental distributions rolled over into another qualified plan.

87 Note the radical departure of this "poor man's flat tax proposal" from the flat tax proposals of Steve Forbes, Jack Kemp and others: Their "make the rich richer" flat tax would exempt from taxation capital gains, dividends, interest, inheritances, and gifts, and insulate the rich from contributing from their property incomes to the regressive, pay-as-you-go Social Security and Medicare systems. Under our flat tax, the poverty level worker and his employer would pay no Social Security or Medicare taxes, because all revenues to meet Social Security and Medicare promises would come from a flat tax.

88 The tax-favored payout of corporate dividends advocated here *should not be labeled "tax subsidies,"* any more than deductible wage costs are "subsidies" to employers. Tax-deductible profit distributions under Capital Homesteading represent structural reform of the tax system. These tax deductions are designed to eliminate the unjust "double tax" penalty on corporate profits, by integrating the corporate income tax with the per-

sonal income tax, while exempting reasonable property accumulations to meet the Nation's income security goals.

IX. Other Policy Reforms

89 See "Capital Homesteading for DC Citizens: A Federal Reserve Demonstration for Funding Economic Empowerment." Norman G. Kurland. Occasional Paper, Arlington: Center for Economic and Social Justice, 1995.

X. A New Social Contract

90 Scott McCartney, "United's Woes Can be Traced to Shortsighted Employees," *The Wall Street Journal,* December 4, 2002. Available online at: http://online.wsj.com/article_print/0,,SB1038430684859691828,00.html.

91 Philip P. Pan, "Workers in China Fail as Owners of Factories," *The Washington Post,* December 4, 2002, p.A1.

92 A similar case of clinging to old mindsets was the tragic demise of the South Bend Lathe Company, which instituted the world's first 100% leveraged ESOP by 100% of the workers and saved 500 jobs. Neither the union nor management was able to break out of their traditional, top-down, conflict-oriented, wage system mode of labor-management relations. When finally forced to be sold after 17 years of employee ownership, this shining ESOP success story became mocked in the press as a fable where "owners had gone on strike against themselves." See "What Can We Learn From an ESOP 'Failure'?", Chapter 5 in *Journey to an Ownership Culture: Insights from the ESOP Community,* Dawn K. Brohawn, ed., Lanham, MD: Scarecrow Press, 1997.

93 Growing evidence indicates that the most healthy, productive and profitable companies are those which share ownership, profits, information, and power with all workers so that each can become more fully involved and actively connected to the company's performance. See "The Performance Effects of Employee Ownership Plans," a study by Michael A. Conte and Jan Svejnar, which appears in *Paying for Productivity: A Look at the Evidence,* Alan S. Blinder, ed. (Washington, D.C.: The Brookings Institution, 1990). These findings have been confirmed in various studies by the National Center for Employee Ownership (Oakland, CA), which recently found that in terms of productivity ESOP companies grew 2.3% per year faster than they would have without an ESOP, and the gains increase if the companies make employee ownership a part of the corporate culture.

94 See "Value-Based Management: A Framework for Equity and Efficiency in the Workplace" by Dawn K. Brohawn. This essay appeared in the compendium *Curing World Poverty: The New Role of Property,* John H. Miller, ed., Social Justice Review: St. Louis, MO, 1994. As articulated by CESJ, "Justice-Based Management[SM]" (formerly referred to by CESJ as "Value-Based Management[SM]") reflects the principles of economic and social justice in the structuring of a company's constitution, operations and governance. First, JBM[SM] seeks to instill within the company's core values and code of ethics, the dignity, development and empowerment of each person affected by the company—every worker, customer, vendor, and stakeholder. Second, JBM[SM] recognizes that the financial success of the company depends on consistently delivering the highest possible value to the customer (*i.e.,* the highest possible quality at the lowest possible price). Third, JBM[SM] embodies the principle that a person's share of the fruits produced by the enterprise should be linked to the value he contributes, both as a worker and as an owner.

One reason for CESJ's abandoning the term "Value-Based Management," was that this label has been used elsewhere to describe a strategic management approach aimed at increasing economic value for a corporation's shareholders. (See, for example, *Manag-*

ing for Value: A Guide to Value-Based Strategic Management by Bernard C. Reimann, Oxford, OH: The Planning Forum, 1987.) While this objective is, in and of itself, laudable, it ignores the moral imperative and business rationale for bringing workers and other nonowning stakeholders into the ownership structure of the company. In fact, its single-minded focus on increasing shareholder value for existing owners has led to abuses of the workforce that have been satirized in the popular "Dilbert" comic strip.

95 J.P. Morgan reputedly stated that he would never pay his top-level executives more than 8 times more than the lowest paid worker. Today in some companies the pay differential (including stock options and other corporate perquisites) exceeds a ratio of 400:1. Such an unbridgeable gap in compensation cannot help but create a culture that separates people, destroying any sense of community between workers and their leaders.

96 What constitutes a "significant" level of ownership does not necessarily depend on a specific percentage of equity owned by a particular employee or employees as a group. There is, however, a threshold level of ownership where a person perceives that he has something valuable to lose. Helping workers reach this threshold of "ownership consciousness" is a critical objective within a justice-based ESOP company, for example, where workers acquire their ownership using the profits of their corporation, rather than by expending their personal savings or income. A JBM^SM company should aim at enabling all workers to accumulate a minimum level of assets (which could be mixture of company shares and other assets) of at least 8 to 10 times their salary. Such a target amount could generate a second income from the accumulated assets equivalent to a worker's annual income from labor.

97 One of the best examples of Justice-Based Management^SM can be found at Fastener Industries in Berea, Ohio, described by the Ohio Employee Ownership Center as "a national model for what employee ownership can achieve. It is one of the most productive and profitable companies in its industry." See "How Have Employee-Owned Companies Fared?", *Owners at Work,* Winter 1999/2000, p. 13. Fastener was one of three companies awarded the CESJ Global Award for [Justice]-Based Management^SM in 1991. Another example of a highly successful company that has been gradually integrating Justice-Based Management^SM into its operations, risk-and-reward system and long-range strategic plan, is Western Building Products in Milwaukee, Wisconsin. See "Western Building Products, Inc.: Organized for the Common Good," by William L. Nicholson and George W. Lorenz, *Social Justice Review,* January/February 2002, pp. 14-16.

98 "Unions, After the Fall," *The Washington Times* (May 2, 1993) A14. Also see Tables, "Union Affiliation of Employed Wage and Salary Workers by Occupation and Industry," *News,* Bureau of Labor Statistics, U.S. Department of Labor, available at web site: www.bls.gov, November 29, 2002.

99 Barry Bluestone and Irving Bluestone, *Negotiating the Future: A Labor Perspective on American Business* (New York: HarperCollins Publishers, Inc., 1992) xiv.

100 See "Changing the 'Us-vs-Them' Mentality," by James H. Dayley, *Social Justice Review,* September/October 2002, pp. 147-148.

101 See discussion of distributive justice in Appendix 6, "Defining Economic and Social Justice.

102 Norman G. Kurland, "What Can We Learn from an ESOP 'Failure'?", article in *Journey to an Ownership Culture: Insights from the ESOP Community,* Dawn K. Brohawn, ed., Lanham, MD: Scarecrow Press and The ESOP Association, 1997.

103 John M. Berry, "Greenspan Praises Markets' Flexibility: Fed Chief Says Changes Buoyed Economy," *The Washington Post,* November 20, 2002, p. E1.

XI. Recommendations for Next Steps

104 Norman G. Kurland, "Dinner at the Madison: Louis Kelso Meets Russell Long," *Owners at Work,* Ohio Employee Ownership Center, Winter 1997/1998, pp. 5-8.

105 Norman G. Kurland, "How to Win a Revolution...And Enjoy It," occasional paper, Arlington, VA: Center for Economic and Social Justice, 1972, updated 1989.

106 Dawn K. Brohawn, "Value-Based Management A Framework for Equity and Efficiency in the Workplace, published in *Curing World Poverty: The New Role of Property,* John H. Miller, ed., Social Justice Review: St. Louis, MO, 1994.

107 See William Ferree, S.M., Ph.D., *Introduction to Social Justice,* originally published by Paulist Press, 1948, republished by the Center for Economic and Social Justice (with new foreword by Norman G. Kurland), Arlington, Virginia, 1998. Also see William Ferree, *The Act of Social Justice,* Washington DC: The Catholic University of America Press, 1942.

108 Norman G. Kurland, "The Abraham Federation: A New Framework for Peace in the Middle East." Originally published in *World Citizen News,* Dec. 1978. Updated and republished in *American-Arab Affairs* (now *Middle East Policy*), Spring 1991, a publication of the Middle East Policy Council. Updated and republished in *Curing World Poverty: The New Role of Property, op.cit.*

XII. Conclusion: Building a Nation of Owners

109 Under a national Capital Homesteading program, the development of nonpolluting, renewable sources of energy would help break America's dependence on foreign oil and would reduce the depletion of America's precious natural resources. More decentralized, broadly owned power systems would also provide a higher degree of national security, and would be less prone to regional power outages as suffered recently by people living on the West Coast.

110 See Chapter 2, "Economic Freedom: Property and Leisure," *The Capitalist Manifesto,* Louis O. Kelso and Mortimer, J. Adler, *op.cit.*

GLOSSARY

Appropriation. The legislative process by which funds (tax revenues or government borrowings) are allocated to government programs on a discretionary rather than a formula-determined basis. An appropriation differs from an entitlement in that funds allocated via an entitlement program are automatic, whereas an appropriation must be approved each time. Legislators can hide government spending through the use of tax credits, tax subsidies, rebates, exemptions and other tax breaks to individuals and companies, rather than exposing these "tax expenditures" to the light of the appropriations process. Such practices decrease government's accountability to taxpayers and add to the complexity, costs of administration and unfairness in tax policy.

Bank. A financial institution that takes deposits and makes loans.

Bank of Issue. A financial institution that makes loans by printing currency backed by the assets financed with the proceeds of the loan. In other words, a bank of issue "monetizes" assets. These "assets" may be either productive and self-liquidating (as required under Capital Homesteading) or nonproductive (such as government or consumer debt paper).

Bank, Central. A "bank for banks." A central bank functions as a bank of issue for a region's commercial banks, usually being the only financial institution permitted to "monetize" assets for circulation as currency. A central bank differs from a commercial bank or other financial institution in that it purchases loans and other assets (usually financial) that have already been made or issued by other banks and financial institutions. A central bank purchases such assets by printing currency, striking coin or creating demand deposits denominated in units of the currency, which are destroyed or retired when the loans purchased are redeemed by the borrower. Because a central bank purchases the assets at less than face value or at a discount, this process is called "discounting," a power provided by Congress to the Federal Reserve Banks in the U.S. under Section 13 of the Federal Reserve Act. Members of the general public are not usually permitted to discount their personal loans at a central bank, a privilege reserved for "member" banks of the financial system over which the central bank exercises a regulatory function. The central bank controls the creation of money and credit, and sets interest rate policy.

Bank, Commercial. A financial institution that takes deposits and makes loans to facilitate commercial transactions. A commercial bank buys and sells money for carrying on a society's economic transactions. If permitted by law, it may have the power to create money. It is then called a "bank of issue." A commercial bank may also function as a savings bank offering personal financial services to individuals.

Bank, Investment. A financial institution that buys and sells securities (*e.g.*, shares of company stock and corporate debt instruments). It frequently acts as a middleman between the primary or original issuer of a security and the ultimate secondary purchaser.

Barrier. In terms of binary economics, a barrier is anything in the "invisible architecture" of society's laws, or in the rules or customs of an institution, that inhibits or prevents full participation in the economic process for any or all otherwise qualified individuals.

Binary Economics. The "post-scarcity" theory developed by lawyer-economist Louis O. Kelso in the 1950s. "Binary" means "consisting of two parts." Kelso divided the factors of production into two all-inclusive categories — the human ("labor"), and the non-human ("capital"). The central tenet of binary economics is that there are two components to productive output and to income: (1) that generated by human labor, and (2) that generated by capital. Classical economic theory, on the other hand, regards all output and income to be derived from labor whose productivity is enhanced by capital.

In contrast to traditional schools of economics which assume that scarcity is inevitable, binary economics views shared abundance — sustainable economic growth and the equitable distribution of future wealth and income throughout society — as achievable. Binary economics holds that broad-based affluence and economic freedom, as opposed to financial insecurity and economic dependency for the many, is made possible through the widespread ownership of constantly improved capital instruments and social institutions to produce more and more consumable goods with less and less input and resources.

Binary economists Robert Ashford and Rodney Shakespeare identify three distinguishing concepts within binary theory — *binary productiveness,* the *binary property right,* and *binary growth.* These components interact and reinforce one another, allowing for maximum rates of sustainable growth within a modern, globalized economy.

Binary economics recognizes a natural synergy, as opposed to an unavoidable trade-off, between economic justice and efficiency within a global free marketplace. Rejecting pure *laissez-faire* assumptions, binary economics holds that a truly free and just global market requires (1) effective broad-based ownership of capital, (2) the restoration of and universalized access to the full rights of private property, (3) limited economic power of the state (whose main role should be to eliminate special privileges, monopolies and other barriers to equal participation) and (4) free and open markets for determining just wages, just prices, and just profits.

The market theory of binary economics is underpinned by three interrelated principles of economic justice:

(1) *Participative justice,* the input principle which demands as a fundamental human right, equal opportunity for every person to contribute to the production of society's marketable wealth both as a worker and as an owner of productive assets.

(2) *Distributive justice,* the outtake principle which holds that the contribution of labor to the economic process should be compensated at the market-determined rate (or "just wage") for each particular type of human contribution to the production of marketable wealth. This principle dictates that the contribution of capital should be compensated by the "just profit" generated by the project or enterprise. (Profit is determined by the market-based rental value of contributed capital assets, or by the gross revenues resulting from market-determined "just prices" less the market-based cost of the factors of production, including labor.)

(3) *Harmony,* the feedback principle that balances and restores participation and distribution within the economic system. This principle was referred to by Louis Kelso and Mortimer Adler as the "principle of limitation" and by others as "social justice," as it calls for the restructuring of the economic system to restore participative and distributive justice.

Binary Growth. Within binary theory, this concept holds that economies grow steadily larger as private capital acquisition is distributed more broadly among the population on market principles.

Binary Productiveness. This concept states that while humans contribute to economic growth through all forms of labor, capital assets such as machines and technological processes are making an even bigger, ever-increasing contribution to overall output, in relation to that contributed by human labor.

Binary Property Right. This concept refers to the right of every person to acquire, on market principles, private (individual and joint) ownership of wealth-creating capital assets.

Capital. In binary economics, all non-human factors of production, including land, plant and equipment, advanced technological tools, rentable space, physical infrastructure, and intangibles, such as patents, copyrights and advanced management systems.

Capital Homestead. An analogue of the nineteenth century American programs enacted to bring about a broad distribution of the ownership of land. Capital Homesteading expands the concept to include ownership of advanced technologies, including management, marketing and distribution systems, through equity shares in enterprises capable of competing without special protections within a free and just global economy.

Capital Credit Reinsurance Corporation (CCRC). An "insurer of last resort" for loans made under Capital Homesteading. The CCRC would "insure the insurers" of loans discounted by the Federal Reserve, further spreading the risk of loan defaults throughout the system. "Risk premiums" for Capital Homestead credit would be covered by debt servicing charges.

Capital Homestead Account (CHA). (*See* Capital Homestead Act.)

Capital Homestead Act. A national economic policy based on the binary growth model, designed to lift barriers in the present financial and economic system and universalize access to the means of acquiring and possessing capital assets. The Capital Homestead Act would allow every man, woman and child to accumulate in a tax-sheltered Capital Homestead Account, a target level of assets sufficient to generate an adequate and secure income for that person without requiring the use of existing pools of savings or reductions in current levels of consumption. Formerly called the "Industrial Homestead Act."

Capital Homestead Exemption. The amount that a Capital Homestead participant could accumulate without paying taxes on his or her capital accumulations or on the dividend income used to pay for the capital.

Capitalism. An economic/financial system where a relatively small number of individuals own the vast bulk of capital assets, and where the majority of the population is employed at a wage and owns little or no capital. As a socio-political system, "capitalism" represents the institutionalization of greed, concentrated power and monopoly.

Louis Kelso used the term "capitalism" (or "universal capitalism") to describe a free market system where capital (as opposed to labor) is the predominant factor of production, and where there exists the widest possible distribution of private ownership of capital among the households of the economy. However, a growing number of binary economists have rejected, for semantic and philosophical reasons, any use of the term "capitalism" to describe the logical alternative to traditional capitalism and socialism. (*See* Just Third Way.)

The term "capitalism" was invented as a pejorative by socialists, not by Adam Smith or other pioneers of free market economics. Expressed as an "ism," "capital-ism" connotes an ideology or value system that places its highest value on capital (or "things"), ranking it higher in importance than labor (or human beings). From the standpoint of binary theory itself, the term fails to acknowledge the interdependence and respective contributions of *both* capital and labor, with the distribution of incomes to both factors determined by market principles as well as principles of economic justice. While the term "capitalism" retains some degree of respectability within the United States and other developed countries, it has become increasingly disparaged by opponents of globalization and many citizens in the developing world.

Capitalism is often confused with "free markets" or "democracy," but in practice has historically resulted in mercantilism. So-called "democratic capitalism," as some have labeled America's socio-economic system, has fostered an unstable, mercantilist, conflict-prone and class-divided combination of political democracy and economic plutocracy. While many defenders of democratic capitalism share with binary economists support for limited economic power of government, establishment of free markets and free trade, and restoration of private property rights, they generally treat universal access to capital owner-ship as irrelevant politically and economically.

Charity. The virtue or moral habit by which we love our neighbor as ourselves. Charity is often popularly understood as "almsgiving," the applied virtue of charity in which one gives out of human compassion, without any expectation of anything in return. It is inspired by love and respect for the inherent dignity and worth of every human person. The principle of distribution for charity is "to each according to his need." This stands in sharp contrast to the principle of distribution for justice, "to each according to his contribution." Both prin-ciples are valid and complementary, but, as we are reminded by moral philoso-phers, charity should never be a substitute for justice. According to the Talmu-dic scholar Moses Maimonides, the highest form of charity is to enable the poor man to lift himself out of poverty (for example, by helping him go into business), so that the poor person can become economically self-reliant and capable of being charitable to others.

Charity, Social. Social charity is the virtue or moral habit, analogous to indi-vidual charity, that guides us in how we behave toward our institutions. It is the "soul" of social justice. This social virtue inspires us to "love our institutions as we love our friends," acknowledging their faults but seeking to help in their per-fection and transformation rather than in their destruction. Social charity is the preliminary step of properly orienting and educating oneself in order to organize with others in acts of social justice to restructure unjust or ineffective laws and institutions. Social charity is different from organized charity, which is a form of individual charity (*i.e.,* directed at human persons rather than social institutions).

Chicago Plan. A proposal from the 1930s to implement a 100% reserve re-quirement (*i.e.,* full asset backing behind all bank loans) as a means of address-ing the financial chaos resulting from speculative loans that resulted in the stock market crash of 1929.

Collateral. Existing wealth pledged as security for a loan, *i.e.,* a guarantee that a loan will be repaid. If the loan is in default, the lender may seize the pledged wealth.

Collective. As a noun, the collective is an abstraction of the aggregate of activi-ties of a group of human beings acting in concert. It does not recognize the individuals making up the group, nor is it synonymous with the common good. (*See* Common Good.)

Collectivism. As used in socialist theory, collectivism or collective ownership denies the right of any individual to acquire a personal ownership stake in land, natural resources or other means of production. Instead, collectivism recognizes only ownership by the group or legally recognized entity that reflects the inter-ests of group members. It differs radically from joint ownership where many persons, as in a modern corporation or in many cooperatives, may acquire a direct personal stake in and share ownership rights, power and profits over modern productive assets, as under a binary economic system.

Common Good. The common good is that network of institutions and social systems that gives form and structure to society, within which the individual may exercise his rights to the fullest degree possible consistent with the demands of justice and the needs of his fellow human beings. It establishes the conditions for the exercise of the natural freedoms indispensable for the development of human initiatives and the good of every member of society. The common good also describes the social and cultural environment that governs human interactions. The common good aims toward the dignity and development of each human person, as well as the well-being, just ordering and development of society. The common good may further be defined as "the sum total of social conditions, laws and institutions that allow people, either as individuals or as groups, to reach their fulfillment more fully and effectively."

The late social philosopher Rev. William Ferree, S.M., Ph.D. described the direct relationship that each individual has with the common good: "When it is realized that the Common Good consists of that whole vast complex of institutions, from the simplest 'natural medium' of a child's life, to the United Nations itself, then a very comforting fact emerges: Each of these institutions from the lowest and most fleeting 'natural medium' to the highest and most enduring organization of nations is the Common Good *at that particular level.* Therefore everyone, from the smallest and weakest child to the most powerful ruler in the world, can have direct care of the Common Good at his level."

Community Investment Corporation (CIC). An expanded ownership mechanism designed as a for-profit, professionally managed real estate planning and development corporation that can borrow on behalf of its shareholders (the citizens of a local or regional area) to purchase land, plan its use, and develop the land for productive purposes. The citizen-shareholders thus gain a definable ownership interest in local real estate, sharing in appreciated land values, and profits from leases, etc., as well as have a voice in future land development. CICs differ from Community Development Corporations (CDCs), which are nonprofit entities in which citizens have no direct control and do not have any direct and personal ownership interest.

Consumption Income. Income expended on the purchase of consumer goods and services, rather than on direct investment or savings.

Corporation. Also referred to as a "joint stock corporation." The modern business corporation is an institution or legal entity that can be used to limit the liability and any claims on non-corporate personal assets of its owners when the corporation enters into contracts, borrows money, carries out its operations, and serves consumers in local as well as global markets. The corporation is a creation of the law (*i.e.*, a "legal person"). Its purpose is to acquire, aggregate and coordinate technological and financial capital with labor inputs. It facilitates access to financial markets, while insulating its shareholders from the risk of default on corporate debts and obligations. All the assets of a corporation are owned collectively by the corporation itself, with the shareholders owning shares of the company's stock. Except upon dissolution of the corporation, no shareholder or creditor may make a personal claim on any particular capital assets owned by the corporation, unless those assets are pledged as collateral on a corporate loan.

From the advent of the industrial revolution, and increasingly so in today's Information Age, the corporation has become the arena for growing abuses by those who manage and control them, and has failed to live up to its potential for serving as society's most important institution for balancing the untapped productive growth of a market economy with the purchasing power needed to absorb the goods and services the private sector is capable of producing. Most, if not all, of these drawbacks of the corporation can be overcome by democratizing corporate accountability and transparency systems and increasing corporate dividend distributions to a broadened base of corporate shareholders, especially its workers.

Cost. The aggregate of all charges, tangible and intangible, associated with production of marketable goods and services. Usually expressed or measured in units of currency.

Credit. A loan of money to be repaid, usually with an added amount of interest, transaction fees, or, under Islamic banking, through a risk-sharing, profit-sharing loan.

Credit, Capital. Funds lent or borrowed to finance feasible, "self-liquidating" projects that are expected to generate an income and repay the loan out of that future income. Capital credit is designed to advance outside funds to be repaid with *future* savings. It is a modern social tool for enabling people without sufficient past savings to become capital owners voluntarily on market principles. Also referred to as "Productive Credit" and "Procreative Credit."

Credit, Consumer. Funds lent or borrowed to expend on consumer goods and services; that is, things that do not pay for themselves.

Credit, Non-Recourse. Loans in which the borrower is insulated from the risk of default and his personal assets cannot be seized in the event of loan default. Instead the loan will generally be secured by the assets standing behind the loan, by loan default insurance, or by a guarantee of a third party or the corporation itself. Under one example of nonrecourse credit, a loan to a corporation is nonrecourse to the shareholders of that corporation, unless the shareholders personally guarantee the loan. Another example is with a leveraged Employee Stock Ownership Plan, where the workers who benefit from loans made to an ESOP Trust are not personally liable in the event of default. Under Capital Homesteading, the proposed capital credit insurance provides a substitute for collateral to enable the lender to recover funds lent, thus insulating from risk any personal assets of the borrower.

Credit, Pure. Extension of interest-free credit (generally through the central banking system) backed by a financially feasible project, as opposed to using existing accumulations of savings or other wealth unrelated to the project being financed. Instead of compound interest charges, pure credit costs would be covered by service fees (*see* Bank, Central), transaction fees of intermediate financial institutions, and loan default risk insurance premiums to capital credit insurers and reinsurers.

Credit, Self-Liquidating. Loans expected to cover the costs of capital assets out of future profits realized from the productiveness of those assets.

Credit System, Two-Tiered. A key monetary reform under Capital Homesteading that distinguishes between "good" uses of money and credit (*i.e.,* used to finance broadly owned private sector growth and production) and "bad" uses of credit (*i.e.,* used for fueling nonproductive consumer and government debt, or speculation). The Fed's discount window would be available exclusively to member banks and members of the Farm Credit system for discounting "eligible" paper for feasible, ownership-expanding industrial, commercial, and agricultural projects.

Under this policy, credit and "new money" for Capital Homesteading, *i.e.,* feasible business projects linked to broadened ownership (Tier 1), would be generated "interest-free" through the discount mechanism of the central bank, at a service charge based on the cost to the central bank of creating new money and regulating the lending institutions (0.5% or less). Credit and money for nonproductive, ownership-concentrating uses (Tier 2) would come from past savings ("old money"), and would be charged an interest rate determined by normal market yields on such savings. Under Capital Homesteading, local lenders would add their normal transaction fees and risk premiums for servicing capital acquisition loans, and the new loans would be collateralized by newly issued shares and newly acquired capital assets. Premiums paid to capital credit insurers and reinsurers would be pooled to spread the risk of default.

Currency. Standardized tokens of value circulated as money within an economy or region. (*See* Legal Tender.)

Customer Stock Ownership Plan or Consumer Stock Ownership Plan (CSOP). An expanded capital ownership vehicle for providing self-liquidating, productive credit to the regular customers of public utilities, marketing cooperatives, mass transit systems, family health care systems, etc., linking them as owners to the enterprise's future investment opportunities and capital growth. For his patronage, the regular customer would get back ownership rights, represented by shares released to his CSOP account as the CSOP's debt is repaid with pretax earnings paid in the form of tax-deductible dividends on CSOP-held shares. Released shares would be allocated among users according to their relative patronage of the system. Future dividends on CSOP stock would be used to offset each user's monthly bill. The CSOP would also create an internal market for repurchasing shares when there is no public market for the shares.

Default. The failure or inability of a borrower to repay a loan under terms agreed upon by a lender and borrower.

Deflation. Fewer units of currency "chasing" an unchanged amount of goods and services. Also defined as a contraction in the volume of available money or credit resulting in a decline of the general price level. Backing the currency in a rapidly growing economy with a commodity (such as gold or silver) or otherwise restricting the amount of currency available, are the most common causes of deflation. Backing the currency with productive assets directly financed with the creation of new money would allow the money supply to expand as needed to finance feasible capital investments.

Demand. Demand is the want or desire to possess a good or service, with the goods, services, or financial instruments necessary to make a legal transaction for those goods or services.

Demand Deposit. Demand deposits are a category of money made up of bank deposits subject to checking on demand (*i.e.,* a checking account). For example, if you have $1,000 in your checking account, that deposit can be regarded as money, since you can pay for purchases with checks drawn upon it. When "pure credit" (newly created money) is used to buy newly issued shares to fund corporate growth, the lending bank increases the demand deposits of the Capital Homesteader to use for buying the new shares.

Demand, Aggregate. Aggregate demand is the sum of all demand in an economy. This can be computed by adding the expenditures on consumer goods and services, investment, and net exports (total exports minus total imports).

Demand, Derived. A secondary demand dependent on a primary demand. The demand for capital goods, for example, is dependent on effective consumer demand.

Demand, Effective. In Keynesian terms, income to be used for consumption, as opposed to income diverted for reinvestment.

Dilution, Economic. A decrease in an enterprise's share or asset values that occurs when new shares are added without a corresponding increase in the productiveness of the capital assets or net profits of that enterprise. Economic dilution constitutes an erosion of property rights for existing shareholders. Where share or asset values increase despite an issuance of new shares, there may be political dilution in equity ownership, but no economic dilution.

Dilution, Political. The just diffusion of economic power in an enterprise when new shareholders are added in ways that do not violate the property rights of existing shareholders. Political dilution is not a dilution of property rights as long as the economic values of existing shareholders are not diminished by the issuance of new shares. (*See* Dilution, Economic.)

Discount Rate. The percentage by which a central bank reduces the amount of cash printed or demand deposit created to purchase qualified loans from qualified banks and financial institutions. Under binary economic policy, this rate takes the form of a service fee, estimated at 0.5%, to cover all central banking and regulatory costs of monetizing Capital Homesteading loans made by commercial banks and other qualified financial institutions for broadening the ownership of new capital.

Discount Window. Not an actual "window," but the mechanism whereby a central bank carries out the process of discounting. (*See* Bank, Central.)

Discounting. The process by which a central bank purchases qualified loans from commercial banks by printing currency or creating demand deposits. The amount paid for the loans is usually less than face value, or at a "discount," thus accounting for the description of this process as "discounting." For example, on a $10,000 loan discounted at 0.5%, the lender would give the borrower $9,950 ($10,000-$50) in cash. In the Federal Reserve System, the discount rate refers to the interest rate that the Fed charges its member banks.

Distributism. An economic system proposed by G. K. Chesterton and Hilaire Belloc that called for widely distributed small holdings of land and other productive assets. This system aimed at securing and protecting individual rights by enabling ordinary citizens to acquire a moderate ownership stake of income-generating property. Distributism was mainly concerned with breaking up current accumulations of wealth. It paid little attention to the ability of the modern corporation and the money- and credit-creating powers of central banks to accelerate growth and spread out ownership of newly added and transferred capital on credit repayable with future savings.

Dividend. Profits paid to the owner or shareholder of a corporation. Under current U.S. law and custom, dividends must be proposed and approved by the Board of Directors of a corporation, thus taking away from the owner his property right or entitlement to receive the full stream of income from his capital. Under Capital Homesteading, shareholders would receive a full distribution of their share of profits (*i.e.,* full dividend payouts on their Capital Homestead shares) and management would have to solicit from shareholders the reinvestment of those dividends, or use new borrowings, in order to finance corporate growth.

Duty. A legally enforceable obligation to do or not to do an act. A duty on the part of one person, persons, or institution is always the result of a right held by another person, persons, or institution.

Employee Stock Accumulation Plan (ESAP). A term used to describe a employee benefit plan that enables workers to accumulate shares in their employer company, but which withholds the rights of first-class shareholders over those shares, particularly the right to vote one's own shares on standard shareholder issues or to elect a representative to the board of directors. Except on certain major corporate issues, ESOPs today are permitted by law to withhold pass-through of the vote on shares held by the ESOP for employee-owners. In practice today, most ESOPs operate as ESAPs. Capital Homesteading policies would offer credit and tax incentives to encourage companies with ESOPs to pass through full ownership rights to their worker-shareholders.

Employee Stock Ownership Plan (ESOP). An expanded ownership mechanism now "qualified" under U.S. retirement law, which can borrow on behalf of employees as a group to acquire equity shares in the employer company repayable with pre-tax profits or dividends. ESOPs today may be either leveraged (designed to borrow to acquire company shares) or unleveraged (contributed by the employer). Typically an ESOP does not require employees to use their own savings or wages to acquire their shares, or to pledge their personal assets as collateral in a leveraged transaction.

Entitlement. An automatic allocation of funds by a government program in the form of a cash payment subsidy or a reduction or rebate of taxes due the government. This differs from an "appropriation" in that funds allocated via an appropriation must be approved each time, whereas an entitlement is automatic and requires positive action to change.

Ephemeralization. A term invented by R. Buckminster Fuller to describe the process of "doing more with less" as a continuing process of redesigning technology and structures of the physical world through more effective uses of existing natural resources, recycled materials and energy sources. In terms of binary economics, ephemeralization refers to the process of increasing the productiveness of capital relative to that of labor.

Feasible. When used in reference to the funding of an acquisition or transfer of capital on borrowed money, the quality of a capital project that can generate, or reasonably be expected to generate, an income sufficient to repay the loan, within a reasonable period. (*See* Credit, Capital.)

Federal Capital Credit Corporation (FCCC). A private or public institution designed to promote capital ownership among all citizens, by aggregating many Capital Homestead loans for discounting by the Federal Reserve. The FCCC is modeled after "Fannie Mae" (Federal National Mortgage Association) and "Freddie Mac" (Federal Home Mortgage Corporation), which were established to allow more Americans to obtain home mortgages. The FCCC would purchase qualified Capital Homesteading loans from lenders, bundle these loans and take the securitized CHA loans to the discount window of the regional Federal Reserve Bank. The Federal Reserve would treat the insured, dividend-backed CHA securities as it now treats government debt paper, using them as substitute backing for the currency.

Federal Capital Insurance Corporation (FCIC). A private or public institution that would provide Capital Homestead credit insurance, similar to FHA home mortgage insurance. The FCIC would offer commercial insurance to bank lenders against the risk of default on Capital Homestead credit and would offer, for a premium paid by Capital Homestead participants, some "downside risk" portfolio insurance. Such risks could be spread further through a reinsurance facility (*see* CCRC) established either by the private sector or by the public sector.

Federal Funds Rate. The interest rate that commercial banks charge one another for very short-term ("overnight") loans, as determined by the Board of Governors of the Federal Reserve.

Federal Reserve Act of 1913. The legislation establishing a central bank of the United States.

Federal Reserve System. The system of central banks of the United States. The Federal Reserve System includes the Board of Governors of the Federal Reserve Board and twelve regional Federal Reserve Banks. The Federal Reserve Banks were originally designed to serve as regional development banks to meet the productive credit needs of agriculture, industry and commerce where local savings was inadequate to meet local capital needs for feasible private sector projects. Today the Federal Reserve System's main monetary objective is to control inflation and maintain a stable value for the U.S. dollar. The regional Federal Reserve Banks serve primarily as research centers. Only the Federal Reserve Bank of New York is directly involved in monetary policy through its Open Market Operations, increasing and decreasing the money supply through its purchase and sale of Federal debt paper. In general, the discount operation of the Federal Reserve System has been limited to saving enterprises that are "too big to fail" or foreign economies unable to service their foreign debt.

Fractional Reserve Policy. *(See* Reserve Policy, Fractional.*)*

Global Justice Movement. A free enterprise movement launched in the United States, Canada and the United Kingdom, aimed at restructuring global money and the global marketplace in ways consistent with binary economics and the principles of economic and social justice. *(See* Just Third Way.)

Imputed Rent. The rental value of a person's home that is treated by some economists as the equivalent of the income one would receive if he rented out his personal residence.

Individual Stock Ownership Plan (ISOP). The name originally used to describe a Capital (or "Industrial") Homestead Account.

Industrial Homestead Act. A national economic policy for building widespread capital ownership that was developed in 1964 by Louis Kelso and David Lawrence and promoted in 1975 by then-governor of California Ronald Reagan. This economic program was later slightly modified by the Center for Economic and Social Justice and more fully developed as a comprehensive economic program of monetary, tax and fiscal forms, at the request of the Chief Economist of the National Security Council in 1982. In 1995 it was renamed the "Capital Homestead Act." *(See* Capital Homestead Act.)

Inflation. A general rise in the price level. There are two principal types of inflation. "Demand/Pull" inflation results from more units of currency "chasing" the same or fewer goods and services. This can result from creating money not backed by productive assets (*i.e.*, by assets that generate the goods and services for the new money to purchase), or by a decline in goods and services produced in the economy without a concurrent decrease in the money supply. "Cost/Push" inflation results from artificial increases in labor costs or market-driven increases in the costs of production, *e.g.*, having to drill more expensive wells to produce the same amount of oil. Demand/Pull inflation is controllable through fiscal and monetary policy. Cost/Push inflation can be overcome through substitution, technological advances, or ephemeralization, or by removing artificial pressures to increase unit labor costs.

Insurance, Capital Credit. Insurance to protect commercial lenders against the possibility of default on the part of the borrower. Commercial capital credit insurance is a substitute for collateral, the lack of which is typically a barrier for most borrowers with little or no savings or income. Such insurance would be provided under the Capital Homesteading proposal to safeguard a lender against the risk that the debt to enable citizens to purchase newly issued corporate growth shares may not be serviced out of future enterprise profits.

Interest. Derived from "ownership interest." A portion of the profits of a productive project due to the provider of the financing as his share of the project. More popularly, "interest" is any charge for the use of money, often construed as the "rent" of money, but this is not technically accurate in terms of binary economics. When "interest" is charged on a loan of money created without using existing pools of savings (*i.e.*, instead, using "pure credit"), the more accurate term is a "service charge" and/or a "transaction fee."

Issuance, Primary (*also* "Primary Security"). Newly issued equity shares or bonds reflecting new capital, and purchased directly from the issuer. These may be issued by private companies or the state. When issued by a government, they are referred to as "primary government securities."

Issuance, Secondary (*also* "Secondary Security"). Outstanding equity shares or bonds reflecting existing securities being resold, which are purchased from someone other than the original issuer. Secondary issuances are securities that are normally traded on stock exchanges, with their values determined by speculation among security traders. These instruments may be issued originally by private companies or the government. Under today's financial system, most people who purchase secondary shares expect to realize a gain from a change in the value of the underlying asset, rather than through realizing a stream of income from that asset.

"Secondary government securities" are government securities like Treasury bonds that are purchased from someone other than the government. Under Capital Homesteading, there would be a prohibition against using "pure credit" (*i.e.*, new money) created by the Fed for speculative purchases of secondary issuances or any government securities (which represent government debt, not productive assets). In those cases, speculation in secondar\y issuances and government debt could only be purchased with "old money," representing already accumulated savings.

"Just Third Way." A free market system that economically empowers all individuals and families through the democratization of money and credit for new production, with universal access to direct ownership of income-producing capital. This socio-economic paradigm offers the logical "third alternative" to the two predominant socio-economic paradigms today — *capitalism* and *socialism/communism*.

In capitalism, economic power and private ownership of capital are concentrated in a small percentage of the population (*i.e.*, a few own). In socialism/communism, the state owns and/or controls productive capital (*i.e.*, nobody owns). In the "Just Third Way," widespread dispersion of capital ownership functions as the economic check against the potential for corruption and abuse, including by the government. Restoration of the full rights of property and extension of private property to every individual, serves as the basis for economic democracy, the necessary foundation for effective political democracy.

The "Just Third Way" differs markedly from other versions of the "Third Way," such as the version espoused by Bill Clinton and Tony Blair, which attempts to give moral legitimacy to the Wall Street capitalist approach to economic globalization and blends political democracy with economic plutocracy.

The new paradigm views as a virtue healthy self-interest (*i.e.*, where individual good is directed toward, or in harmony with, the common good). It views greed and envy, on the other hand, as vices, both destructive of a moral and just society. In contrast to capitalism which institutionalizes *greed*, or socialism which institutionalizes *envy*, the "Just Third Way" institutionalizes *justice*.

Justice. Functionally, justice is a set of universal principles that guide people in judging what is right and what is wrong, no matter what culture and society they live in. It is one of the cardinal individual virtues of classical moral philosophy, along with fortitude (courage), temperance (self-control), and prudence (effectiveness). Justice is based on the maxim of *suum cuique*, "to each his due," or, "to each his own." Justice as a moral virtue disposes one person to respect the rights of others and to establish in human relationships the harmony that promotes equity and fairness with regard to other persons and to the common good. The basis of justice is the dignity of each human person. Justice reflects the qualities of balance and equivalence. It holds that each person deserves to be rewarded for his virtues/good habits and good actions and penalized for his vices/bad habits and bad actions.

Justice, Commutative. Also referred to under classical philosophy as "strict justice," commutative justice deals with exchanges of equal or equivalent value between individuals or groups of individuals. In reference to exchanges between parties to a transaction, it imposes a duty of an exact measurement that must be discharged with something having that exact, objective value. That is, a debt of five dollars must be repaid with five dollars.

Justice, Distributive. Defined by Aristotle in his *Ethics*, the classic concept of distributive justice is based on a proportionality of value given and received, rather than on a strict equality of results. It deals with a distribution or division of something among various people interacting cooperatively with one another, in shares proportionate to the value of each one's relative contribution to the outcome.

Justice, Economic. Economic justice is a subset of social justice. It encompasses the moral principles that guide people in creating, maintaining and perfecting economic institutions. These institutions determine how each person earns a living, enters into contracts, exchanges goods and services with others and otherwise produces an independent material foundation for economic subsistence. The ultimate purpose of economic justice is to free each person economically to develop to the full extent of his or her potential, enabling that person to engage in the unlimited work beyond economics, the work of the mind and the spirit done for its own intrinsic value and satisfaction. (*See Work, Leisure.*) The triad of interdependent principles of economic justice that serve as the moral basis of binary economics are the principle of *Participation* (or

Participative Justice), the principle of *Distribution* (or *Distributive Justice*), and the principle of *Harmony* (sometimes referred to as *Social Justice*).

Justice, Individual. Those moral principles and virtues that apply to and guide interactions between individuals. In contrast, "social justice" governs how we, as members of groups, relate to our institutions and social systems, particularly whether each of us is able to participate fully in the common good.

Justice, Participative. Participative justice refers to the right that everyone has to participate fully in all institutions of the common good, including a right of access to the means to participate. George Mason, in the 1776 *Virginia Declaration of Rights*, specified as one of the fundamental human rights, access to "the means of acquiring and possessing property." As first identified and defined by Louis O. Kelso and Mortimer J. Adler as the "input principle" in economic justice, participative justice refers to the ordering of our economic institutions. This principle requires that every person have access to the means and opportunity to contribute economic value through both labor and capital inputs. In economic justice, distribution follows participation. What each person is entitled to receive is determined by his or her relative contribution/participation. As advancing technology begins to contribute a proportionately greater share than human labor to the production of marketable goods and services, participative justice demands the elimination of barriers to capital ownership. Participative justice also requires the universalization of access to such social goods as capital credit through a well-organized banking and legal system.

Justice, Social. Social justice is the particular virtue whose object is the common good of all human society, rather than, as with individual justice, the individual good of any member or group. It is one of the basic social virtues in the field of social morality. Social justice guides humans as social beings in creating and perfecting organized human interactions, or institutions. It is the principle for restoring moral balance and harmony in the social order. Social justice imposes on each member of society a personal responsibility to work with others to design and continually perfect our institutions as tools for personal and social development. To the extent an institution violates the human dignity of any person or group, organized acts of social justice are required to correct the defects in that institution. Actions such as "social justice tithing," for example, recognize a personal responsibility to devote a certain amount of time toward working with others to improve the organizations and institutions in which we live and work.

Justice-Based Management ("JBM"). A leadership philosophy and management system organized in accordance with universal principles of economic and social justice to create a sustainable ownership culture within all economic enterprises and institutions. The objective of JBM within a productive enterprise is to increase long-term corporate profitability by maximizing value to the customer. Its ultimate purpose is to empower each person economically as a worker and as an owner. JBM embodies two precepts of equity: 1) that people are entitled to a proportionate share of what they helped to produce both with their labor and their productive assets, and 2) that all people are entitled to live in a culture that offers them equality of dignity and opportunity, with equal access to the means of acquiring property and power to secure their fundamental rights. Originally called "Value-Based Management" ("VBM").

Labor. The human factor of production, also generally understood as "work for pay." In binary economics, labor refers to all forms of physical, mental and entrepreneurial work that humans contribute to the economic process. Binary theory would view the term "human capital" as a misnomer, referring not to "capital" as such, but to improvements in human labor or human productive capability.

Legal Tender. Currency in such amounts and denominations as the law authorizes a debtor to tender and requires a creditor to receive in payment of money obligations.

Limitation, Principle of. The third principle put forth by Louis Kelso and Mortimer Adler in their triad of economic justice, which operates as the feedback principle for ensuring that participative and distributive justice are in balance and working properly. The principle of limitation prevents such concentrations of capital ownership as are injurious to the economic rights of others, *i.e.*, their right of effective participation in production and to earn thereby a viable income in the form of the distributive share to which they are justly entitled by the value of their contribution.

Kelso and Adler point out that the principle of limitation has significance only for an economy based on the institution of private property in the means of production and on the joint participation of a number of independent contributors to the production of wealth. It has no meaning in an economy where every person owns only his or her labor (and there is no chattel slavery), or where the distributive share that an individual receives bears no relation to the value of the contribution he makes (such as an economic system based on distribution according to need).

Some binary economists, for semantic and philosophical reasons, later renamed this third principle of economic justice as "the principle of harmony" or "the principle of social justice." This was not to deny the negative concept of limitation, but to recognize the positive duty demanded by social justice for every citizen to organize with others to restructure all institutions of the economic system to allow participative and distributive justice to function properly for all members of society.

Market Glut. Production that cannot be cleared at market prices.

Market, Primary. A marketing arrangement for purchasing financial instruments from the original issuers.

Market, Secondary. A marketing arrangement for purchasing financial instruments from other than the original issuers. The New York Stock Exchange, for example, is a secondary market, as are all securities exchanges.

Maslow's Hierarchy of Needs. Based on the writings of Abraham Maslow, a recognition and categorization of various levels of human needs for reaching one's fullest human potential, ranked from the most urgent (survival and security) to social needs such as recognition by others (a necessary aspect of justice), to the most important (self-esteem and ultimately, self-actualization).

Mercantilism. A system where those holding concentrated economic power employ the powers of government to perpetuate monopolies, special privileges, subsidies and trade protections for their advantage at the expense of their competitors and most citizens. Historically, a national economic goal under mercantilism was the accumulation of specie (gold and silver) by importing raw materials cheaply and selling manufactured goods to the suppliers of the raw materials. To achieve these goals, businessmen turned to government to provide them with trade protections, special privileges and monopolies, arguing that such policies were needed to protect domestic jobs. Mercantilist policies have given rise to an unfree and unjust global market, and have helped to widen the gap between wealthy and poor nations, and wealthy and poor citizens.

Monetization. The process of creating general media of exchange ("money"). This process can be carried out by any individual capable of making a promise, but is most often carried out by banks of issue and central banks. Under fractional reserve banking, the commercial banking system as a whole creates money. For example, under a 20% reserve requirement, an individual bank may be able to lend out 80% of its reserves, and as those funds are deposited and reloaned many times over in the same nation, the ultimate effect of the process is to create five times as much money as is backed by reserves.

Money. Money is (1) a medium of exchange, (2) a store of value, (3) a standard of value, and (4) a common measure of value. Money is a "social good," an artifact of civilization invented to facilitate economic transactions for the common good. Like any other human tool or technology, this societal tool can be used justly or unjustly. As binary economist Louis Kelso has pointed out, "Money is not a part of the visible sector of the economy. People do not consume money. Money is not a physical factor of production, but rather a yardstick for measuring economic input, economic outtake and the relative values of the real goods and services of the economic world. Money provides a method of measuring obligations, rights, powers and privileges. It provides a means whereby certain individuals can accumulate claims against others, or against the economy as a whole, or against many economies. It is a system of symbols that many economists substitute for the visible sector and its productive enterprises, goods and services, thereby losing sight of the fact that a monetary system is a part only of the invisible sector of the economy, and that its adequacy can only be measured by its effect upon the visible sector."

Money, Old. The pool of past accumulations or savings available for new capital formation, lent out at a market-determined interest rate.

Money, New. Newly created money that is independent of past accumulations. Under Capital Homesteading, new money (backed by newly created wealth financed through "interest-free" pure credit) would be extended through the Federal Reserve System and its member banks for private sector growth linked to capital democratization.

Negative Income Tax. A proposal advocated by monetarist and Nobel economist Milton Friedman to use the tax system to subsidize basic subsistence incomes directly by redistributing incomes from all taxpayers to all persons who earn below a certain income level; also known as reverse income taxation.

Non-Recourse Credit. (*See* Credit, Non-Recourse.)

Open Market Committee. The basic unit of the Federal Reserve System, operated by the Federal Reserve Bank of New York, that governs the U.S. money supply. It increases the money supply by buying Treasury securities (representing Federal debt and deficit spending) from major securities dealers and increasing demand deposits. It decreases the money supply by selling Treasury securities through the same dealers and decreasing demand deposits.

Paper, Agricultural. Financial instruments (such as promissory notes) secured by agricultural assets, usually the value of crops to be harvested within a year.

Paper, Commercial. Financial instruments, usually unsecured (that is, with no specific collateral other than the general credit worthiness of a firm) issued by a financial institution or private company. These are usually short-term liabilities of less than a year and, in the United States, usually in multiples of $100,000.

Paper, Industrial. Financial instruments secured by industrial assets, usually the value of the assets purchased on credit, and inventory.

Post Scarcity. (*See* Scarcity, Post.)

Power. The ability to do or to effect change. Legally, power means an ability on the part of a person to produce a change in a given legal relation by doing or not doing a given act.

Price, Just. The transaction value reached voluntarily by an informed buyer and an informed seller after a series of implicit or explicit offers and counteroffers, with neither under any compulsion to buy or sell.

Price. The value of the goods or money that is given to acquire a good or service. In a market economy, "price" is the transaction value reached voluntarily by the buyer and seller, with neither under any compulsion to buy or sell. In a centrally planned economy, prices are set by government without regard to the value of the item to the buyer or the cost of the item to the seller.

Prime Rate. The interest rate commercial banks charge their best customers. It includes a markup over the cost of the money to the commercial bank.

Privilege. Privilege is a legal freedom on the part of one person as against another person, group of persons, association, or institution to do a given act, or a legal freedom not to do a given act. From the standpoint of the person or persons against whom privilege operates, privilege means the absence of right.

The one against whom privilege operates has no power to prevent the one who holds the privilege from engaging in a particular course of action or nonaction.

Procreative Credit. (*See* Credit, Capital.)

Productive Credit. (*See* Credit, Capital.)

Productiveness. An expression of the *pro rata* contribution of an economic factor to production, as measured by the market-determined value each factor contributes to the overall production process. In contrast, the commonly accepted term, "productivity," measures economic output strictly in terms of one factor (labor) alone, while treating the contribution of technology and other forms of productive capital as irrelevant for income distribution.

Profits. The financial gain resulting from the use of capital in a transaction after all expenses are paid. Also, the "return to capital" determined by subtracting all costs, including labor costs, from the revenues received from the sale of marketable goods and services by the enterprise.

Propensity to Consume, Average. The proportion of disposable income that the average individual or family unit spends on goods and services.

Propensity to Consume, Marginal. The amount that consumption changes in response to an incremental change in disposable income. It is equal to the change in consumption divided by the change in disposable income that produced the consumption change. The marginal propensity to consume of a rich person is lower than that of a poor person. The rich person, having satisfied his consumption needs, will tend to invest the remainder of his income in income-producing assets (capital) rather than purchasing more consumer goods from producers. As Louis Kelso observed, today's "closed system" of financing capital formation is unable to channel capital ownership and capital incomes to the poor, whose higher propensity to consume would enable "excess" production to be cleared from the market.

Property. Property is an aggregate of the rights, powers and privileges, recognized by the laws of the nation, which an individual may possess with respect to various objects. Property is not the object owned, but the sum total of the "rights" which an individual may "own" in such an object. These in general include the rights of (1) possessing, (2) excluding others, (3) disposing or transferring, (4) using, (5) enjoying the fruits, profits, product or increase, and (6) destroying or injuring, if the owner so desires. In a civilized society, these rights are only as effective as the laws which provide for their enforcement. English common law, adopted into the fabric of American law, recognizes that the rights of property are subject to the limtations that (1) things owned may not be so used as to injure others or the property of others, and (2) they may not be used in ways contrary to the general welfare of the people as a whole. From this definition of private property, a purely functional and practical understanding of the nature of property becomes clear. Property in everyday life is the right of control.

Rediscounting. (*See* Discounting.)

Reserve Policy, 100%. A requirement that for every dollar created for lending purposes by a commercial bank, the bank would have to retain a corresponding dollar's worth of financial or tangible assets to support the loan. Under a 100% reserve requirement, funds to loan out can only be obtained by the bank printing money, if permitted by the banking laws, or by discounting (selling) the loans it makes immediately to the central bank for funds to cover 100% of the demand deposits of a borrowing enterprise or farm. There would thus be a direct link between new money created in a region served by a central bank and the ability to satisfy the region's needs for capital credit for feasible projects. Under 100% reserves, every dollar of new money would be backed by productive assets, adding to the economy in the form of new plant and equipment, new rentable space, and new physical infrastructure and other forms of procreative capital. As the loan principal is repaid, the newly created money would be taken out of circulation or used to make new asset-backed loans.

Reserve Policy, Fractional. The amount of cash or cash equivalents (usually government bonds) a commercial bank is required to have on hand to cover demand for cash on deposit. This is usually expressed as a ratio or percentage of reserves to deposits. For example, a 20% reserve requirement would mean that for every dollar deposited with the bank, the bank would have to retain 20¢ on hand that could not be loaned out. Since each loan is circulated through the banking system, creating new deposits and more loans, each new dollar of deposits under a 20% fractional reserve policy allows the banking system as a whole to create "out of thin air" five dollars of new loans, whether those loans are for nonproductive or speculative uses, for covering public sector deficits, or for productive uses. Contrast with *Reserve Policy, 100%.*

Reserves. Cash or cash equivalents (usually government securities) that a commercial bank has on hand to cover demand for cash on deposit.

Right. A legally enforceable claim of one person against another (*i.e.,* some other individual, group of individuals, association, or institution), that the other shall do a given act or shall not do a given act. A right describes a relation or relationship between the person who has the right, and the other who has the correlative duty — the person against whom the right exists.

Risk Premium. An amount generally added by a lender to insure against anticipated risks that the outstanding principal on a loan may not be repaid or is not backed by sufficient collateral. Under Capital Homesteading such risk premiums could be "pooled" by capital credit insurers and reinsurers to offer a substitute for collateral.

Savings, Forced. The method by which productive assets are purchased with cash accumulated by reducing potential purchases of consumer goods and services.

Savings, Future. The process by which capital is financed on pure credit and the acquisition loan repaid out of the future stream of income generated by the asset.

Savings, Past. The term in binary economics for existing pools of savings. Described as "past" because such savings were generated by reductions in consumption in the past instead of the present or future.

Say's Law of Markets. A recognition that production and consumption should be in balance in a market economy. Another way of expressing this is that the economic values of all goods and services equals the aggregate incomes resulting to all producers. Therefore, as Jean-Baptiste Say said, "It is then in strict reality with their productions that they make their purchases; it is impossible for them to buy any articles whatever to a greater amount than that which they have produced either by themselves, or by means of their capitals and lands." (Jean-Baptiste Say, *Letters to Mr. Malthus On Several Subjects of Political Economy And On The Causes Of The Stagnations of Commerce*. London: Sherwood, Neely, and Jones, 1821, p. 2.) Thus "demand" (income) in an economy governed by competitive market forces is supposed to generate its own "supply" (production), and supply its own demand. Because most workers have only their labor to sell in competition with labor-saving technologies and workers in other labor markets willing or forced to perform the same work at lower wages, and the ownership incomes from technological advances are highly concentrated among already affluent individuals, Say's Law has been negated by anti-market political policies and laws. Binary economics was developed to restore the systems equilibrium of Say's Law by creating a more free and just market economy, with all consumers sharing profits from their direct ownership stakes in enterprises that employ such technologies.

Scarcity. (*See* Scarcity, Economic.)

Scarcity, Economic. In economic terminology, "scarcity" refers to the fact that the same resource — regardless of its quantity — cannot be put to more than a single use at a time. Scarcity in an economic sense refers simply to the choice as to what use to put a specific resource, not to the quantity available. Most schools of economics, following the paradigm of Thomas Malthus, implicitly equate economic scarcity with insufficiency, and erroneously conclude that insufficiency is inevitable. Technological change, however, according to critics of Malthus, makes shared abundance a plausible goal of development theory, offering hope that world poverty is a solvable problem.

Scarcity, Effective. The popular understanding of "scarcity;" that is, the quality or condition of insufficiency. In non-binary economics, effective scarcity exists as an unyielding constraint on growth and development. Binary economics holds that the constraints of scarcity can be overcome by invention and more efficient exploitation of existing resources through the process of "ephemeralization," the redesign of our technologies to "do more with less." (*See* Ephemeralization.)

Scarcity, Post. Any arrangement or transformation of an economic system that helps overcome the constraints of insufficiency or effective scarcity. This is not a rejection of *economic* scarcity, but a refutation of the assumption that *effective* scarcity is inevitable. In binary economies, any insufficiency resulting from economic scarcity can be overcome through substitution or improvements in technology. Thus, Louis Kelso can be termed a "post scarcity" economist for devising a logical framework and comprehensive strategy for harnessing voluntary private-sector initiatives to overcome the artificial constraints to shared abundance. The post-scarcity challenge of the 21st Century is to restructure the social order through acts of social justice to overcome basic social and economic problems.

Security, Primary. (*See* Issuance, Primary.)

Security, Secondary. (*See* Issuance, Secondary.)

Share.   A unit of equity ownership in a corporation, generally referred to as "common stock," which stands last in line against others with claims on a corporate enterprise. This ownership is represented by a stock certificate, which names the company and the shareowner. The number of shares a corporation is authorized to issue is detailed in its corporate charter.

Socialism.   A system of political economy in which the state (or a collective) assumes either ownership or control (and thus effective ownership) of the means of production, thus centralizing the power to regulate wages, prices, profits and all economic institutions.

Sovereignty.   Intrinsic possession of and ability to exercise inalienable rights. "Sovereignty" is that bundle of rights within the common good that accrue to people as fundamental human rights.

Sovereignty, Economic.   That aspect of individual sovereignty requiring that each human being, as an entity with inalienable rights, be given full and equal access to the institutions of the economic common good as a matter of right. Economic sovereignty also refers to the exercise of the ability to function in the economy as a financially independent person. This is often misstated as the right to a living wage, but is more properly construed as the right of access to all means to acquire income through contributions to the economic process, whether through ownership of one's labor, or the ownership of one's capital, or preferably both. Economic sovereignty may thus be briefly stated as the right to private property, and is thus the moral foundation of both a sound economic order and social order as a whole.

Sovereignty, Political.   That aspect of individual sovereignty which regulates the role of the state and the individual's interaction with the state. Just as private property is essential for one's economic sovereignty, access to the political ballot by economically sovereign citizens is essential to safeguard one's political sovereignty against the potential abuses of the coercive powers that reside in government. The ultimate check on government power is to make government economically dependent on the people, not vice versa. The state does not possess political sovereignty intrinsically, but only by delegation from the members of society. This delegation may be revoked for just cause and under certain conditions, but must then be vested in a more just form of government.

Subsidiarity.   The principle stating that those most closely involved at a particular level of the common good are charged with the immediate responsibility of monitoring and reforming the level of the common good in which they live, work, function, etc. The "Principle of Subsidiarity," is defined by the late social philosopher Rev. William Ferree, S.M., Ph.D. in two parts: First, no higher organization may arrogate to itself a function which a lower organization can adequately perform; second, no lower organization may usurp a higher one for its own particular purposes. In management terms, subsidiarity refers to the delegation of decision-making power over a particular area of operation by those working directly in that area.

Subsistence. In social and economic terms, a state of "pre-development" in which a predominantly labor-intensive economic process and extremely primitive tools produce barely enough for survival for most members of a society. As the tools of that economy improve to more capital-intensive levels, the economy will move to greater levels of abundance, and from subsistence to affluence. A binary economy would produce even greater affluence and faster growth rates than a capital-intensive economy where ownership is concentrated, as capital incomes widely dispersed throughout the population would increase mass purchasing power and effective demand for consumer goods, thereby stimulating higher demand for new capital formation.

Supply, Aggregate. The total value of the goods and services produced in a country, plus the value of imported goods, less the value of exports.

Supply. The total quantity of a good or service available for purchase at a given price.

Synergy. The force resulting from mutually cooperating action of separate units which together produce an effect greater than any component acting alone. "Win-win" concept in game theory. Contrast with "zero-sum."

Tax Credit. A tax subsidy that allocates funds without either legislating an entitlement or approving an appropriation. A tax credit allocates funds by permitting tax payers to retain funds normally remitted as taxes if they engage in approved activities at their own expense, thus circumventing the legislative process. A tax credit is similar to an entitlement, but without the collection and dispersal of cash by the state. This permits "hidden" expenditures to advance selected programs without the amount being subject to public scrutiny.

Tax, Payroll. Not a tax, *per se*, but a collection or advance payment of an individual's income tax burden taken out of salary or wages.

Third Way. (*See* Just Third Way.)

Two-Tiered Credit System. (*See* Credit System, Two-Tiered.)

Value. In economic terms, the worth of any tangible or intangible good or service, usually expressed in units of currency, as determined by market forces.

Value-Based Management (VBM). The term originally used by some binary economists to describe a 21st Century servant leadership philosophy and management system for creating and sustaining an expanded ownership culture within business corporations, based on the integration of moral values and market concepts of "value." The term was later changed to "Justice-Based Management (JBM)" when "Value-Based Management (VBM)" began being used by Wall Street and various business schools to describe the purchase of marketable securities or capital assets based on speculation that those assets are undervalued in the market. (*See* Justice-Based Management.)

Voting Passthrough. The equivalent of the right to vote one's shares in a "beneficial" ownership arrangement such as an ESOP, where shares are legally owned by a trust for the benefit of employee participants, rather than owned directly by them. Participants may, if the trust is so designed, have the power to direct the Trustee of an ESOP to vote on their behalf company shares held in their ESOP accounts. Current ESOP law requires pass-through of the vote on major issues such as the sale of the company, but does not require passing through the vote on typical shareholder issues or to elect representatives to the Board of Directors.

Wage System. An economic arrangement of society where a determinant number of people generate the bulk of their income solely through the mechanism of wages, and where the ownership, control over, and property incomes from productive capital is highly concentrated in a tiny percentage of people. Because most people in a wage system have only their labor to sell, in competition with advancing technology and lower-wage workers, the wage system leads inevitably to economic plutocracy, conflict between haves and have-nots, political manipulation of the marketplace, and concentrations of power throughout society.

Wages. Compensation for human labor. Subsistence on wages alone tends to make the wage earner dependent on the employer and leaves him economically vulnerable in the global marketplace.

Work, Leisure. Aristotle's term for "the work of civilization," or the unpaid work outside of economics that is done for its own sense of satisfaction or for its intrinsic value to society. The idea of leisure work can be construed as human activity geared toward fulfilling human needs above the level of security and subsistence on Maslow's hierarchy. It is oriented toward all creative activity and initiatives by which every human being can develop toward self-actualization. In a binary economy where most people could earn the bulk of their subsistence incomes from the ownership of capital, those people could afford to shift from economic work ("toil") to leisure work.

Work. Generally construed as labor, *i.e.*, human activity geared toward production of economic goods and services. In a broader sense, work also includes the idea of what Aristotle termed "leisure work," that is, unpaid human activity whose object is personal, social, or spiritual development.

Zero-Sum. The notion in game theory, or in an economic system, that one person can only win or gain if someone else loses. The opposite of "zero-sum" or "win-lose," is synergy or "win-win."

BIBLIOGRAPHY

Books and Reports

Adler, Mortimer J. and Gorman, William, *The American Testament,* New York: Praeger Press, 1975.

Ashford, Robert H. A., and Shakespeare, Rodney, *Binary Economics: The New Paradigm,* University Press of America: Lanham, Maryland, 1999.

Bach, G. L., *Federal Reserve Policy-Making: A Study in Government Economic Policy Formation,* New York: Knopf Printing, 1950.

Bagehot, Walter, *Lombard Street,* 1873.

Belloc, Hilaire, *The Crisis of Civilization, Being the Matter of a Course of Lectures Delivered at Fordham University, 1937,* Rockford, Illinois: TAN Books and Publishers, Inc., 1991.

Blasi, Joseph R., *Employee Ownership: Revolution or Ripoff?* , Cambridge, Massachusetts: Ballinger Publishing Company, 1988.

Blasi, Joseph R. and Kruse, Douglas L., *The New Owners: The Mass Emergence of Employee Ownership in Public Companies and What It Means to American Business,* New York: Harper Business, 1991.

Bluestone, Barry, and Bluestone, Irving, *Negotiating the Future: A Labor Perspective on American Business* , New York: HarperCollins Publishers, Inc., 1992.

Blum, Walter and Kalven, Harry, *The Uneasy Case for Progressive Income Taxation,* University of Chicago Press, 1954.   ·

Board of Governors of the Federal Reserve System and the U.S. Treasury Department, *The Federal Reserve and the Treasury, Answers to Questions from the Commission on Money and Credit,* Englewood Cliffs, New Jersey: Prentice-Hall, 1963.

Brohawn Dawn K., ed., *The Role of Property in Building Economic and Social Justice: Questions and Answers for Participants, CESJ Seminar, De La Salle Conference Center (Rome),* Arlington, Virginia: Center for Economic and Social Justice, 1991.

Brohawn, Dawn K., ed., *Every Worker an Owner: A Revolutionary Free Enterprise Challenge to Marxism,* orientation writings for the 1986 Presidential Task Force on Project Economic Justice, Arlington, Virginia: Center for Economic and Social Justice, 1987.

Council of Economic Advisors, *2002 Economic Report of the President,* available in .pdf format at: http://w3.access.gpo.gov/eop/.

Currie, Lauchlin, *The Supply and Control of Money in the United States,* Cambridge, Massachusetts: Harvard University Press, 1934.

DePree, Max, *Leadership is an Art,* East Lansing: Michigan State University Press, 1987.

Ferree, William, *Introduction to Social Justice,* Arlington, Virginia: Center for Economic and Social Justice, 1998.

Ferree, William, *The Act of Social Justice*, Washington DC: The Catholic University of America Press, 1942.

Friedman, Kathy, *Legitimation of Social Rights and the Western Welfare State*, Chapel Hill: University of North Carolina Press, 1981.

Fuller, R. Buckminster, *Utopia or Oblivion: The Prospects for Humanity*, New York: Bantam Books, 1969.

Gates, Jeff, *Democracy at Risk: Rescuing Main Street from Wall Street*, New York: Perseus Publishing, April 2000.

Gates, Jeff, *The Ownership Solution: Toward a Shared Capitalism for the 21ˢᵗ Century*, Reading, MA: Addison-Wesley, 1998.

Gorga, Carmine, The *Economic Process*, Gloucester, Massachusetts: The Somist Institute Press, 1978.

Government Printing Office, *Economic Report of the President*, February 2002.

Greider, William, *One World, Ready or Not: The Manic Logic of Global Capitalism*, New York: Simon and Schuster, 1997.

Greider, William, *Secrets of the Temple: How the Federal Reserve Runs the Country*, New York: Simon and Schuster, 1988.

Habiger, Matthew, *Papal Teaching on Private Property 1891-1981*, Lanham, Maryland: University Press of America, 1990.

Halstead, Ted and Lind, Michael, *The Radical Center: The Future of American Politics*, New York: Doubleday, 2001.

Hanke, Steve H., ed., *The Political Economy of Privatization*, New York: The Academy of Political Science, 1986.

Jevons, William Stanley, "The Functions of Money," *Money and the Mechanism of Exchange*, New York: D. Appleton and Company, 1898.

Joint Economic Committee of Congress, *The 1976 Joint Economic Report*, March 10, 1976.

Joint Economic Committee, U.S. Congress, *Broadening the Ownership of New Capital: ESOPs and Other Alternatives*, staff study, June 17, 1976.

Joint Economic Committee, U.S. Congress, *Employee Stock Ownership Plans (ESOPs)*, Hearings (2 volumes), December 12, 1975.

Kelso, Louis O. and Adler, Mortimer J., *The Capitalist Manifesto*, New York: Random House, 1958.

Kelso, Louis O. and Adler, Mortimer J., *The New Capitalists*, New York: Random House, 1961.

Kelso, Louis O. and Kelso, Patricia Hetter, *Democracy and Economic Power: Extending the ESOP Revolution*, Cambridge, Massachusetts: Balinger Publishing Company, 1986.

Kelso, Louis O. and Hetter, Patricia, *Two-Factor Theory: The Economics of Reality*, New York: Random House, 1967.

Knight, Frank, *The Economic Organization*, Chicago, Illinois: The University of Chicago, 1933.

Kuhn, Thomas S, *The Structure of Scientific Revolutions*, Second Edition, London, U.K.: The University of Chicago Press, 1970.

Levering, Robert; Moskowitz, Milton, and Katz, Michael, *The 100 Best Companies to Work for in America*, New York: Plume, 1984.

Lieber, James B., *Friendly Takeover: How an Employee Buyout Saved a Steel Town*, New York: Penguin Group, 1995.

Logue, John; Glass, Richard; Patton, Wendy; Teodosio, Alex; and Thomas, Karen, *Participatory Employee Ownership: Best Practices in Employee Ownership*, Kent, OH: Worker Ownership Institute and Ohio Employee Ownership Center, 1998.

Maaloe, Erik, *The Employee Owner: Organizational and Individual Change within Manufacturing Companies as Participation and Sharing Grow and Expand*, Copenhagen: Academic Press, 1998.

Meade, J.E., *Efficiency, Equality and the Ownership of Property*, London: Geo. Allen & Unwin Ltd., 1964.

Metzger, Burt L., *Increasing Productivity through Profit Sharing*, Evanston, Ill.: Profit Sharing Research Foundation, 1980.

Miller, Rev. John H., S.T.D., ed., *Curing World Poverty: The New Role of Property*, St. Louis, Missouri: Social Justice Review, 1994.

Morrison, Charles, *An Essay on the Relations Between Labour and Capital*, London: Longman, Brown, Green, and Longmans, 1854.

Moulton, Harold G., *The Formation of Capital*, Washington, DC: The Brookings Institution, 1935.

Moulton, Harold G.; Edwards, George W.; Magee, James D.; Lewis, Cleona, *Capital Expansion, Employment, and Economic Stability*, Washington, DC: The Brookings Institution, 1940.

Moulton, Harold, G., *Financial Organization and the Economic System*, New York: McGraw Hill Book Company, 1938.

O'Rourke, P. J., *Eat the Rich: A Treatise on Economics*, Atlantic Monthly Press: New York, 1998.

Peters, Thomas J. and Austin, Nancy, *A Passion for Excellence*, New York: Random House, 1985.

Peters, Thomas J. and Waterman, Robert H. Jr., *In Search of Excellence*, New York: Harper & Row, 1982.

Powers, Treval C., *Leakage: The Bleeding of the American Economy*, New Canaan, CT: Benchmark Publications, 1996.

Presidential Task Force on Project Economic Justice, *High Road to Economic Justice*, Arlington: Center for Economic and Social Justice, 1986.

President's Commission on Strengthening Social Security, *Strengthening Social Security and Creating Personal Wealth for All Americans*, December 11, 2001.

Proudfoot, G. Wilfred and Shakespeare, Rodney A., *The Two Factor Nation: Or How to Make the People Rich*, Yorkshire, England: Two Factor Companies, 1997

Quarrey, Michael; Blasi, Joseph; and Rosen, Corey, *Taking Stock: Employee Ownership at Work*, Cambridge, Massachusetts: Ballinger Publishing Company, 1986.

Quarter, Jack, *Beyond the Bottom Line: Socially Innovative Business Owners*, Westport, CT: Quorum Books, 2000.

Ragland, Robert A., *Employee Stock Ownership Plans: An Assessment of the Contribution of ESOPs to Private Wealth, Business Productivity and Economic Growth*, Washington, DC: National Chamber Foundation, 1989.

Rockefeller III, John D. *The Second American Revolution: Some Personal Observations*. New York, Harper and Row, 1973.

Rosen, Corey; Klein, Katherine J. and Young, Karen, *Employee Ownership in America: The Equity Solution*, Lexington, Massachusetts: Lexington Books, 1985.

Sabre Foundation, *Expanded Ownership*, Fond du Lac, Wisconsin, 1972.

Schumpeter, Joseph A., *The Theory of Economic Development*, New Brunswick: Transaction Publishers, 1993.

Shakespeare, Rodney and Challen, Peter, *Seven Steps to Justice*, London, England: New European Publications, 2002.

Simmons, John and Mares, William, *Working Together*, New York: Knopf, 1983.

Simons, Henry C., *Economic Policy for a Free Society*, Chicago, Illinois: University of Chicago Press, 1948.

Sithole, Ndabaningi, *The Secret of American Success: Africa's Great Hope*, Washington, DC: Gazaland Publishers, 1988.

Smiley, Robert W. Jr. and Gilbert, Ronald J., eds., *Employee Stock Ownership Plans: Business Planning, Implementation, Law & Taxation*, Larchmont, New York: Maxwell Macmillan/Rosenfeld Launer, 1989.

Solow, R. M., K. J. Arrow, S. Karlin, and P. Suppes, eds., *Mathematical Methods in the Social Sciences, 1959*, 89-104, Stanford University Press, 1960.

Sowell, Thomas, *Say's Law: An Historical Analysis*, Princeton, New Jersey: The Princeton University Press, 1972.

Stack, Jack, *The Great Game of Business: The Only Sensible Way to Run a Business*, New York: Currency Books, 1992.

Tanner, Michael, "Privatizing Social Security: A Big Boost for the Poor," report by the Cato Institute's *Project on Social Security Privatization*, SSP No. 4, July 26, 1996.

U.S. Congress, House Banking and Currency Committee, *A Primer on Money*, August 5, 1964.

U.S. Congressional House Committee on Banking and Currency, *Report of the Committee Appointed Pursuant to House Resolutions 429 and 504 to Investigate the Concentration of Control of Money and Credit*. Washington, DC: U.S. Government Printing Office, 1913.

U.S. Congress, Joint Economic Committee, *Hearings on ESOPs*, 1976.

Weitzman, Martin L., *The Share Economy*, Cambridge, Massachusetts: Harvard University Press, 1984.

Articles
Aaron, Henry, "To Fix Social Security," *The Washington Post*, April 8, 1998.

Aaron, Henry J. and Reischauer, Robert D., "Tune It Up, Don't Trade It In," *The Washington Post*, April 19, 1998.

Aaron, Henry J. and Rivlin, Alice, "Social Security Boosts Nation's Wealth," *The Washington Post*, June 12, 2000.

Aeppel, Timothy, "Workers Not Included," *The Wall Street Journal*, November 19, 2002, B1.

Angell, James W., "The 100 Per Cent Reserve Plan," The Quarterly Journal of Economics, November 1935, pp. 1-35.

"Artificial Intelligence," *Business Week*, March 8, 1982.

Apfel, Kenneth S., "Social Security Standoff," *The Washington Post*, April 11, 2001, A27.

Ashford, Robert, "The Binary Economics of Louis Kelso," *Curing World Poverty: The New Role of Property*, John H. Miller, ed., St. Louis: Social Justice Review, 1994.

Bailey, Norman A., "A Nation of Owners: A Plan for Closing the Growing U.S. Knowledge and Capital Asset Gaps,"

The International Economy, September/October 2000.

Bailey, Norman A., "Central Bank Funding of Economic Growth and Economic Justice Through Expanded Capital Ownership," speech presented at the Capital Ownership Group Conference on Globalization, Four Points Sheraton Hotel, Washington, D.C., October 9-11, 2002.

Bailey, Norman A., "Fed Should Share the Wealth," *The Journal of Commerce*, May 15, 1989.

Bailey, Norman A., "The American Economy: Power and Paradox," *The Yale Review*, New Haven: Yale University Press, 1966.

Bailey, Norman A., "The Role and Function of Monetary Policy in the Promotion of Expanded Capital Ownership," paper presented at a panel on "Latin America and Economic Empowerment," sponsored by the World Institute for Development and Peace, September 26, 1997.

Ball, Robert, "Reflections on Social Security," *The Wall Street Journal*, May 2, 1973.

Balz, Dan, "Social Security Reform Becomes Defining Issue," *The Washington Post*, May 15, 2000.

Barone, Michael, "The Deeper Currents," The National Interest column, *U.S. News and World Report*, November 11, 2002, p. 34.

Berkowitz, Edward D., "The Insecurity of Privatization," *The Washington Post*, Outlook Section, December 8, 1996, p. C1.

Berry, John M., "Fed Proposal Would Remove 'Stigma' from Discount Windows," *The Washington Post*, p. E1.

Berry, John M., "Greenspan Praises Markets' Flexibility: Fed Chief Says Changes Buoyed Economy," *The Washington Post*, November 20, 2002, p. E1.

Betancourt, Antonio L., "Curing World Poverty Through the Democratization of Access to Money and Credit," paper presented at the Asian Convention on World Peace on "Projections for an Asian Community," Manila, Philippines, November 1999.

Brohawn, Dawn K., "Value-Based Management A Framework for Equity and Efficiency in the Workplace, published in *Curing World Poverty: The New Role of Property*, John H. Miller, ed., Social Justice Review: St. Louis, MO, 1994.

Bush, George, "Remarks by President Bush and President Putin to Russian Exchange Students and Students of Crawford High School," Crawford High School, Crawford, Texas, November 15, 2001, Office of the White House Press Secretary. (Complete text available from http://www.usembassy.it/file2001_11/alia/a1111504.htm)

Center for Economic and Social Justice, "A New Model of Nation-Building for Citizens of Iraq," occasional paper, update of May 12, 2003.

Collins, Chuck, Hartman, Chris, and Sklar, Holly, "Divided Decade: Economic Disparity at the Century's Turn," United for a Fair Economy, December 15, 1999, URL: ufenet.org/press/divided_decade.html.

Columbia Law Review, Vol. 20, 93 (Dodge v. Ford Motor Company).

Dayley, James H., "Changing the 'Us-vs-Them' Mentality," *Social Justice Review,* September/October 2002, pp. 147-148.

Davenport, John, "The Testament of Henry Simons" *Fortune,* January, 1946, pp. 116 - 119.

Denison, Edward, "Accounting for United States Economic Growth: 1929-69," Washington, DC: Brookings Institution, 1974.

Denison, Edward, *Accounting for Slower Economic Growth: The United States in the 1970s,* Washington, DC: Brookings Institution, 1979.

Dionne, Jr., E.J., "Low-Income Taxpayers: New Meat for the Right," *The Washington Post,* November 26, 2002, p. A29.

Dodge v. Ford Motor Company, 204 Mich. 459 (1919), 170 N.W. 668, 3 A.L.R. 413.

Dolley, James C., "The Industrial Advance Program of the Federal Reserve System," *Quarterly Journal of Economics,* February 1936, pp. 229 - 274.

Eisner, Robert, "No Need to Sacrifice Seniors or Children," *The Wall Street Journal,* February 2, 1996.

Fauntroy, The Hon. Rev. Walter E., "Learning From an Old Example: A Plan to Address America's Problem," *National Black Monitor,* Part 1 (March 1996, pp. 5-6) and Part 2 (April 1996, pp. 6-7).

Fauntroy, The Hon. Rev. Walter E., "The Most Serious Problem Confronting the Nation and the World Today and the Economic Paradigm for the 21st Century That Will Solve It," speech presented at the 18th Annual Luncheon of the Philadelphia Martin Luther King, Jr. Association for Nonviolence, January 17, 2000.

Feldstein, Martin, "Let's Really Save Social Security," *The Wall Street Journal,* February 10, 1998.

Friedman, Kathy V., "Capital Credit: The Ultimate Right of Citizenship," Paper presented at the 86th Annual Meeting of the American Sociological Association, August 23-27, 1991. Reprinted in *Curing World Poverty* cited below.

Government Printing Office, *Strengthening Social Security and Creating Personal Wealth for All Americans,* report of the President's Commission, December 11, 2001.

"Greenspan Backs Use Of Surpluses to Keep Social Security Afloat," *The Wall Street Journal,* January 30, 1998.

Grosscup, Peter Stenger, "How to Save the Corporation," *McClure's Magazine,* February, 1905, reprinted in *Curing World Poverty: The New Role of Property,* St. Louis, Missouri: Social Justice Review, 1994.

Grunwald, Michael, "Terror's Damage: Calculating the Devastation," *The Washington Post,* October 28, 2001, p. A12.

Halstead, Ted, "The Big Tax Bite You Don't Even Think About," *The Washington Post,* April 23, 2000.

Hausman, Tate, "'Booming' Economy Benefits the Rich, Busts the Rest," AlterNet. URL: www.alternet.org/PublicArchive/Hausman924.html.

Humphrey, Hubert H., "Broadening Capital Ownership," letter to the editor from Senator Hubert H. Humphrey, Chairman of the Joint Economic Committee, published in the *Washington Post,* July 20, 1976.

Ip, Greg, "Fed is Overhauling Procedure for Discount-Window Loans," *The Wall Street Journal*, May 20, 2002, p. A2.

Kelso, Louis O., "Karl Marx: The Almost Capitalist," *American Bar Association Journal*, March 1957.

Kelso, Louis O. and Hetter, Patricia, "Invisible Violence of Corporate Finance," The Washington Post, Business Section, June 18, 1972, p. F1.

Kelso, Louis O. and Hetter, Patricia, "Uprooting World Poverty: A Job for Business," *Business Horizons*, Graduate School of Business, Indiana University, Fall 1964.

Kendrick, John W., "Productivity Trends and Recent Slowdown: Historical Perspective, Causal Factors, and Policy Options," *Contemporary Economic Problems*, Washington, DC: American Enterprise Institute, 1979.

Klein, Joe, "If Chile Can Do It," *Newsweek*, December 12, 1994.

Kurland, Norman G., "A New Look at Prices and Money: The Kelsonian Binary Model for Achieving Rapid Growth Without Inflation," *Journal of Socio-Economics*, December, 2001, 495-515.

Kurland, Norman, "An Illustrated Guide for Statesmen: A Two-Pronged Strategy for Implementing ESOP Privatizations in a Developing or Transforming Economy," occasional paper, Arlington, Virginia: Center for Economic and Social Justice, 1991.

Kurland, Norman G., "Beyond ESOPs: Steps Toward Tax Justice." *The Tax Executive*, April and July 1977.

Kurland, Norman G., "Capital Homesteading for D.C. Citizens: A Federal Reserve Demonstration for Funding Economic Empowerment." occasional paper, Arlington, VA: Center for Economic and Social Justice, 1995.

Kurland, Norman G., "Dinner at the Madison: Louis Kelso Meets Russell Long," *Owners at Work*, Ohio Employee Ownership Center, Winter 1997/1998, pp. 5-8.

Kurland, Norman. "Future of the Multinational Corporation: Who Will Own It?", occasional paper, Arlington, Virginia: Center for Economic and Social Justice, 1988.

Kurland, Norman G., "How to Win a Revolution...And Enjoy It," occasional paper, Arlington, VA: Center for Economic and Social Justice, 1972, updated 1989.

Kurland, Norman G., "Kelsonian Monetary Weapons for Fighting Inflation," paper presented at the panel on "Kelsonian Economics," 1977 Annual Meeting of the Eastern Economics Association. Reprinted in the Hearings on H.R. 3056, Small Business Employee Ownership, Subcommittee on Access to Equity Capital and Business Opportunities, Committee on Small Business, U.S. House of Representatives, May 8, 15, 1979, pp. 15-29.

Kurland, Norman G., "The Abraham Federation: A New Framework for Peace in the Middle East." Originally published in *World Citizen News*, December, 1978. Updated and republished in *American-Arab Affairs* (now *Middle East Policy*), Spring 1991, a publication of the Middle East Policy Council.

Kurland, Norman G., "The Capital Homestead Act: National Infrastructural Reforms to Make Every Citizen A Shareholder," Washington, D.C.: Center for Economic and Social Justice, 1996 (revised from 1982 paper originally entitled "The Industrial Homestead Act: National Infrastructural Reforms to Make Every Citizen A Shareholder").

Kurland, Norman, "The Community Investment Corporation (CIC): A Vehicle for Economic and Political Empowerment of Individual Citizens at the Community Level," occasional paper, Arlington, Virginia: Center for Economic and Social Justice, 1992.

Kurland, Norman G., "The Elusive Third Way," letter to the editor, *The Washington Post*, September 22, 1998, p. A16.

Kurland, Norman G., "The Federal Reserve Discount Window," *The Journal of Employee Ownership Law and Finance*, Vol. 10, No. 1, Oakland, California: National Center for Employee Ownership, Winter 1998.

Kurland, Norman G., "What Can We Learn from an ESOP 'Failure'?", article in *Journey to an Ownership Culture: Insights from the ESOP Community*, Dawn K. Brohawn, ed., Lanham, MD: Scarecrow Press and The ESOP Association, 1997.

Leggett, William, "Municipal Docks," *Plaindealer*, December 3, 1836.

Longman, Phillip, "Justice Between Generations," *The Atlantic Monthly*, June, 1985.

Myers, Robert J., "Social Security's Hidden Hazards," *The Wall Street Journal*, July 28, 1972.

New York Stock Exchange, Office of Economic Research, *People and Productivity: A Challenge to Corporate America*, November 1982.

Nicholson, William L. and Lorenz, George W., "Western Building Products, Inc.: Organized for the Common Good," *Social Justice Review*, January/February 2002, pp. 14-16.

Penny, Tim, "Case for Return to Original Intent of Social Security, *The Wall Street Journal*, July 11, 1988.

Penny, Timothy J., "Save Social Security From Big Spenders," *The Wall Street Journal*, March 9, 1998.

Reagan, Ronald, "Tax Plan No. 1," *Viewpoint with Ronald Reagan*, radio show (Ronald Reagan urges ESOP financing), February 1975.

Reagan, Ronald, speech before the Young Americans for Freedom, San Francisco, CA, July 20, 1974.

Rossett, Claudia, "Greenspan's Dilemma," Wall Street Journal, December 12, 1997, p. A18.

Rudman, Warren B., "Social Security Shell Game," *The Washington Post*, January 12, 1994.

Saint Phalle, Thibaut de, "How the Fed Lets the Deficits Flourish," *Business Week*, May 20, 1985.

Samuelson, Robert J., "Justice Among Generations," *The Washington Post*, January 15, 1997.

Sheen, Fulton J. Sheen, "New Slavery: Freedom Without Property is Incomplete," from a collection of essays, *On Being Human: Reflections on Life and Living*, New York: Doubleday & Co., 1982

Slater, Stanley F., and Olson, Eric M., "A Fresh Look at Industry and Market Analysis," *Business Horizons*, Indiana University Graduate School of Business, Jan.-Feb. 2002, 15.

Social Security Board, "Security in Your Old Age," Washington, DC: Government Printing Office, 1935.

Stein, Herbert, "The Social Security Surplus Confusion," *The Wall Street Journal*, March 27, 1990.

Thompson, Bennie and Greenspan, Alan. Exchanges of March 24, 1995 and April 7, 1995. Reprinted in "The Federal Reserve Discount Window," occasional paper, Arlington: Center for Economic and Social Justice, 1995.

"Two Firms Keep American Dream Alive," *The Washington Times*, September 14, 2001, F1.

United States Department of the Treasury, "Daily Treasury Statement: Cash and debt operations of the United States Treasury, November 22, 2002," Table III-C. Financial Management Service (FMS) website at www.fms.treas.gov.dts.

Wolff, Edward N., "Recent Trends in Wealth Ownership," a paper for the conference on "Benefits and Mechanisms for Spreading Asset Ownership in the United States," New York University, December 10-12, 1998.

Yergin, Daniel, "Herd on the Street: A Quarterly Stampede," *The Washington Post*, June 6, 2002, p. B1.

Zwick, Charles J., and Lewis, Peter A., "Apocalypse Not: Social Security Crisis is Overblown," *The Wall Street Journal*, April 11, 2001, p. A18.

Web Sites

On the Just Third Way, Binary Economics and Justice-Based Management SM

Center for Economic and Social Justice: www.cesj.org

Global Justice Movement: www.globaljusticemovement.org

The Kelso Institute: www.kelsoinstitute.org

On Employee Stock Ownership Plans and Participatory Management

National Center for Employee Ownership: www.nceo.org

The ESOP Association: www.esopassociation.org

Ohio Employee Ownership Center: www.kent.edu/oeoc

Capital Ownership Group: http://cog.kent.edu

The Shared Capitalism Institute: www.sharedcapitalism.org

Virtual Union: www.virtualunions.info

On Advanced Waste-to-Energy Technologies

Equitech International, LLC: www.equitechllc.com

Intellergy Corporation: www.intellergy.com

Other Sources

Social Security Administration: www.ssa.gov

President's Commission to Strengthen Social Security: www.csss.gov

Economic Report of the President: http://w3.access.gpo.gov/eop/

U.S. Census Bureau: www.census.gov

Federal Reserve Board: www.federalreserve.gov

U.S. Department of Labor: www.dol.gov

U.S. Department of Commerce: www.commerce.gov

APPENDICES

1. Original Social Security Handout from 1935

2. Extract from Section 13 of the Federal Reserve Act of 1913

3. What Capital Homesteading Would Mean to the Average American: Projected Wealth and Income Accumulations Under Capital Homesteading

4. A New Look at Prices and Money: The Kelsonian Binary Model for Achieving Rapid Economic Growth Without Inflation

5. Statistics on Wealth and Income Distribution

6. Defining Economic and Social Justice

7. Matrix Comparing Capitalism, Socialism, and the "Just Third Way"

8. The Elusive Third Way

9. A New Model of Nation-Building for Citizens of Iraq (Executive Summary)

10. About CESJ

11. About the Authors

APPENDIX 1
ORIGINAL SOCIAL SECURITY HANDOUT FROM 1935

SECURITY IN   YOUR OLD AGE

SOCIAL SECURITY BOARD
Washington. D. C.

To Employees of Industrial and Business Establishments

FACTORIES · SHOPS · MINES · MILLS · STORES OFFICES AND OTHER PLACES OF BUSINESS

The United States Government will, in the near future, set up a Social Security account for you, if you are eligible. To understand your obligations, rights, and benefits you should read the following general explanation.

THERE is now a law in this country which will give about 26 million working people something to live on when they are old and have stopped working. This law, which gives other benefits, too, was passed last year by Congress and is called the Social Security Act.

Under this law the United States Government will send checks every month to retired workers, both men and women, after they have passed their 65th birthday and have met a few simple requirements of the law.

WHAT THIS MEANS TO YOU

THIS means that if you work in some factory, shop, mine, mill, store, office, or almost any other kind of business or industry, you will be earning benefits that will come to you later on. From the time you are 65 years old, or more, and stop working, you will get a Government check every month of your life, if you have worked some time (one day or more) in each of any 5 years after 1936, and have earned during that time a total of $2,000 or more.

The checks will come to you as a right. You will get them regardless of the amount of property or income you may have. They are what the law calls "Old-Age Benefits" under the Social Security Act. If you prefer to keep on working after you are 65, the monthly checks from the Government will begin coming to you whenever you decide to retire.

The Amount of Your Checks

How much you will get when you are 65 years old will depend entirely on how much you earn in wages from your industrial or business employment between January 1, 1937, and your 65th birthday. A man or woman who gets good wages and has a steady job most of his or her life can get as much as $85 a month for life after age 65. The least you can get in monthly benefits, if you come under the law at all, is $10 a month.

IF YOU ARE NOW YOUNG

Suppose you are making $25 a week and are young enough now to go on working for 40 years. If you make an average of $25 a week for 52 weeks in each year, your check when you are 65 years old will be $53 a month for the rest of your life. If you make $50 a week, you will get $74.50 a month for the rest of your life after age 65.

IF YOU ARE NOW MIDDLE-AGED

But suppose you are about 55 years old now and have 10 years to work before you are 65. Suppose you make only $15 a week on the average. When you stop work at age 65 you will get a check for $19 each month for the rest of your life. If you make $25 a week for 10 years, you will get a little over $23 a month from the Government as long as you live after your 65th birthday.

IF YOU SHOULD DIE BEFORE AGE 65

If you should die before you begin to get your monthly checks, your family will get a payment in cash, amounting to 3½ cents on every dollar of wages you have earned after 1936. If, for example, you should die at age 64, and if you had earned $25 a week for 10 years before that time, your family would receive $455. On the other hand, if you have not worked enough to get the regular monthly checks by the time you are 65, you will get a lump sum, or if you should die your family or estate would get a lump sum. The amount of this, too, will be 3½ cents on every dollar of wages you earn after 1936.

TAXES

THE same law that provides these old-age benefits for you and other workers, sets up certain new taxes to be paid to the United States Government. These taxes are collected by the Bureau of Internal Revenue of the U. S. Treasury Department, and inquiries concerning them should be addressed to that bureau. The law also creates an "Old-Age Reserve Account" in the United States Treasury, and Congress is authorized to put into this reserve account each year enough money to provide for the monthly payments you and other workers are to receive when you are 65.

YOUR PART OF THE TAX

The taxes called for in this law will be paid both by your employer and by you. For the next 3 years you will pay maybe 15 cents a week, maybe 25 cents a week, maybe 30 cents or more, according to what you earn. That is to say, during the next 3 years, beginning January 1, 1937, you will pay 1 cent for every dollar you earn, and at the same time your employer will pay 1 cent for every dollar you earn, up to $3,000 a year. Twenty-six million other workers and their employers will be paying at the same time.

After the first 3 years—that is to say, beginning in 1940—you will pay, and your employer will pay, 1½ cents for each dollar you earn, up to $3,000 a year. This will be the tax for 3 years, and then, beginning in 1943, you will pay 2 cents, and so will your employer, for every dollar you earn for the next 3 years. After that, you and your employer will each pay half a cent more for 3 years, and finally, beginning in 1949, twelve years from now, you and your employer will each pay 3 cents on each dollar you earn, up to $3,000 a year. That is the most you will ever pay.

YOUR EMPLOYER'S PART OF THE TAX

The Government will collect both of these taxes from your employer. Your part of the tax will be taken out of your pay. The Government will collect from your employer an equal amount out of his own funds.

This will go on just the same if you go to work for another employer, so long as you work in a factory, shop, mine, mill, office, store, or other such place of business. (Wages earned in employment as farm workers, domestic workers in private homes, Government workers, and on a few other kinds of jobs are not subject to this tax.)

OLD-AGE RESERVE ACCOUNT

Meanwhile, the Old-Age Reserve fund in the United States Treasury is drawing interest, and the Government guarantees it will never earn less than 3 percent. This means that 3 cents will be added to every dollar in the fund each year.

Maybe your employer has an old-age pension plan for his employees. If so, the Government's old-age benefit plan will not have to interfere with that. The employer can fit his plan into the Government plan.

What you get from the Government plan will always be more than you have paid in taxes and usually more than you can get for yourself by putting away the same amount of money each week in some other way.

Note.—"Wages" and "employment" wherever used in the foregoing mean wages and employment as defined in the Social Security Act.

WHERE TO GET MORE INFORMATION

If you want more information, write to the *Social Security Board, Washington, D. C.*, or get in touch with one of the following offices:

REGION I—Maine, New Hampshire, Vermont, Massachusetts, Rhode Island, and Connecticut:
Social Security Board
120 Boylston Street
Boston, Mass.

REGION II—New York:
Social Security Board
45 Broadway
New York, N. Y.

REGION III—New Jersey, Pennsylvania, and Delaware:
Social Security Board
Widener Building
Juniper and Chestnut Streets
Philadelphia, Pa.

REGION IV—Virginia, West Virginia, North Carolina, Maryland, and District of Columbia:
Social Security Board
National Theatre Building
Washington, D. C.

REGION V—Kentucky, Ohio, and Michigan:
Social Security Board
Bulkley Building
1501 Euclid Avenue
Cleveland, Ohio

REGION VI—Illinois, Indiana, and Wisconsin:
Social Security Board
211 West Wacker Drive
Chicago, Ill.

REGION VII—Tennessee, Mississippi, Alabama, Georgia, Florida, and South Carolina:
Social Security Board
1829 First Avenue North
Birmingham, Ala.

REGION VIII—Iowa, Minnesota, North Dakota, South Dakota, and Nebraska:
Social Security Board
New Post Office Building
Minneapolis, Minn.

REGION IX—Missouri, Kansas, Arkansas, and Oklahoma:
Social Security Board
Dierks Building
1006 Grand Avenue
Kansas City, Mo.

REGION X—Louisiana, Texas, and New Mexico:
Social Security Board
Smith-Young Tower Building
San Antonio, Tex.

REGION XI—Montana, Idaho, Utah, Colorado, Arizona, and Wyoming:
Social Security Board
Patterson Building
1706 Welton Street
Denver, Colo.

REGION XII—California, Oregon, Washington, and Nevada:
Social Security Board
Humboldt Bank Building
785 Market Street
San Francisco, Calif.

INFORMATIONAL SERVICE CIRCULAR No. 9

APPENDIX 2
EXCERPTS FROM THE FEDERAL RESERVE ACT OF 1913

(as Amended; Source: US Code Collection of Cornell University)

Title 12
Chapter 3
Subchapter IX

Sec. 342. — Deposits; exchange and collection; member and nonmember banks or other depository institutions; charges.

Any Federal Reserve bank may receive from any of its member banks, or other depository institutions, and from the Unites States, deposits of current funds in lawful money, national—bank notes, Federal reserve notes, or checks, and drafts, payable upon presentation or other items, and also, for collection, maturing notes and bills; or, solely for purposes of exchange or of collection may receive from other Federal reserve banks deposits of current funds in lawful money, national—bank notes, or checks upon other Federal reserve banks, and checks and drafts, payable upon presentation within its district or other items, and maturing notes and bills payable within its district; or, solely for the purposes of exchange or of collection, may receive from any nonmember bank or trust company or other depository institution deposits of current funds in lawful money, national—bank notes, Federal reserve notes, checks and drafts payable upon presentation or other items, or maturing notes and bills: Provided, Such nonmember bank or trust company or other depository institution maintains with the Federal Reserve bank of its district a balance in such amount as the Board determines taking into account items in transit, services provided by the Federal Reserve bank, and other factors as the Board may deem appropriate: Provided further, That nothing in this or any other section of this chapter shall be construed as prohibiting a member or nonmember bank or other depository institution from making reasonable charges, to be determined and regulated by the Board of Governors of the Federal Reserve System, but in no case to exceed 10 cents per $100 or fraction thereof, based on the total of checks and drafts presented at any one time, for collection or payment of checks and drafts and remission therefor by exchange or otherwise; but no such charges shall be made against the Federal reserve banks.

Sec. 343. — Discount of obligations arising out of actual commercial transactions

Upon the indorsement of any of its member banks, which shall be deemed a waiver of demand, notice and protest by such bank as to its own indorsement exclusively, any Federal reserve bank may discount notes, drafts, and bills of exchange arising out of actual commercial transactions; that is, notes, drafts, and bills of exchange issued or drawn for agricultural, industrial, or commercial purposes, or the proceeds of which have been used, or are to be used, for such purposes, the Board of Governors of the Federal Reserve System to have the right to determine or define the character of the paper thus eligible for discount, within the meaning of this chapter. Nothing in this chapter contained shall be construed to prohibit such notes, drafts, and bills of exchange, secured by staple agricultural products, or other goods, wares, or merchandise from being eligible for such discount, and the notes, drafts, and bills of exchange of factors issued as such making advances exclusively to producers of staple agricultural products in their raw state shall be eligible for such discount; but such definition shall not include notes, drafts, or bills covering merely investments or issued or drawn for the purpose of carrying or trading in stocks, bonds, or other investment securities, except bonds and notes of the Government of the United States. Notes, drafts, and bills admitted to discount under the terms of this paragraph must have a maturity at the time of discount of not more than ninety days, exclusive of grace.

In unusual and exigent circumstances, the Board of Governors of the Federal Reserve System, by the affirmative vote of not less than five members, may authorize any Federal reserve bank, during such periods as the said board may determine, at rates established in accordance with the provisions of section 357 of this title, to discount for any individual, partnership, or corporation, notes, drafts, and bills of exchange when such notes, drafts, and bills of exchange are indorsed or otherwise secured to the satisfaction of the Federal reserve bank: Provided, That before discounting any such note, draft, or bill of exchange for an individual or a partnership or corporation the Federal reserve bank shall obtain evidence that such individual, partnership, or corporation is unable to secure adequate credit accommodations from other banking institutions. All such discounts for individuals, partnerships, or corporations shall be subject to such limitations, restrictions, and regulations as the Board of Governors of the Federal Reserve System may prescribe.

Sec. 344. — Discount or purchase of bills to finance agricultural shipments

Upon the indorsement of any of its member banks, which shall be deemed a waiver of demand, notice, and protest by such bank as to its own indorsement exclusively, and subject to regulations and limitations to be prescribed by the Board of Governors of the Federal Reserve System, any Federal reserve bank may discount or purchase bills of exchange payable at sight or on demand which grow out of the domestic shipment or the exportation of nonperishable, readily marketable agricultural and other staples and are secured by bills of lading or other shipping documents conveying or securing title to such staples: Provided, That all such bills of exchange shall be forwarded promptly for collection, and demand for payment shall be made with reasonable promptness after the arrival of such staples at their destination: Provided further, That no such bill shall in any event be held by or for the account of a Federal reserve bank for a period in excess of ninety days. In discounting such bills Federal reserve banks may compute the interest to be deducted on the basis of the estimated life of each bill and adjust the discount after payment of such bills to conform to the actual life thereof.

Sec. 345. — Rediscount of notes, drafts, and bills for member banks; limitation of amount

The aggregate of notes, drafts, and bills upon which any person, copartnership, association, or corporation is liable as maker, acceptor, indorser, drawer, or guarantor, rediscounted for any member bank, shall at no time exceed the amount for which such person, copartnership, association, or corporation may lawfully become liable to a national banking association under the terms of section 84 of this title: Provided, however, That nothing in this section shall be construed to change the character or class of paper now eligible for rediscount by Federal reserve banks.

Sec. 346. — Discount of acceptances

Any Federal reserve bank may discount acceptances of the kinds hereinafter described, which have a maturity at the time of discount of not more than ninety days' sight, exclusive of days of grace, and which are indorsed by at least one member bank: Provided, That such acceptances if drawn for an agricultural purpose and secured at the time of acceptance by warehouse receipts or other such documents conveying or securing title covering readily marketable staples may be discounted with a maturity at the time of discount of not more than six months' sight exclusive of days of grace

Sec. 347. — Advances to member banks on their notes

Any Federal reserve bank may make advances for periods not exceeding fifteen days to its member banks on their promissory notes secured by the deposit or pledge of bonds, notes, certificates of indebtedness, or Treasury bills of the United States, or by the deposit or pledge of debentures or other such obligations of Federal intermediate credit banks which are eligible for purchase by Federal reserve banks under section 350 of this title, or by the deposit or pledge of bonds issued under the provisions of subsection (c) of section 1463 [1] of this title; and any Federal reserve bank may make advances for periods not exceeding ninety days to its member banks on their promissory notes secured by such notes, drafts, bills of exchange, or bankers' acceptances as are eligible for rediscount or for purchase by Federal reserve banks under the provisions of this chapter or secured by such obligations as are eligible for purchase under section 355 of this title. All such advances shall be made at rates to be established by such Federal reserve banks, such rates to be subject to the review and determination of the Board of Governors of the Federal Reserve System. If any member bank to which any such advance has been made shall, during the life or continuance of such advance, and despite an official warning of the reserve bank of the district or of the Board of Governors of the Federal Reserve System to the contrary, increase its outstanding loans secured by collateral in the form of stocks, bonds, debentures, or other such obligations, or loans made to members of any organized stock exchange, investment house, or dealer in securities, upon any obligation, note, or bill, secured or unsecured, for the purpose of purchasing and/or carrying stocks, bonds, or other investment securities (except obligations of the United States) such advance shall be deemed immediately due and payable, and such member bank shall be ineligible as a borrower at the reserve bank of the district under the provisions of this section for such period as the Board of Governors of the Federal Reserve System shall determine: Provided, That no temporary carrying or clearance loans made solely for the purpose of facilitating the purchase or delivery of securities offered for public subscription shall be included in the loans referred to in this section.

Sec. 347a. — Advances to member bank groups; inadequate amounts of eligible and acceptable assets; liability of individual banks in group; distribution of loans among banks of group; rate of interest; notes accepted for advances as collateral security for Federal reserve notes; foreign obligations as security for advances

Upon receiving the consent of not less than five members of the Board of Governors of the Federal Reserve System, any Federal reserve bank may make advances, in such amount as the board of directors of such Federal reserve bank may determine, to groups of five or more member banks within its district, a majority of them independently owned and controlled, upon their time or demand promissory notes, provided the bank or banks which receive the proceeds of such advances as herein provided have no adequate amounts of eligible and acceptable assets available to enable such bank or banks to obtain sufficient credit accommodations from the Federal reserve bank through rediscounts or advances other than as provided in section 347b [1] of this title. The liability of the individual banks in each group must be limited to such proportion of the total amount advanced to such group as the deposit liability of the respective banks bears to the aggregate deposit liability of all banks in such group, but such advances may be made to a lesser number of such member banks if the aggregate amount of their deposit liability constitutes at least 10 per centum of the entire deposit liability of the member banks within such district. Such banks shall be authorized to distribute the proceeds of such loans to such of their number and in such amount as they may agree upon, but before so doing they shall require such recipient banks to deposit with a suitable trustee, representing the entire group, their individual notes made in favor of the group protected by such collateral security as may be agreed upon. Any Federal reserve bank making such advance shall charge interest or discount thereon at a rate not less than 1 per centum above its discount rate in effect at the time of making such advance. No such note upon which advances are made by a Federal reserve bank under this section shall be eligible under section 412 of this title as collateral security for Federal reserve notes.

No obligations of any foreign government, individual, partnership, association, or corporation organized under the laws thereof shall be eligible as collateral security for advances under this section.

Member banks are authorized to obligate themselves in accordance with the provisions of this section.

Sec. 347b.—Advances to individual member banks on time or demand notes; maturities; time notes secured by mortgage loans covering one-to-four family residences

(a) In general

Any Federal Reserve bank, under rules and regulations prescribed by the Board of Governors of the Federal Reserve System, may make advances to any member bank on its time or demand notes having maturities of not more than four months and which are secured to the satisfaction of such Federal Reserve bank.

Notwithstanding the foregoing, any Federal Reserve bank, under rules and regulations prescribed by the Board of Governors of the Federal Reserve System, may make advances to any member bank on its time notes having such maturities as the Board may prescribe and which are secured by mortgage loans covering a one-to-four family residence. Such advances shall bear interest at a rate equal to the lowest discount rate in effect at such Federal Reserve bank on the date of such note.

(b) Limitations on advances

(1) Limitation on extended periods

Except as provided in paragraph (2), no advances to any undercapitalized depository institution by any Federal Reserve bank under this section may be outstanding for more than 60 days in any 120-day period.

(2) Viability exception

(A) In general

If —

(i) the head of the appropriate Federal banking agency certifies in advance in writing to the Federal Reserve bank that any depository institution is viable; or

(ii) the Board conducts an examination of any depository institution and the Chairman of the Board certifies in writing to the Federal Reserve bank that the institution is viable, the limitation contained in paragraph (1) shall not apply during the 60-day period beginning on the date such certification is received.

(B) Extensions of period

The 60-day period may be extended for additional 60-day periods upon receipt by the Federal Reserve bank of additional written certifications under subparagraph (A) with respect to each such additional period.

(C) Authority to issue a certificate of viability may not be delegated

The authority of the head of any agency to issue a written certification of viability under this paragraph may not be delegated to any other person.

(D) Extended advances subject to paragraph (3)

Notwithstanding paragraph (1), an undercapitalized depository institution which does not have a certificate of viability in effect under this paragraph may have advances outstanding for more than 60 days in any 120-day period if the Board elects to treat —

(i) such institution as critically undercapitalized under paragraph (3); and

(ii) any such advance as an advance described in subparagraph (A)(i) of paragraph (3).

(3) Advances to critically undercapitalized depository institutions

(A) Liability for increased loss

Notwithstanding any other provision of this section, if —

(i) in the case of any critically undercapitalized depository institution —

(I) any advance under this section to such institution is outstanding without payment having been demanded as of the end of the 5-day period beginning on the date the institution becomes a critically undercapitalized depository institution; or

(II) any new advance is made to such institution under this section after the end of such period; and

(ii) after the end of that 5-day period, any deposit insurance fund in the Federal Deposit Insurance Corporation incurs a loss exceeding the loss that the Corporation would have incurred if it had liquidated that institution as of the end of that period, the Board shall, subject to the limitations in subparagraph (B), be liable to the Federal Deposit Insurance Corporation for the excess loss, without regard to the terms of the advance or any collateral pledged to secure the advance.

(B) Limitation on excess loss

The liability of the Board under subparagraph (A) shall not exceed the lesser of the following:

(i) The amount of the loss the Board or any Federal Reserve bank would have incurred on the increases in the amount of advances made after the 5-day period referred to in subparagraph (A) if those increased advances had been unsecured.

(ii) The interest received on the increases in the amount of advances made after the 5-day period referred to in subparagraph (A).

(C) Federal Reserve to pay obligation

The Board shall pay the Federal Deposit Insurance Corporation the amount of any liability of the Board under subparagraph (A).

(D) Report

The Board shall report to the Congress on any excess loss liability it incurs under subparagraph (A), as limited by subparagraph (B)(i), and the reasons therefore, not later than 6 months after incurring the liability.

(4) No obligation to make advances

A Federal Reserve bank shall have no obligation to make, increase, renew, or extend any advance or discount under this chapter to any depository institution.

(5) Definitions

(A) Appropriate Federal banking agency

The term "appropriate Federal banking agency" has the same meaning as in section 1813 of this title.

(B) Critically undercapitalized

The term "critically undercapitalized" has the same meaning as in section 1831 of this title.

(C) Depository institution

The term "depository institution" has the same meaning as in section 1813 of this title.

(D) Undercapitalized depository institution

The term "undercapitalized depository institution" means any depository institution which —

(i) is undercapitalized, as defined in section 1831o of this title; or

(ii) has a composite CAMEL rating of 5 under the Uniform Financial Institutions Rating System (or an equivalent rating by any such agency under a comparable rating system) as of the most recent examination of such institution.

(E) Viable

A depository institution is "viable" if the Board or the appropriate Federal banking agency determines, giving due regard to the economic conditions and circumstances in the market in which the institution operates, that the institution—

(i) is not critically undercapitalized;

(ii) is not expected to become critically undercapitalized; and

(iii) is not expected to be placed in conservatorship or receivership

Sec. 347c. — Advances to individuals, partnerships, and corporations; security; interest rate

Subject to such limitations, restrictions, and regulations as the Board of Governors of the Federal Reserve System may prescribe, any Federal reserve bank may make advances to any individual, partnership, or corporation on the promissory notes of such individual, partnership, or corporation secured by direct obligations of the United States or by any obligation which is a direct obligation of, or fully guaranteed as to principal and interest by any agency of the United States. Such advances shall be made for periods not exceeding 90 days and shall bear interest at rates fixed from time to time by the Federal reserve bank, subject to the review and determination of the Board of Governors of the Federal Reserve System.

Sec. 347d. — Transactions between Federal Reserve banks and branch or agency of foreign bank; matters considered

Subject to such restrictions, limitations, and regulations as may be imposed by the Board of Governors of the Federal Reserve System, each Federal Reserve bank may receive deposits from, discount paper endorsed by, and make advances to any branch or agency of a foreign bank in the same manner and to the same extent that it may exercise such powers with respect to a member bank if such branch or agency is maintaining reserves with such Reserve bank pursuant to section 3105 of this title. In exercising any such powers with respect to any such branch or agency, each Federal Reserve bank shall give due regard to account balances being maintained by such branch or agency with such Reserve bank and the proportion of the assets of such branch or agency being held as reserves under section 3105 of this title. For the purposes of this paragraph, the terms "branch", "agency", and "foreign bank" shall have the same meanings assigned to them in section 3101 of this title.

Sec. 348. — Discount of obligations given for agricultural purposes or based upon livestock; collateral security for Federal reserve notes

Upon the indorsement of any of its member banks, which shall be deemed a waiver of demand, notice, and protest by such bank as to its own indorsement exclusively, any Federal reserve bank may, subject to regulations and limitations to be prescribed by the Board of Governors of the Federal Reserve System, discount notes, drafts, and bills of exchange issued or drawn for an agricultural purpose, or based upon livestock, and having a maturity, at the time of discount, exclusive of days of grace, not exceeding nine months, and such notes, drafts, and bills of exchange may be offered as collateral security for the issuance of Federal reserve notes under the provisions of section 16 of this Act: Provided, That notes, drafts, and bills of exchange with maturities in excess of six months shall not be eligible as a basis for the issuance of Federal reserve notes unless secured by warehouse receipts or other such negotiable documents conveying or securing title to readily marketable staple agricultural products or by chattel mortgage upon livestock which is being fattened for market.

Sec. 348a. — Transactions with foreign banks; supervision of Board of Governors of the Federal Reserve System

The Board of Governors of the Federal Reserve System shall exercise special supervision over all relationships and transactions of any kind entered into by any Federal reserve bank with any foreign bank or banker, or with any group of foreign banks or bankers, and all such relationships and transactions shall be subject to such regulations, conditions, and limitations as the Board may prescribe. No officer or other representative of any Federal reserve bank shall conduct negotiations of any kind with the officers or representatives of any foreign bank or banker without first obtaining the permission of the Board of Governors of the Federal Reserve System. The Board of Governors of the Federal Reserve System shall have the right, in its discretion, to be represented in any conference or negotiations by such representative or representatives as the Board may designate. A full report of all conferences or negotiations, and all understandings or agreements arrived at or transactions agreed upon, and all other material facts appertaining to such conferences or negotiations, shall be filed with the Board of Governors of the Federal Reserve System in writing by a duly authorized officer of each Federal reserve bank which shall have participated in such conferences or negotiations.

Sec. 349. — Rediscount for intermediate credit banks of obligations given for agricultural purposes; discount of notes made pursuant to section 1031

Any Federal reserve bank may, subject to regulations and limitations to be prescribed by the Board of Governors of the Federal Reserve System, rediscount such notes, drafts, and bills mentioned in section 348 of this title for any Federal intermediate credit bank, except that no Federal reserve bank shall rediscount for a Federal intermediate credit bank any such note or obligation which bears the indorsement of a nonmember State bank or trust company which is eligible for membership in the Federal reserve system in accordance with subchapter VIII of this chapter. Any Federal reserve bank may also, subject to regulations and limitations to be prescribed by the Board of Governors of the Federal Reserve System, discount notes payable to and bearing the indorsement of any Federal intermediate credit bank covering loans or advances made by such bank pursuant to the provisions of section 1031 [1] of this title which have maturities at the time of discount of not more than nine months, exclusive of days of grace, and which are secured by notes, drafts, or bills of exchange eligible for rediscount by Federal Reserve banks.

Sec. 350. — Purchase and sale of debentures and like obligations of intermediate credit banks and agricultural credit corporations

Any Federal reserve bank may also buy and sell debentures and other such obligations issued by a Federal intermediate credit bank or by a national agricultural credit corporation, but only to the same extent as and subject to the same limitations as those upon which it may buy and sell bonds issued under title I of the Federal Farm Loan Act.

Sec. 351. — Obligations of cooperative marketing association as issued or drawn for agricultural purposes

Notes, drafts, bills of exchange, or acceptances issued or drawn by cooperative marketing associations composed of producers of agricultural products shall be deemed to have been issued or drawn for an agricultural purpose, within the meaning of sections 348 and 349 to 352 of this title, if the proceeds thereof have been or are to be advanced by such association to any members thereof for an agricultural purpose, or have been or are to be used by such association in making payments to any members thereof on account of agricultural products delivered by such members to the association, or if such proceeds have been or are to be used by such association to meet expenditures incurred or to be incurred by the association in connection with the grading, processing, packing, preparation for market, or marketing of any agricultural product handled by such association for any of its members: Provided, That the express enumeration in this section of certain classes of paper of cooperative marketing associations as eligible for rediscount shall not be construed as rendering ineligible any other class of paper of such associations which is now eligible for rediscount.

Sec. 352. — Limitation on amount of obligations of certain maturities which may be discounted and rediscounted

The Board of Governors of the Federal Reserve System may, by regulation, limit to a percentage of the assets of a Federal reserve bank the amount of notes, drafts, acceptances, or bills having a maturity in excess of three months, but not exceeding six months, exclusive of days of grace, which may be discounted by such bank, and the amount of notes, drafts, bills, or acceptances having a maturity in excess of six months, but not exceeding nine months, which may be rediscounted by such bank.

Notes on Sec. 352a.

Section, act Dec. 23, 1913, ch. 6, Sec. 13b, as added June 19, 1934, ch. 653, Sec. 1, 48 Stat. 1105; amended Aug. 23, 1935, ch. 614, title III, Sec. 323, 49 Stat. 714, authorized Federal Reserve Banks to make loans to industrial and commercial businesses and to discount or purchase industrial obligations from financial institutions, and created an industrial advisory committee

EFFECTIVE DATE OF REPEAL

Section 601 of Pub. L. 85—699 provided that the repeal of this section is effective one year after Aug. 21, 1958

SAVINGS PROVISION

Section 601 of Pub. L. 85—699 provided that the repeal of this section shall not affect the power of any Federal Reserve bank to carry out, or protect its interest under, any agreement theretofore made or transaction entered into in carrying on operations under this section

FUND FOR MANAGEMENT COUNSELING Section 602(a), (b) of Pub. L. 85—699 provided that: "(a) Within sixty days after the enactment of this Act (Aug. 21, 1958), each Federal Reserve bank shall pay to the United States the aggregate amount which the Secretary of the Treasury has heretofore paid to such bank under the provisions of section 13b of the Federal Reserve Act (this section); and such payment shall constitute a full discharge of any obligation or liability of the Federal Reserve bank to the United States or to the Secretary of the Treasury arising out of subsection (e) of said section 13b (subsec. (e) of this section) or out of any agreement thereunder. "(b) The amounts repaid to the United States pursuant to subsection (a) of this section shall be covered into a special fund in the Treasury which shall be available for grants under section 7(d) of the Small Business Act (section 636(d) of Title 15, Commerce and Trade). Any remaining balance of funds set aside in the Treasury for payments under section 13b of the Federal Reserve Act (this section) shall be covered into the Treasury as miscellaneous receipts.

Sec. 353. — Purchase and sale of cable transfers, acceptances and bills

Any Federal reserve bank may, under rules and regulations prescribed by the Board of Governors of the Federal Reserve System, purchase and sell in the open market, at home or abroad, either from or to domestic or foreign banks, firms, corporations, or individuals, cable transfers and bankers' acceptances and bills of exchange of the kinds and maturities by this chapter made eligible for rediscount, with or without the indorsement of a member bank.

Sec. 354. — Transactions involving gold coin, bullion, and certificates

Every Federal reserve bank shall have power to deal in gold coin and bullion at home or abroad, to make loans thereon, exchange Federal reserve notes for gold, gold coin, or gold certificates, and to contract for loans of gold coin or bullion, giving therefor, when necessary, acceptable security, including the hypothecation of United States bonds or other securities which Federal reserve banks are authorized to hold

Sec. 355. — Purchase and sale of obligations of National, State, and municipal governments; open market operations; purchases and sales from or to United States; maximum aggregate amount of obligations acquired directly from or loaned directly to United States.

Every Federal Reserve bank shall have power:

(1)

To buy and sell, at home or abroad, bonds and notes of the United States, bonds issued under the provisions of subsection (c) of section 1463 [1] of this title and having maturities from date of purchase of not exceeding six months, and bills, notes, revenue bonds, and warrants with a maturity from date of purchase of not exceeding six months, issued in anticipation of the collection of taxes or in anticipation of the receipt of assured revenues by any State, county, district, political subdivision, or municipality in the continental United States, including irrigation, drainage and reclamation districts, and obligations of, or fully guaranteed as to principal and interest by, a foreign government or agency thereof, such purchases to be made in accordance with rules and regulations prescribed by the Board of Governors of the Federal Reserve System. Notwithstanding any other provision of this chapter, any bonds, notes, or other obligations which are direct obligations of the United States or which are fully guaranteed by the United States as to principal and interest may be bought and sold without regard to maturities but only in the open market.

(2)

To buy and sell in the open market, under the direction and regulations of the Federal Open Market Committee, any obligation which is a direct obligation of, or fully guaranteed as to principal and interest by, any agency of the United States.

Sec. 356. — Purchase of commercial paper from member banks and sale of same

Every Federal reserve bank shall have power to purchase from member banks and to sell, with or without its indorsement, bills of exchange arising out of commercial transactions, as hereinbefore defined.

Sec. 357. — Establishment of rates of discount

Every Federal reserve bank shall have power to establish from time to time, subject to review and determination of the Board of Governors of the Federal Reserve System, rates of discount to be charged by the Federal reserve bank for each class of paper, which shall be fixed with a view of accommodating commerce and business, but each such bank shall establish such rates every fourteen days, or oftener if deemed necessary by the Board.

Sec. 358. — Establishment of accounts for purposes of open-market operations; correspondents and agencies

Every Federal reserve bank shall have power to establish accounts with other Federal reserve banks for exchange purposes and, with the consent or upon the order and direction of the Board of Governors of the Federal Reserve System and under regulations to be prescribed by said Board, to open and maintain accounts in foreign countries, appoint correspondents, and establish agencies in such countries wheresoever it may be deemed best for the purpose of purchasing, selling, and collecting bills of exchange, and to buy and sell, with or without its indorsement, through such correspondents or agencies, bills of exchange (or acceptances) arising out of actual commercial transactions which have not more than ninety days to run, exclusive of days of grace, and which bear the signature of two or more responsible parties, and, with the consent of the Board of Governors of the Federal Reserve System, to open and maintain banking accounts for such foreign correspondents or agencies, or for foreign banks or bankers, or for foreign states as defined in section 632 of this title. Whenever any such account has been opened or agency or correspondent has been appointed by a Federal reserve bank, with the consent of or under the order and direction of the Board of Governors of the Federal Reserve System, any other Federal reserve bank may, with the consent and approval of the Board of Governors of the Federal Reserve System, be permitted to carry on or conduct, through the Federal reserve bank opening such account or appointing such agency or correspondent, any transactions authorized by this section under rules and regulations to be prescribed by the board.

Sec. 359. — Purchase and sale of acceptances of intermediate credit banks and agricultural credit corporations

Every Federal reserve bank shall have power to purchase and sell in the open market, either from or to domestic banks, firms, corporations, or individuals, acceptances of Federal intermediate credit banks and of national agricultural credit corporations, whenever the Board of Governors of the Federal Reserve System shall declare that the public interest so requires.

Notes on Sec. 359a.

Section, act Dec. 23, 1913, ch. 6, Sec. 14(h), as added June 8, 1979, Pub. L. 96—18, Sec. 2, 93 Stat. 35, which authorized the Secretary of the Treasury to borrow and sell in open market, and required the repurchase and return of obligations to Federal Reserve Banks, was effective only during the two—year period that began June 8, 1979, as provided by section 3(a) of Pub. L. 96—18.

Sec. 360. — Receiving checks and drafts on deposit at par; charges for collections, exchange, and clearances

Every Federal reserve bank shall receive on deposit at par from depository institutions or from Federal reserve banks checks and other items, including negotiable orders of withdrawal and share drafts and drafts drawn upon any of its depositors, and when remitted by a Federal reserve bank, checks and other items, including negotiable orders of withdrawal and share drafts and drafts drawn by any depositor in any other Federal reserve bank or depository institution upon funds to the credit of said depositor in said reserve bank or depository institution. Nothing herein contained shall be construed as prohibiting a depository institution from charging its actual expense incurred in collecting and remitting funds, or for exchange sold to its patrons. The Board of Governors of the Federal Reserve System shall, by rule, fix the charges to be collected by the depository institutions from its patrons whose checks and other items, including negotiable orders of withdrawal and share drafts are cleared through the Federal reserve bank and the charge which may be imposed for the service of the clearing or collection rendered by the Federal reserve bank.

Sec. 361. — Bills receivable, bills of exchange, acceptances; regulations by Board of Governors

The discount and rediscount and the purchase and sale by any Federal reserve bank of any bills receivable and of domestic and foreign bills of exchange, and of acceptances authorized by this chapter, shall be subject to such restrictions, limitations, and regulations as may be imposed by the Board of Governors of the Federal Reserve System.

Section 362, act June 1, 1955, ch. 113, title I, 69 Stat. 72, which related to reimbursement of Federal Reserve banks and branches for necessary expenses incident to deposit of withheld taxes in Government depositories, was from the Treasury—Post Office Appropriation Act, 1956, and was not repeated in subsequent appropriation acts.

Similar provisions were contained in the following prior appropriation acts: May 28, 1954, ch. 242, title I, 68 Stat. 144. June 18, 1953, ch. 132, title I, 67 Stat 67. June 30, 1952, ch. 523, title I, 66 Stat. 289. Aug. 11, 1951, ch. 301, title I, 65 Stat. 182. Sept. 6, 1950, ch. 896, Ch. IV, title I, 64 Stat. 634. June 30, 1949, ch. 286, title I, 63 Stat. 358. June 14, 1948, ch. 466, title I, 62 Stat. 409.

Section 363, act June 1, 1955, ch. 113, title I, 69 Stat. 72, which related to reimbursement of Federal Reserve banks and branches for necessary expenses incident to verification and destruction of unfit United States paper currency, was from the Treasury—Post Office Appropriation Act, 1956, and was not repeated in subsequent appropriation acts.

Similar provisions were contained in the following prior appropriation act: May 28, 1954, ch. 242, title I, 68 Stat. 144.

Section 364, act Sept. 26, 1970, Pub. L. 91—422, title II, 84 Stat. 875, which related to reimbursement of Federal Reserve banks and branches for expenditures as fiscal agents of the United States on account of Post Office Department operations, was from the Treasury, Post Office, and Executive Office Appropriation Act, 1971, and was not repeated in subsequent appropriation acts.

APPENDIX 3

WHAT CAPITAL HOMESTEADING WOULD MEAN TO THE AVERAGE AMERICAN: PROJECTED WEALTH AND INCOME ACCUMULATIONS UNDER CAPITAL HOMESTEADING

Parameters (Assumptions)

Accumulation Beginning at Age:	0
Annual Capital Credit Allocation:	$3,000.00
Annual Service and Risk Fees on Outstanding Principal:	3.00%
"Pre-Tax" Rate of Return on "Full-Payout" Shares:	15.00%
Term of Acquisition Loan in Years:	9

Age	Homestead Accumulation	Annual Earnings	Acquisition Debt Balance	Payments of Principal	Service & Risk Fees	Total Debt Service	Residual to Homesteader
0	$3,000.00	$450.00	$2,666.67	$333.33	$90.00	$423.33	$26.67
1	6,000.00	900.00	5,000.00	666.67	170.00	836.67	63.33
2	9,000.00	1,350.00	7,000.00	1,000.00	240.00	1,240.00	110.00
3	12,000.00	1,800.00	8,666.67	1,333.33	300.00	1,633.33	166.67
4	15,000.00	2,250.00	10,000.00	1,666.67	350.00	2,016.67	233.33
5	18,000.00	2,700.00	11,000.00	2,000.00	390.00	2,390.00	310.00
6	21,000.00	3,150.00	11,666.67	2,333.33	420.00	2,753.33	396.67
7	24,000.00	3,600.00	12,000.00	2,666.67	440.00	3,106.67	493.33
8	27,000.00	4,050.00	12,000.00	3,000.00	450.00	3,450.00	600.00
9	30,000.00	4,500.00	12,000.00	3,000.00	450.00	3,450.00	1,050.00
10	33,000.00	4,950.00	12,000.00	3,000.00	450.00	3,450.00	1,500.00
11	36,000.00	5,400.00	12,000.00	3,000.00	450.00	3,450.00	1,950.00
12	39,000.00	5,850.00	12,000.00	3,000.00	450.00	3,450.00	2,400.00
13	42,000.00	6,300.00	12,000.00	3,000.00	450.00	3,450.00	2,850.00
14	45,000.00	6,750.00	12,000.00	3,000.00	450.00	3,450.00	3,300.00
15	48,000.00	7,200.00	12,000.00	3,000.00	450.00	3,450.00	3,750.00
16	51,000.00	7,650.00	12,000.00	3,000.00	450.00	3,450.00	4,200.00
17	54,000.00	8,100.00	12,000.00	3,000.00	450.00	3,450.00	4,650.00
18	57,000.00	8,550.00	12,000.00	3,000.00	450.00	3,450.00	5,100.00
19	60,000.00	9,000.00	12,000.00	3,000.00	450.00	3,450.00	5,550.00
20	63,000.00	9,450.00	12,000.00	3,000.00	450.00	3,450.00	6,000.00
21	66,000.00	9,900.00	12,000.00	3,000.00	450.00	3,450.00	6,450.00
22	69,000.00	10,350.00	12,000.00	3,000.00	450.00	3,450.00	6,900.00
23	72,000.00	10,800.00	12,000.00	3,000.00	450.00	3,450.00	7,350.00
24	75,000.00	11,250.00	12,000.00	3,000.00	450.00	3,450.00	7,800.00
25	78,000.00	11,700.00	12,000.00	3,000.00	450.00	3,450.00	8,250.00
26	81,000.00	12,150.00	12,000.00	3,000.00	450.00	3,450.00	8,700.00
27	84,000.00	12,600.00	12,000.00	3,000.00	450.00	3,450.00	9,150.00
28	87,000.00	13,050.00	12,000.00	3,000.00	450.00	3,450.00	9,600.00
29	90,000.00	13,500.00	12,000.00	3,000.00	450.00	3,450.00	10,050.00
30	93,000.00	13,950.00	12,000.00	3,000.00	450.00	3,450.00	10,500.00
31	96,000.00	14,400.00	12,000.00	3,000.00	450.00	3,450.00	10,950.00
32	99,000.00	14,850.00	12,000.00	3,000.00	450.00	3,450.00	11,400.00
33	102,000.00	15,300.00	12,000.00	3,000.00	450.00	3,450.00	11,850.00
34	105,000.00	15,750.00	12,000.00	3,000.00	450.00	3,450.00	12,300.00
35	108,000.00	16,200.00	12,000.00	3,000.00	450.00	3,450.00	12,750.00

Continued on next page

WHAT CAPITAL HOMESTEADING WOULD MEAN TO THE AVERAGE AMERICAN:
PROJECTED WEALTH AND INCOME ACCUMULATIONS UNDER CAPITAL HOMESTEADING

Age	Homestead Accumulation	Annual Earnings	Acquisition Debt Balance	Payments of Principal	Service & Risk Fees	Total Debt Service	Residual to Homesteader
36	$111,000.00	$16,650.00	$12,000.00	$3,000.00	$450.00	$3,450.00	$13,200.00
37	114,000.00	17,100.00	12,000.00	3,000.00	450.00	3,450.00	13,650.00
38	117,000.00	17,550.00	12,000.00	3,000.00	450.00	3,450.00	14,100.00
39	120,000.00	18,000.00	12,000.00	3,000.00	450.00	3,450.00	14,550.00
40	123,000.00	18,450.00	12,000.00	3,000.00	450.00	3,450.00	15,000.00
41	126,000.00	18,900.00	12,000.00	3,000.00	450.00	3,450.00	15,450.00
42	129,000.00	19,350.00	12,000.00	3,000.00	450.00	3,450.00	15,900.00
43	132,000.00	19,800.00	12,000.00	3,000.00	450.00	3,450.00	16,350.00
44	135,000.00	20,250.00	12,000.00	3,000.00	450.00	3,450.00	16,800.00
45	138,000.00	20,700.00	12,000.00	3,000.00	450.00	3,450.00	17,250.00
46	141,000.00	21,150.00	12,000.00	3,000.00	450.00	3,450.00	17,700.00
47	144,000.00	21,600.00	12,000.00	3,000.00	450.00	3,450.00	18,150.00
48	147,000.00	22,050.00	12,000.00	3,000.00	450.00	3,450.00	18,600.00
49	150,000.00	22,500.00	12,000.00	3,000.00	450.00	3,450.00	19,050.00
50	153,000.00	22,950.00	12,000.00	3,000.00	450.00	3,450.00	19,500.00
51	156,000.00	23,400.00	12,000.00	3,000.00	450.00	3,450.00	19,950.00
52	159,000.00	23,850.00	12,000.00	3,000.00	450.00	3,450.00	20,400.00
53	162,000.00	24,300.00	12,000.00	3,000.00	450.00	3,450.00	20,850.00
54	165,000.00	24,750.00	12,000.00	3,000.00	450.00	3,450.00	21,300.00
55	168,000.00	25,200.00	12,000.00	3,000.00	450.00	3,450.00	21,750.00
56	171,000.00	25,650.00	12,000.00	3,000.00	450.00	3,450.00	22,200.00
57	174,000.00	26,100.00	12,000.00	3,000.00	450.00	3,450.00	22,650.00
58	177,000.00	26,550.00	12,000.00	3,000.00	450.00	3,450.00	23,100.00
59	180,000.00	27,000.00	12,000.00	3,000.00	450.00	3,450.00	23,550.00
60	183,000.00	27,450.00	12,000.00	3,000.00	450.00	3,450.00	24,000.00
61	186,000.00	27,900.00	12,000.00	3,000.00	450.00	3,450.00	24,450.00
62	189,000.00	28,350.00	12,000.00	3,000.00	450.00	3,450.00	24,900.00
63	192,000.00	28,800.00	12,000.00	3,000.00	450.00	3,450.00	25,350.00
64	195,000.00	29,250.00	12,000.00	3,000.00	450.00	3,450.00	25,800.00
65	198,000.00	29,700.00	12,000.00	3,000.00	450.00	3,450.00	26,250.00

"RESIDUAL" RECEIVED BY HOMESTEADER DURING PERIOD OF ACCUMULATION	$780,450.00
Gross Benefits to Homesteader by Age 65 (Homestead Accumulation plus "Residual"):	$978,450.00
Cost to Government/Taxpayers (Taxes avoided on "tax free" Homestead Accumulation (28%)):	$55,440.00
Taxes on Dividend Income (28% marginal rate, all Homestead Income assumed marginal):	$218,526.00
Net Tax Benefit to Government due to Homestead Program:	$163,086.00
Net Benefits to Homesteader by Age 65:	$759,924.00

"RETIREMENT (NO FURTHER ADDITIONS, BEGIN ACCELERATED PAYMENTS OF PRINCIPAL)"

Age	Homestead Accumulation	Annual Earnings	Acquisition Debt Balance	Payments of Principal	Service & Risk Fees	Total Debt Service	Residual to Homesteader
66	$198,000.00	$29,700.00	$9,000.00	$3,000.00	$360.00	$3,360.00	$26,340.00
67	198,000.00	29,700.00	6,000.00	3,000.00	270.00	3,270.00	26,430.00
68	198,000.00	29,700.00	3,000.00	3,000.00	180.00	3,180.00	26,520.00
69	198,000.00	29,700.00	-	3,000.00	90.00	3,090.00	26,610.00
70	198,000.00	29,700.00	-	-	-	-	29,700.00
71	198,000.00	29,700.00	-	-	-	-	29,700.00
72	198,000.00	29,700.00	-	-	-	-	29,700.00

APPENDIX 4
A NEW LOOK AT PRICES AND MONEY:
The Kelsonian Binary Model for Achieving Rapid Growth Without Inflation

by Norman G. Kurland
© 1972, revised 2001, 2003.

Published in *The Journal of Socio-Economics,* 2001 (Vol. 30).

Introduction

What is money? In his 1967 book coauthored with his wife Patricia Hetter Kelso, *Two-Factor Theory: The Economics of Reality,* the late Louis O. Kelso described money:

> Money is not a part of the visible sector of the economy; people do not consume money. Money is not a physical factor of production, but rather a yardstick for measuring economic input, economic outtake and the relative values of the real goods and services of the economic world. Money provides a method of measuring obligations, rights, powers and privileges. It provides a means whereby certain individuals can accumulate claims against others, or against the economy as a whole, or against many economies. It is a system of symbols that many economists substitute for the visible sector and its productive enterprises, goods and services, thereby losing sight of the fact that a monetary system is a part only of the invisible sector of the economy, and that its adequacy can *only* be measured by its effect upon the visible sector.[1]

What is clear from this description is that money is a "social good," an artifact of civilization invented to facilitate economic transactions for the common good. Like any other human tool or technology, this societal tool can be used justly or unjustly. It can be used by a few who control it to suppress the natural creativity of millions of people, or it can be used to achieve economic liberation and prosperity for all affected by the money economy.

How important is money? Meyer Amschel Rothschild, the founding father of one of the world's most powerful financial dynasties, has been quoted, perhaps apocryphally, as having said:

> Let me issue and control a nation's money and I care not who writes the laws.[2]

Confirming the relationship between money power, access to property, and political power, is the clear-sighted observation of Benjamin Watkins Leigh in the 1829 Virginia debates on the U.S. Constitution:

> Power and property may be separated for a time, by force or fraud — but divorced, never. For, as soon as the pang of separation is felt … property will purchase power, or power will take property.[3]

It takes no genius to understand the relationship between money and market prices. "Too many dollars chasing too few goods" is the classic definition of inflation. And history is replete with cases where money has been politically controlled to benefit the few at the expense of the many.

In this paper a case will be made for a prudent and humane transformation of any nation's monetary system. In the future, it will be shown, new money could be created in ways that can unharness the full productive potential of society, while closing what *The Wall Street Journal* (September 13, 1999, p. A1) recognizes as the growing wealth gap between the richest 10% and the rest of society.[4] Furthermore, such reforms could be undertaken voluntarily without the need to redistribute existing wealth. Under the proposed model of development, prices, wages and interest rates would be determined completely by competitive market forces, not by the whim of central bankers, politicians or organized power blocs.

This paper will show that Say's Law of Markets — that supply can create its own demand and demand its own supply — can be made to work. Higher rates of sustainable growth could be achieved, assuming: (1) capital credit is universally accessible and (2) profits are fully distributed to raise overall consumption, savings and investment levels. Reforms based on this new economic paradigm, first developed by Louis O. Kelso and later refined by Robert Ashford and Rodney Shakespeare,[5] would result in an asset-backed money supply that would provide sufficient liquidity to banks and other financial institutions for financing an expanding portion of the new productive assets which are added each year to grow the economy.

Unutilized productive capacity, concentrated capital ownership and widespread unmet needs and wants characterize, in different degrees, every economy in the world. In this context, the potential for substantial ownership-linked "binary growth" calls for a fundamental reconsideration of monetary policy and its relevance to Say's Law.

The term "binary", when used by Kelso and those embracing his theories, refers to two all-encompassing categories — people (or "labor") and things (or "capital") — to describe every kind of physical and intangible input to the productive process. Binary economics involves the study of how technological change impacts the relationship between labor and capital. As a socio-economic paradigm, it reveals the impact on income and asset distribution, as well as the moral, political and social implications, of universal access to capital ownership under theoretically free market conditions.

While this author recognizes that both Karl Marx and John Maynard Keynes, and their many followers in academia, have rejected Say's Law of Markets, this paper will point out how the binary economic model originally conceived by Louis Kelso refutes the criticisms of Marx and Keynes and offers a more sound moral and economic framework for promoting sustainable development within a market system. The Kelso model — recognizing both labor and capital as direct and interdependent sources of mass purchasing power — would be structured to create a more just and more productive system than any market system in the history of modern civilization.

Wealth distribution assumes wealth creation. According to recent studies, productive capital (i.e., technological and systems advances and improved land uses) accounts for almost 90% of productivity growth in the modern world.[6] Thus, balanced growth in a market economy depends on incomes distributed through widespread individual ownership of productive capital, i.e., all non-human means of production. The technological sources of production growth would then be automatically linked by free market forces to the ownership-based consumption incomes needed to purchase new products from the market. Thus, Say's Law of Markets — which both Marx and Keynes attempted to refute — would become a practical reality for the first time since the Industrial Revolution began.

As Ashford and Shakespeare have explained, binary economics reconciles Say's Law to the persistent coexistence of unutilized productive capacity and unmet needs and wants. This new perspective recognizes that "supply (in the form of increasing capital productiveness) will generate demand in proportion to its distribution."[7]

The challenge this paper will present, especially to academic economists, is in its mathematical demonstration of how Say's Law of Markets can be reconciled both with the classical quantity theory of money and various measures of net national product (NNP) to permit accelerated rates of growth without inflation, as predicted by binary economic theory. A side-effect of this proof is to relegate the Phillips' curve — asserting that inflation and unemployment are inextricably linked — to the dustbin of economic history.

The ultimate aim of this paper is to present a logical and unified market system that is structured to combine economic efficiency with fundamental principles of economic justice.[8] Implicit in this position is that no known economy in the history of civilization, particularly since the advent of modern technology, has offered both genuine justice for all, and optimum rates of productive efficiency. If this author is correct, those frustrated by today's unfree and unjust market economies are urged to come together for serious study and discussion of an alternative model of development — the new paradigm of binary economics.

Problems Not Effectively Addressed by Conventional Economics

How will the U.S. economy finance the $2 trillion required each year (at 2000 rates of growth)[9] to meet the nondefense capital requirements of the U.S. private and public sectors in the form of new plant and equipment, new hardware and software technologies, new rentable space and new physical infrastructure?

Assuming we can solve this problem, who will own the massive amounts of new capital brought into existence to meet our needs for energy self-sufficiency, new communities, and new housing, mass transit, new communications systems, resource recycling and conservation, expanded food and fiber production, etc.? Will those assets be owned by the same top 10% of U.S. families who own and control 90% of directly owned U.S. corporate stock? Will those assets be owned by government and quasi-government agencies? Will those assets, in the words of Peter Drucker, be "socialized" in the hands of money managers, pension funds or foundation bureaucrats? Or will that new capital become owned by many people whose incomes today depend almost exclusively on their (often subsidized) jobs, paternalistic government welfare and subsidy handouts, and private charity?

Can such massive investments be made without foreign oil dollars, or, for that matter, without exclusive dependency on the past savings accumulated by the rich or the reservoirs of accumulated small savings of the middle class and the poor? Can capital be acquired on expanded bank credit ("pure credit") secured by the future income (or future savings) derived from such new investments?

Can the Federal Reserve System become the "lender of last resort" so that the "full faith and credit" of "We, the People" can pump newly issued money into the banking system on a self-liquidating and asset-backed basis? And can this newly created credit be channeled under the supervision of local banks into *unsubsidized*, self-liquidating, commercially insured loans at 2-4% borrowing costs to fund feasible projects of enterprises that voluntarily want to acquire their future capital needs in ways that broaden the base of U.S. capital ownership in the process?

Why is the Asset Gap Growing Between A Wealthy Elite and Other Citizens?

What explains the growing maldistribution of capital ownership in America and throughout the global economy? Why is there a massive and growing capital gap between the already wealthy and those who have little or no capital assets and generally live from paycheck to paycheck, or even from hand to mouth? Why is it easier for a Bill Gates to increase his capital from $10 billion to over $90 billion in a few years than for the average American to accumulate in net worth enough to live on for two or three months?

Let us examine some of the structural root causes that enable the rich to get richer and the poor to become increasingly vulnerable to the forces of global change. Wealthy people can attract capital credit (i.e., other people's money) to add new and more powerful productive assets to their existing ownership stakes, because wealthy people can pledge their previous accumulations as collateral, thus eliminating the potential risk to lenders in the event that the loan cannot be repaid. Most citizens, especially the poor, have no assets to pledge as collateral. Therefore, most people cannot qualify for capital credit to purchase, on the same terms as the already wealthy, newly added self-liquidating productive assets. Once feasibility standards are met, such assets, in the hands of reasonably competent management, will pay for themselves out of future profits or savings and then become a source of additional capital incomes for those with access to capital credit. Thus, those without assets (and therefore by definition people who cannot overcome the traditional collateralization hurdle) remain with little or no hope to share profits from their own assets and gain an independent source for their future consumption incomes.

The Logic of Corporate Finance: A Key Tool for Creating New Owners Simultaneously with New Capital Creation Within a Market Economy

The guiding logic of all corporate finance is that all projects must be self-liquidating. Newly formed capital, such as improved land, new structures and new tools, are never brought into existence by a well-managed enterprise unless the new investments will pay for themselves. Under ordinary circumstances, "payback" for new equipment is generally expected within three to five years. In the corporate sector, it is interesting to note, the corporate umbrella insulates the eventual owners of this new capital, generally the already wealthy, from personal risk in the event the corporation defaults on its loans or goes bankrupt.

Using conventional methods of finance, over $2 trillion of new productive assets (or about $7,500 worth for every man, woman and child) are added annually to both the private sector and public sector of the U.S. economy. Virtually none of this newly created capital is financed in ways that create any new owners when it is formed. Theoretically, all or at least most of these assets could be financed in ways that they could be broadly and privately owned, as suggested by Louis Kelso and other binary economists since the 1950s.

Binary economics would require that inclusionary self-liquidating capital credit be made accessible to corporate employees and other current non-owners of productive capital in order to turn them into economically independent capital owners. And, in the same way that the currently wealthy use credit to increase their wealth, and thus their incomes, this would be done without unreasonable self-deprivation during the working lives of people economically enfranchised under a comprehensive national expanded ownership strategy.

As the logic and techniques of binary corporate finance are extended throughout the economy, all new incremental productive power can automatically be built into individuals who have unsatisfied needs and wants — without diminishing their take-home pay or past accumulation of savings. This will break the monopoly of capital ownership held by the currently wealthy — those with functionally excessive productive power in terms of their consumer needs and wants. The savings of the currently wealthy would then flow into the most risky and speculative ventures, or for insuring capital credit for the non-rich, or for supplying consumer credit and other nonproductive forms of credit.

"Pure credit" can be defined as productive credit extended by a commercial bank, other financial institutions or a central bank in a manner independent of past savings, so that the amount borrowed plus all transaction costs are secured and repayable with future savings from the capital assets acquired with such credit. Limiting the extension of "pure credit" by the central bank to current non-owners and leaving the pool of past savings open for use by the currently wealthy and for nonproductive government and consumer borrowing would result in a noninflationary expansion of the ownership of capital assets. Such high-powered credit would enable private lenders to expand the money supply for feasible private sector projects by discounting their "eligible" asset acquisition loan paper with the central bank. This expansion of the money supply could continue as long as underutilized resources, people and technology are available for supplying more marketable goods and services to the economy. "Pure credit" would thus free the economy to grow to the full physical limits of its workforce, available resources, technology, and the projected additional buying power of new domestic and foreign consumers.

After each increment of new capital has paid for itself from the future earnings (future savings) that it produces, effective demand and effective supply would be synchronized by normal market forces — and this would continue to do so as long as the new capital became a source of an expanded income for the poor and those in the middle-class who today do not have adequate and secure incomes to meet their needs. Binary economics would enable them to produce and earn more as owners of "procreative" capital in order to meet these needs.

From the standpoint of corporate productiveness, the binary economics approach would build all increases in capital productiveness (*i.e.*, value added by capital assets) into workers and other non-owners. New owners would then be entitled to all the income increases attributable to their growing shares of corporate ownership. Artificial pressures for increases in labor and welfare incomes that add to costs and therefore go into the price of products sold (*e.g.*, more pay for less work) would tend to diminish. Removing artificial restraints on capital creation would enable output to soar.

Once the cost of creating such capital is liquidated and the new money is cancelled out, the productive assets continue to produce wealth and incomes for its owners many times their original formation cost. Hence, where capital incomes are distributed broadly within a nation of owners, prices can eventually be reduced, while making the economy as a whole work more efficiently and equitably.

A Two-Tiered Credit Solution for
Separating Good From Bad Uses of Credit

Should the Federal Reserve establish a two-tiered credit system that sharply differentiates between participatory and productive uses of credit and exclusionary and/or nonproductive uses of credit? Under such a system, the lower tier (Tier 1) would be based upon "new money" created exclusively for financing private sector capital expansion in ways that democratize access to future capital ownership and profits, a counter-inflationary process the Center for Economic and Social Justice calls "Capital Homesteading."[10] The higher tier (Tier 2), as at present, would be based on market-determined yields on already accumulated savings available to the economy ("old money"). Interest rates on old money would contain whatever "inflation premium" is appropriate to offset the direct and indirect inflationary effects of present monetary, fiscal, employment and income maintenance policies. As illustrated below, Capital Homesteading would provide all citizens with access to self-liquidating capital credit to purchase new and transferred capital secured by future profits of viable enterprises, as opposed to limiting such access to the fortunate few who own most of today's capital.

The lower tier of expanded bank credit for Capital Homesteading projects would be grounded on a Federal Reserve discount rate or "service fee" of 0.5% or so to cover all central banking costs. The markup above each bank's cost of money (estimated at 2 to 4% for low-risk capital credit) would be market-driven, based wholly on (1) the risk of loan default (the "risk premium"), (2) the cost of administering the loan, and (3) a reasonable profit for the lending institution in competition with other lenders.

Capital Homesteading: A New Vision for the New Millennium

Following the precedent established for decentralizing land ownership under the homestead acts of the 1860s, the nation should now adopt a Capital Homestead Act to share in a totally voluntary way the ever-expanding capital frontier resulting from the continuing advances of modern labor-saving technology. Under Capital Homesteading as a basic pillar of economic policy, the focus of politics will shift to the monetary, banking, insurance, tax and inheritance law reforms needed to create a nation where capital ownership is as accessible to every citizen as the political ballot. As such, the focus would be concentrated on dismantling legal and institutional barriers to more equal ownership opportunities.

All or a major portion of the $2 trillion of the annual "growth ring" of U.S. productive capital can and should be financed through loans made to Trea-

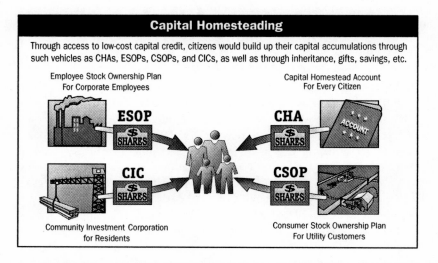

Capital Homesteading

Through access to low-cost capital credit, citizens would build up their capital accumulations through such vehicles as CHAs, ESOPs, CSOPs, and CICs, as well as through inheritance, gifts, savings, etc.

Employee Stock Ownership Plan For Corporate Employees — **ESOP** $ SHARES

Capital Homestead Account For Every Citizen — **CHA** $ SHARES

Community Investment Corporation for Residents — **CIC** $ SHARES

Consumer Stock Ownership Plan For Utility Customers — **CSOP** $ SHARES

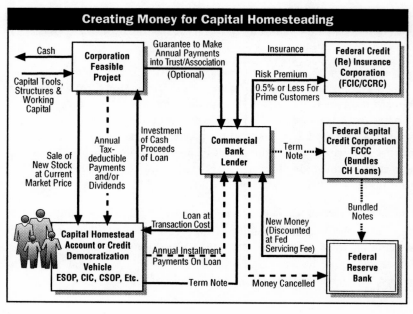

Creating Money for Capital Homesteading

sury-qualified, tax-exempt Employee Stock Ownership Plan (ESOP) trusts and similar Capital Homesteading vehicles, providing a diversified portfolio of newly issued shares secured by future enterprise profits. These other vehicles for democratizing access to capital credit would include Individual Stock Ownership Plans (ISOPs) to enable all American citizens and families to invest in shares in well-managed and economically viable new and expanding enterprises, Community Investment Corporations (CICs) for putting ownership and control over local land in the hands of local citizens and Consumer Stock Ownership Plans (CSOPs) for spreading ownership of natural monopolies among regular customers.

An alternative approach to democratizing the capital credit needs of the U.S. economy is to enable every citizen to establish a Capital Homestead Account or "CHA" (a variation of the ISOP concept) at his or her local bank to receive direct personal access to capital credit as a fundamental right of citizenship. By putting more personal choice in the hands of new owners, their governance rights would likely be enhanced over top-down approaches to Capital Homesteading. With access to monetized credit through a CHA, each citizen from birth would have the funds to invest, with the help of an investment advisor, in full dividend payout shares of 1) the company that he or a member of the family works for, directly or through an ESOP, 2) the companies he regularly buys from, directly or through a CSOP, 3) a community investment corporation to link him to profits from and control over local land development, and 4) a variety of blue-chip growth companies with a history of profits. Capital incomes earned from dividends on one's CHA account offer a private sector supplement to prevent bankruptcy of the pay-as-you-go Social Security system. Under conservative projections, a citizen could accumulate from birth to retirement a tax-sheltered estate of $200,000. Furthermore, over that period, he would receive dividend income totaling over $750,000, and at retirement an estimated annual CHA dividend income of $30,000.[11]

If lack of collateral is one of the major barriers to closing the wealth gap between the rich and the poor through the democratization of capital credit, how can this collateralization barrier be overcome? A substitute is needed for the collateral generally required by lenders to cover the risk of default. That substitute would be a system of credit insurance and reinsurance.

Lenders making "qualified" loans could either self-insure or pool the "risk premium" portion of debt service payments by insuring with commercial capital credit insurers against the risk of default, perhaps 80% to 90% of the unpaid balance. To spread further the risk of loan default, these commercial insurers could come together to establish a Capital Credit Reinsurance Corporation ("CCRC"). Some of the CCRC's reserves could be provided in the form of investments by the already wealthy. Or a portion of the reserves could be provided by the Federal, state or local governments, but only if the CCRC is structured to avoid the unlimited liability that taxpayers were exposed to by making the Federal Government "the insurer of last resort" of failing savings and loan banks in the 1980s.

To further support the CHA, a National Capital Credit Corporation (NCCC) could be set up, similar to Fannie Mae and Freddie Mac, to package and set national standards for insured, self-liquidating capital loans and then discount these loans at the discount window of one of the 12 regional Federal Reserve banks. The Federal Reserve would treat insured CHA loan paper like government debt paper as substitute backing for the U.S. currency.[12]

Legislative Reforms to Create A More Just Market Economy

After hearings devoted to careful scrutiny of Kelsonian concepts and program reforms,[13] the Senate and House Banking Committees should enact legislation designed to:

(1) Establish a public or quasi-public Capital Credit Reinsurance Corporation (or encourage private insurance companies to perform this function) to insure banks, insurance companies, and other lenders who finance loans to Capital Homestead Accounts (CHAs) and similar credit mechanisms, such as the ESOP, ISOP, CSOP and CIC. (This would be similar to the way the Federal Housing Agency insures mortgages on home financing but without making the government the insurer of last resort.)

(2) Amend Section 13 of the Federal Reserve Act to mandate that the Federal Reserve Board and Federal Reserve Banks increase the money supply responsively in ways that enable banks and other qualified lenders to make "qualified" Capital Homesteading loans on feasible (i.e., self-liquidating) projects by discounting the loan paper at a discount rate reflecting real Fed costs (*i.e.,* "pure credit" rates that exclude any inflation premium), pursuant to regulations to be adopted by the Federal Reserve System. The Fed might also require as a condition of eligibility that such loans be insured by capital credit insurers and, for more security, that the insurers pool their risks with a capital credit reinsurance facility.

(3) Establish a counterpart of Fannie Mae and Freddie Mac to set national lending standards and insurance criteria for Capital Homesteading loans, with the power to package loans made by qualified financial institutions for discounting with the Federal Reserve System.[14]

(4) Remove the power that the Federal Reserve now has to change directly the quantity of money in circulation through purchase and sale of government securities via the Open Market Committee, thus preventing future monetization of government deficits and forcing government into the competitive market to fund government debt. It should be noted that the

new money added for Capital Homesteading would substitute dollar-for-dollar with the reduction in open market purchases of government debt paper.

(5) Eliminate the power of the Federal Reserve to control growth of the economy by raising and lowering interest rates, thereby allowing all credit costs above the lender's "cost of money" under the two-tiered credit system to be set entirely by competitive market forces.

In effect, these new policies would amount to launching and promoting a counter-inflationary alternative to today's exclusionary and wealth-concentrating monetary policy. With new consumer power linked directly to the productiveness of new productive assets, the economy would grow at the full extent of its human and nonhuman capacity instead of being artificially constrained by the Federal Reserve System.

In contrast to conventional investment finance, which has systematically perpetuated monopolistic access to the ownership of new productive capital while limiting the economic participation of 95% of U.S. households to their technologically vulnerable labor inputs, ESOP and other Capital Homesteading financing technologies provide a more rational alternative for raising the consumer power of American workers on a direct and individual basis, without violating the overall economy's laws of supply and demand and as a trade-off to unjustified wage increases or perpetual income transfer schemes.

Reconciling Binary Economics with the Classical Quantity Theory of Money

As previously explained, Capital Homesteading depends on the responsiveness of a central bank's discount mechanism to the market-driven demand of the lending community, a demand that originates with the unmet capital credit needs of a more broadly owned private enterprise sector. Some economists have raised the question as to whether such a transformation of monetary and credit policy would cause runaway inflation. This paper is intended to show that economic expansion that is consistent with the logic of binary economics will lead to long-term deflationary effects, but without the adverse consequences upon aggregate demand normally associated with periods of declining prices (e.g., overcapacity, unemployment, and reduced family incomes).

Kelso's binary economic system, in sharp contrast to economies structured to distribute mass purchasing power exclusively through jobs and welfare redistribution, would link income increases directly with the productive contributions from new, expanded or transferred capital. This paper, however, will not discuss why traditional "productivity" theory leads to distortions in income maintenance policies, or why perpetual "cost push" and "demand pull" inflation is inevitable under traditional single-factor policies ("one man-one job"), nor will it explain other fundamental defects of government-subsidized "full employment" policies. (These points are fully covered in the previously cited writings on binary economics.) Rather, it will be demonstrated here that the use of monetized credit for enabling all persons to share equitably in capital ownership and capital incomes would conform to the classical quantity theory of money.

Formula for the Quantity Theory of Money[15]

$M \times V = P \times Q$
(or $M \times V = P \times T$, where Q and T are different symbols for the same variable)

M = Total stock of money in circulation (coin, currency and demand deposits)

V = Velocity of money (the annual rate of use, determined by dividing the Net National Product [NNP] by the total stock of money in circulation [M], or $V = NNP \div M$)

P = Average price level (as defined in the econometric model used by the Federal Reserve)

Q = Number of income transactions (also "T")

Binary Economics is Based on Say's Law of Markets, the Input/Output Logic of a Market Economy

Say's Law confirms the identity in a market economy between the market value of goods and services produced in a given time period and the aggregate purchasing power created out of the process of production and arising in the hands of the participants in production. More simply stated, "For every dollar spent, somebody gets a dollar in economic value." Under binary economics, each of the two basic factors of production — the human factor (labor) and the nonhuman factor (capital) — produce wealth or income in the same physical, economic, political, and ethical senses.

There are thus two ways for an individual to derive an income from a productive activity. The most obvious is wages derived from the contribution of his labor. The other is through ownership of productive land, structures, machines and all tangible and intangible technologies devoted to the production of marketable goods and services. A person's "property right" in the nonhuman factor of production entitles him to receive the entire income or wealth produced by the thing(s) that he owns.

Of course, a free person also owns his own body, and thus has a right to the full fruits of his labor's contribution to the production process, which he can exchange voluntarily for his labor income, or wages. However, binary economics is careful to separate what is human from what is not. The value of the labor or capital contributed to the production process is determined by evaluating all human inputs and all nonhuman or capital inputs through the mechanism of open and competitive markets. These productive inputs can be measured individually by the value each adds as perceived by buyers in a freely competitive market.

Through expansions and transfers of capital under more innovative corporate finance, sounder tax and inheritance policies, and more realistic labor and income maintenance policies, the right to acquire capital and receive income through capital ownership would be made accessible to the masses of mankind, who today are systematically barred from effective ownership of capital.

The logic of an individual enterprise is demonstrated by double-entry bookkeeping. Increased "outtake" (*i.e.*, income) must be based upon increased production or distortions appear — the books (and thus the business enterprise) are "out of balance" — a simple observation about an economic reality. An enterprise increases its profits by increasing production and sales and decreasing costs. Most managers do this by adding new or improved capital instruments, eliminating jobs, or both.

Binary economics carries the logic of double-entry bookkeeping and the nature of a firm's production advances to the level of an entire economic system. Viewing the entire economy, the summation of costs (i.e., prices for all inputs) must always equal the summation of all labor and capital incomes derived from the productive process. In other words, every dollar of cost on one side of the national ledger represents someone's income on the other side. This mathematical identity is the essence of Say's Law of Markets.

At the national level, Say's Law of Markets is expressed in one of two interchangeable ways.

Formulæ for Expressing Say's Law at the National Level

(1) Flow-of-Product Definition of NNP:

$$NNP_F = C + I + G$$

NNP_F = Net National Product (the total money value of the flow of final products of the community)

C =   Total spending for final consumer goods and services

I =   Net capital investment (total capital investment less depreciation ± changes in inventory)

G = Total government expenditures on goods and services (total government disbursements less transfer payments and interest on government obligations)

(2) Earnings or Income Definition of NNP:

NNPᴇ =Eʟ + Ec + Eᴛ

NNPᴇ = Net National Product (the total of factor earnings or income — wages, interest, rents, profits and transfer payments — that are the costs of production of society's final products)

Eʟ = Total after-tax national earnings of labor (wages, salaries, commissions — *i.e.*, employment income)

Ec = Total after-tax earnings of capital (profits, interest, rent — *i.e.*, property income)

Eᴛ = Total net government transfer payments (welfare, social security and other entitlements)

"NNPꜰ" and "NNPᴇ" are simply different ways of expressing the same thing:

NNPꜰ = NNPᴇ = NNP

The Relationship Between the Quantity Theory of Money and Say's Law

There is a direct connection between the quantity theory of money and the various measures of the net national product. Taking the two identities and solving for the common factor in the following way demonstrates how they relate to each other. Thus,

1) V = NNP ÷ M (From the definition of the velocity of money)

2) M x V = P x Q (The Quantity Theory of Money)

3) Substituting for V gives M x NNP ÷ M = P x Q

4) Eliminating M ÷ M (*i.e.*, "1") from the equation leaves NNP = P x Q

5) Substituting identities gives, M x V = NNP

6) And therefore M x V = P x Q = C + I + G = Eʟ + Ec + Eᴛ

Application of the Quantity Theory of Money to an Economy Planned to Operate in Accordance with the System Logic of Binary Economics

Binary economics challenges some of the most fundamental and widely held assumptions underlying conventional schools of economic thought. Among the fallacies exposed by Kelso are:

- the inevitability of effective scarcity,

- the absurdity of "full employment" of workers as an efficient, realistic and morally sound foundation for long-term national income distribution and human development policy,

- the notion that economic growth must be financed by past savings,

- the blind assertion that there is an inevitable trade-off between unemployment and higher prices (the "Phillips Curve"), and many other myths that hide the illogic and structural faults inherent in any market economy that fails to provide for the wide diffusion of ownership of capital — the second, and with advancing technology, the more productive factor of production. When markets are working efficiently, prices are only driven up when there are actual, not artificial or politically induced, shortages of workers, technology and resources.

Few will doubt that there are many system "leakages" in the form of underutilized people, technology and resources. This represents untapped productive capacity that binary economics would add to the productive process.

Let us now match Kelso's assertions with the hard logic of the quantity theory of money.

How was it possible during the World War II era (1940-1945) for the U.S. economy to transform itself from a peacetime Depression economy with unemployment rates never less than 15%, to annual wartime growth rates of at least 13% per year, without causing runaway inflation, with little or no unemployment and with 13 million of America's most able-bodied workers removed from the labor force? Why cannot similar growth rates be sustained in a peacetime economy? The adherents of the so-called Phillips Curve — suggesting that there must be a trade-off between unemployment and inflation — say that this is not theoretically possible. Students of binary economics contend otherwise, pointing to the history of U.S. economic growth from 1865 to 1895, with industrialization blossoming and price levels declining. More compelling is the logic and untapped growth potential of the Kelsonian binary growth model. An economy transformed according to Louis Kelso's binary economic growth model and his principles of economic justice would radically unharness the full productive power of modern technology and create directly the expanded private consumer power for sustaining and justifying vastly accelerated peacetime growth rates.

Kelso offers a two-pronged approach for stemming inflation. First, Kelso logically and directly attacks the multiple causes of inflation under today's inefficient national economic game plan, including ever-rising government costs and the deficit financing of welfare and warfare, plus other nonproductive, resource-wasting activities; excessive consumer debt for people with insufficient present incomes; ever-rising labor costs in the face of decreasing labor (as opposed to capital) productiveness; growing waste of labor and corporate productiveness caused by the demotivation and alienation of millions of potentially productive workers by the injustices, absurdities, and opportunity barriers structured into contemporary economies.

The second prong of Kelso's program would modify our corporate, labor, government planning, taxation, and financing institutions to remove structural barriers to broader capital ownership and revive competitive market forces and faster rates of growth. It would adopt incentives for accelerating capital formation through means that would expand the base of capital ownership and build capital incomes incrementally and in reasonable quantities into the 95% of individuals and families for whom significant capital ownership is virtually impossible to attain today.

Let us now see how the classical quantity theory of money would apply to such a planned ownership program. By combining all the variables in the identity given above, we get,

$$M \times V = P \times Q = NNP = C + I + G = E_L + E_C + E_T$$

Assumptions for Analyzing the Formula

$$M \times V = P \times Q = NNP = C + I + G = E_L + E_C + E_T$$

1. Government spending (G) would be held constant. Any future reductions in welfare and subsidy spending as current recipients begin receiving paychecks and, within a few years, dividend checks under the Capital Homestead Act, might first be applied toward retiring the national debt incurred in the deficit financing of war and welfare over the last 80 years. (In actuality, a strong argument could be made that G would be reduced under a healthier and expanding economy.) Thus, all increases ($\uparrow$) to the nation's output (NNP) would result from added consumer spending (C) and expanded investment (I):

    $$\uparrow NNP = \uparrow C + \uparrow I + G$$

2. Unit costs of labor would be assumed to remain constant for the economy as a whole. The reason is that the new policy would eliminate coercive, mercantilist and monopolistic influences on market wage rates by shifting increases in incomes from fixed wages and entitlements to variable increases based on expanded productiveness of

assets and widespread sharing of ownership profits. Thus, increased purchasing power would be directly tied to increased capital incomes, with prices and wage rates set by market forces, rather than through artificial schemes and income redistribution.

Assuming further that a new ownership-based social contract for workers is in place as a major component of a national Capital Home-steading strategy, the nation's supply of market-oriented productive labor will expand as artificially created and subsidized jobs are elimi-nated, as fixed labor rates become set by global market forces (rather than by political clout), and as barriers to labor mobility and global free trade are lifted. To build a broadly-owned, vastly expanded and more productive market economy, fixed wages would have to be jus-tified by each person's market-determined labor value, opening up enhanced income and profit sharing opportunities for the unem-ployed, the underemployed, the handicapped, the elderly and others whose creative potential is now being suppressed by outdated and confused economic policies.

3.   Total net government transfer payments (T) would be assumed to remain constant.

4.   All future increases in total national incomes or net national product (NNP) would be tied directly to marketable production increases that take the form of increases in employment incomes (E_L) and increases in ownership incomes (E_C), as determined by competitive market forces and free mobility of workers and invested capital:

$$\uparrow NNP = \uparrow E_L + \uparrow E_C + E_T$$

Analysis

Based on the above assumptions, all growth in net national product (NNP) or, in terms of the quantity theory of money, $P \times Q$, would be based on in-creased consumer spending (C) or increased investment (I), or some combi-nation thereof. However, I is a derived demand, dependent wholly on overall projected or perceived increases in C. (See Harold Moulton, *The Formation of Capital*, Brookings Institution, 1935, p. 42.)

Since all increases in labor and property incomes, E_L and E_C, would be sys-tematically channeled under the binary growth economic model to non-afflu-ent persons, overall production could be rapidly expanded to the fullest physical and technological potential of the U.S. economy. The currently "non-wealthy" by definition have a high propensity to consume and a largely unsatisfied pro-prietary desire. Thus underconsumers (whose Capital Homesteading assets would be independently accumulating through "future savings" earned as the assets pay for themselves) should be encouraged to spend all their current incomes to meet unfulfilled consumer needs, with the exception perhaps of a small amount set aside to meet household emergencies. Under Capital Homesteading the new owners would be "forced" to save to acquire their newly issued ownership shares since their future E_c incomes would initially be used to repay the capital acquisition loans.[16] The limits of C would be the sum of projected E_L plus E_c remaining after the formation costs of each new increment of capital are paid. Taking interest payments into account, payback is normally within five to seven years of acquisition.

As was experienced during the 13% annual growth rates during World War II, when maximum market demand for non-consumer-destined production was artificially sustained by government, it is estimated that annual growth rates of at least 6% under the binary growth model would be entirely feasible. Expanded bank credit would become available for expanding productive capacity to the fullest extent of underemployed people and underutilized technology, and U.S. industry itself would be pumping marketing power directly and systematically into its potential private customers through a private sector income distribution system linked to the payrolls and dividend rolls of each firm in the system.

Redistribution of income would become increasingly unnecessary. The accumulated savings of the already affluent who today enjoy monopolistic access to future capital ownership would become free to be channeled through the banking system to provide productive credit for those Capital Homesteading projects which do not meet the requirements for financing through the Fed's pure credit discount mechanism, thus further contributing to expanding the capital ownership base.

As a preliminary step to meeting such industry-generated expanded demands for consumer goods and services, industry would have to increase greatly its capacity to produce more. Expanding to full production can only be achieved by accelerating the rate of new capital formation (I) and by operating new and existing enterprises at their fullest potential.

The Capital Homestead Act offers a workable means for monetizing such expanded investment rates through our national banking system, without relying on the accumulated savings of the already wealthy (who by definition already derive sufficient E_L and E_c to satisfy fully their consumer needs). Without the Capital Homestead Act, all newly created capital would flow automatically into a relatively stationary ownership base, as it has since the beginning of the Industrial Revolution. This does nothing but foment more social disorder and more governmental intervention with every expanded use of technology.

At the microeconomic level, that of the individual business enterprise, capital is never added unless it is expected to pay for its own formation costs out of future earnings of the investment itself (E_c), generally within a few years. Thereafter it continues to produce wealth and income in amounts that may be ten, a hundred, even a thousand times its original investment costs (I). This wealth and income flows to whomever had access to the ownership financing used to formed the new capital. The Capital Homestead Act makes this ownership financing, with its self-liquidating logic and immunity from personal risks of corporate finance, available to the masses, where it was formerly limited to present owners.

Since most increases in wealth production are attributable to unit increases in the productiveness of capital (with a corresponding decrease in the relative productiveness of labor), unit labor costs under the binary growth model would begin to stabilize and might even be reduced as displaced workers began to share the fruits of advanced labor-saving technology. Once unit labor costs become stabilized as workers receive rising dividend incomes after the formation costs of new capital are paid for, a uniquely socially beneficial deflationary effect would result: total output of wealth will have expanded at lower overall production costs. This is because profits (EC) represent a residual of corporate earnings after all other production costs are met. (On the other hand, where there are shortages of certain forms of work that cannot be performed by machines, or where affluent workers choose leisure over economic work, market forces will naturally bid up the costs of those forms of labor.)

With access to two sources of personal income, EL and EC, all potential customers of the overall corporate sector could afford to pay for all new consumer goods and services (including the costs of providing environmental protections and sustainable, nonpolluting energy technologies). The price of each product sold would represent total labor incomes and total capital incomes distributed directly through the enterprises involved to all participants in the productive process. Supply and demand at the market place would be matched, no matter how fast production levels expanded. Prices might even be reduced with no harmful economic effects to the new owners. In fact, an economy might even find itself competitive once again in fields where its labor costs had become out-priced in world markets.

Viewed in the context of the quantity theory of money, increased consumer spending (C) and increased investment (I) would necessarily lead to an increased volume of income transactions (Q) in the overall economy:

$$P \times \uparrow Q = \uparrow C + \uparrow I + G$$

Assuming a national policy to maintain stable or lower prices (P), we can see from the formula $M \times V = P \times Q$ that either the total supply of money in circulation (M), or the velocity of circulation of money (V), or both, would have to increase in order to accommodate increased Q ($\uparrow Q$):

$$\uparrow M \times \uparrow V = P \times \uparrow Q$$

It makes no difference how rapidly **Q** was expanding, as long as **Q** represented new capital goods or new consumer products actually placed on the market where willing customers have sufficient job incomes (**EL**) or sufficient property incomes (**EC**) to purchase such products:

$$P \times \uparrow Q = \uparrow E_L + \uparrow E_C + E_T$$

Anticipating Short-Term Problems in Transition to A Binary Economy

One note of caution is in order, however. While a growing economy needs a growing money supply, there is a slight technical lag between the time that the banking system creates money for new capital acquisitions and the time that such productive assets are actually placed in production and begin to produce income to complete the credit cycle. This has a minor and temporary inflationary effect, but one that is more than offset by the long-term counter-inflationary impact of the binary growth model.

The key to understanding this author's optimism is the recognition that the present economic system fosters many leakages and enormous wastes of human creativity, commercializable advanced technologies and nonproductive uses of natural and man-made resources. The binary growth model would close most of these leakages and reintroduce these wasted resources for the production of marketable goods and services. This very logic of the binary growth model would thus raise the physical production and sales of marketable goods and services far beyond current levels without raising production costs in the short run, and by actually lowering production costs over the mid- to long-term. Moreover, any minor adverse effect would be counterbalanced, even in the short-run, by reducing structural inflationary pressures in today's economy caused by:

- unnecessary and inefficient barriers to enterprise competition,
- vastly underutilized U.S. plant capacity and U.S. manpower,
- costly resistance by organized labor to automation,
- needless strikes, slowdowns, and worker sabotage,
- continually rising labor costs in the face of a continuing displacement of labor inputs resulting from technological improvements,
- more "created" jobs on government and subsidized payrolls to absorb technologically displaced workers who are unwilling or unable to find satisfying private sector jobs,
- higher taxes at all levels of government,
- expanded welfare and unemployment rolls,
- artificial consumer demand created by easy access to consumer credit,
- continuing government deficit spending and rising interest for non-economically productive spending covered by the national debt,

- and many other "demand-pull" and "cost-push" pressures on current price levels.

More enlightened national fiscal and monetary policies, geared to "full ownership" and "full and sustainable production" (instead of artificial and dehumanizing expedients to achieve "full employment") could easily adjust for this minor problem. In no way, however, does it justify any further delays in restoring health to the U.S. economy and greater efficiencies and fairness in how we distribute capital ownership and mass purchasing power.

Conclusion

Kelso's binary economic system and the social technologies that would become available under the Capital Homestead Act offer a new route to accelerated, quality growth without inflation in the U.S. economy. The logic and justice of binary economics offer an improved framework to move America ahead in accordance with its original founding principles, guided by customs, legal principles, institutions and traditions that are embedded in the fabric of this nation. The American Dream offered a revolutionary vision to all citizens to encourage each person and family to gain income self-sufficiency through ownership of productive assets. Binary economics offers a new paradigm to restore that vision, voluntarily and at no one's expense.

Notes

1. Louis O. Kelso and Patricia Hetter, *Two-Factor Theory: The Economics of Reality*, New York: Random House, 1967, p. 54.

2. Frederick Merton, *The Rothschilds, A Family Portrait*, New York: Atheneum, 1962.

3. Benjamin Watkins Leigh, speech on November 3, 1829, *Proceedings and Debates of the Virginia State Convention of 1829-1830*, Volume I, New York: De Capo Press, 1971, p. 156.

4. In his book, *Top Heavy: A Study of Increasing Inequality of Wealth*, New York: Twentieth Century Fund, 1995, Dr. Edward N. Wolff of New York University mentioned that "in 1992, the financial wealth of the top 1 percent was greater than the combined wealth of the bottom 90 percent." Based on his later analysis of the Federal Reserve's *Triennial Survey of Consumer Finances*, Dr. Wolff stated that "the nation's 400 richest families grew by an average of $940 million each from 1997 to 1999, whereas over a recent 12-year period of 1983 to 1995, the modest net worth of the bottom 40 percent of households plummeted 80 percent." (See his paper "Recent Trends in Wealth Ownership" presented at a conference on Asset Ownership in the United States at the New York University, December 10-12, 1998.) Globally, the trends are worse. Jeff Gates in *Democracy at Risk: Rescuing Main Street from Wall Street*, Cambridge, MA: Perseus Publishing, 2000, cited studies showing that "the world's two hundred richest people more than doubled their net worth in the four years to 1999, to more than $1 trillion — an average $5 billion each.... This combined wealth ... now equals the combined annual income of the world's poorest 2.5 billion people" (p. xiv).

5. See *The Capitalist Manifesto*, Louis O. Kelso and Mortimer J. Adler, New York: Random House, 1958; *The New Capitalists: A Proposal for Freeing Growth from the Slavery of Sav-*

ings, Louis O. Kelso and Mortimer J. Adler, New York: Random House, 1961; *Two-Factor Theory: The Economics of Reality,* Louis O. Kelso and Patricia Hetter, New York: Random House, 1967; *Democracy and Economic Power: Extending the ESOP Revolution,* Louis O. Kelso and Patricia Hetter Kelso, Lanham, MD: University Press of America, 1991. (The first two books by Kelso and Adler, and other Kelso writings, are accessible free from the web site of the Kelso Institute for the Study of Economic Systems at www.kelsoinstitute.org.)

See also *Binary Economics: The New Paradigm,* Robert Ashford and Rodney Shakespeare, Lanham, MD: University Press of America, 1999. In the academy, Professor Ashford has pioneered the consideration of binary economics as a distinct economic paradigm, with special emphasis on "The Principle of Binary Growth," which holds that "capital has a potent distributive relationship to growth." According to Professor Ashford, the principle of binary growth distinguishes binary economics from all prior schools of economic thought.

Other articles on binary economics by Robert Ashford include: "A New Market Paradigm for Sustainable Growth: Financing Broader Capital Ownership with Louis Kelso's Binary Economics," Volume XIV, *Praxis,* The Fletcher Journal of Development Studies, pp. 25-59, 1998; "Louis Kelso's Binary Economy," Volume 25, *Journal of Socio-Economics,* pp. 1-53, 1996 (available on westlaw.com in its jjsocecon data base); and "The Binary Economics of Louis Kelso: The Promise of Universal Capitalism," 22 *Rutgers Law Journal* 3, 1990 (available on the web site of the Center for Economic and Social Justice at www.cesj.org and at www.camlaw.rutgers.edu/publications/lawjournal/ashford.htm).

A compendium of writings by many authors on this subject (prepared in collaboration with the Center for Economic and Social Justice) can be found in *Curing World Poverty: The New Role of Property,* John H. Miller, ed., St. Louis, MO: Social Justice Review, 1994. Several articles in *Curing World Poverty* and a broad array of related writings on the moral, political, social and economic implications of the Kelso paradigm are available on the web site of the Center for Economic and Social Justice *op.cit.* at www.cesj.org.

For a sympathetic analysis from a conventional Keynesian perspective, see Stephen V. Kane, "The Theory of Productiveness: A Microeconomic and Macroeconomic Analysis of Binary Growth and Output in the Kelso System," 29 *Journal of Socio-Economics,* 541-563, 2000. For another good presentation on binary economics, see Jerry Gauche, "Binary Economic Models for the Privatization of Public Assets," 27 *Journal of Socio-Economics* 445-459, 1998.

6. John W. Kendrick, "Productivity Trends and Recent Slowdown: Historical Perspective, Causal Factors, and Policy Options," *Contemporary Economic Problems,* Washington, DC: American Enterprise Institute, 1979; also R. M. Solow, in *Mathematical Methods in the Social Sciences, 1959,* pp. 89-104, K. J. Arrow, S. Karlin, and P. Suppes, eds., Palo Alto, CA: Stanford University Press, 1960. Also: Edward Denison, *Accounting for United States Economic Growth: 1929-69,* Washington, DC: Brookings Institution, 1974, and *Accounting for Slower Economic Growth: The United States in the 1970s,* Washington, DC: Brookings Institution, 1979.

7. *Binary Economics: The New Paradigm, op.cit.* at 294. Ashford and Shakespeare further note that "the binary analysis reveals that the law of supply and demand is a natural law, not a political law that can be repealed or evaded to escape its consequences. Just as the law of gravity affects all things material, so too the law of supply and demand affects all things economic. By this law more is produced in open markets than in closed ones. It is thus not only a *natural* law with universal consequences but also a law that manifests itself in differ-

ing ways in different property systems. In state-sponsored communist societies, supply creates very little demand. In the unfree market economies, supply creates considerably more demand, but far from as much as it could. In the open, binary private property system, however, supply will eventually create vastly greater demand." *Ibid.* At 295.

8. See chapter 4 of *Curing World Poverty: The New Role of Property, op cit.*

9. As of the third quarter of 2000, the annual increment added to America's productive asset base of the nondefense economy was $2.07 trillion, consisting of:

New equipment and software, private sector	$1,162.4 billion
Nonresidential structures, private sector	286.6 billion
Residential buildings, private sector	362.3 billion
New equipment and software, public sector	108.0 billion
Structures, public sector	<u>154.5 billion</u>
	$2,073.8 billion

With a U.S. population of 275.3 million in 2000, this amounts to $7527 of new productive assets for each man, woman and child in America. (Source: *The Economic Report of the President*, January 2001, tables B-19 and B-21.)

10. A proposed comprehensive national ownership strategy is described in *The Capital Homestead Act: National Infrastructural Reforms to Make Every Citizen a Shareholder*, Norman G. Kurland, Arlington, VA: Center for Economic and Social Justice, 1999. (Available from CESJ's web site at http://www.cesj.org.)

11. Norman G. Kurland, "Saving Social Security," August 30, 2001, an occasional paper of the Center for Economic and Social Justice available from the CESJ web site, *op. cit.*

12. This idea was first advanced by Dr. Norman A. Bailey, former Special Assistant to President Reagan for International Economic Affairs, in his article, "A Nation of Owners," *The International Economy,* September-October 2000; also available on CESJ web site, *op.cit.*

13. Described in such books as *The New Capitalists* (with Mortimer Adler), *op.cit.,* and *Two-Factor Theory: The Economics of Reality* (with Patricia Hetter), *op.cit.* See also testimony of Mr. Kelso and Norman G. Kurland before the Financial Markets Subcommittee of the Senate Committee on Finance on September 24, 1973. The most detailed description of binary monetary reforms can be found in this author's article, "The Federal Reserve Discount Window," which appeared in the Winter 1998 issue of *The Journal of Employee Ownership Law and Finance*, Oakland, CA: National Center for Employee Ownership. (Also available from the CESJ web site, *op. cit.*)

14. This idea was also conceived by Dr. Norman A. Bailey. See f.12.

15. Paul Samuelson, *Economics*, 6th edition, New York: McGraw-Hill, 1964, chapter 14.

16. In fact, Harold Moulton pointed out in *The Formation of Capital*, Washington, DC: Brookings Institution, 1935, pp. 117-8, that forcing the non-wealthy to reduce their consumption incomes to acquire capital assets is counterproductive. In contrast to "pure credit" repayable with "future savings", the self-denial approach to asset accumulation reduces the feasibility of all growth assets (I), whose financing was based on the assumption of increased consumer demand (C). Cf. Samuelson, *op.cit.,* p. 47.

APPENDIX 5
STATISTICS ON WEALTH AND INCOME DISTRIBUTION

(Excerpted with permission from the Shared Capitalism Institute,
www.sharedcapitalism.org)

- The financial wealth of the top one percent of households now exceeds the combined wealth of the bottom 95 percent.[1]

- The wealth of the Forbes 400 richest Americans grew by an average $940 million each from 1997-1999,[2] while over a recent 12-year period the net worth of the bottom 40 percent of households declined 80 percent.[3]

- For the well-to-do, that's an average increase in wealth of $1,287,671 per day.[4] If that were wages earned over a 40-hour week, that would be $225,962 an hour or 43,876 times the $5.15 per hour minimum wage.

- From 1983-1997, only the top five percent of households saw an increase in their net worth while wealth declined for everyone else.[5]

- As of 1997, the median household financial wealth (marketable assets less home equity) was $11,700, $1,300 lower than in 1989.[6]

- Anticipated Social Security payments are now the largest single "asset" for a majority of Americans. Funded by a levy on jobs, the Social Security payroll tax is now the largest tax paid by a majority of Americans (the largest for 90 percent of GenXers), funded with a flat tax of 12.4 percent on earnings up to $84,900.

- In 1982, inclusion on the Forbes 400 required personal wealth of $91 million. The list then included 13 billionaires. By 2002, $550 million was required for inclusion on a list that included 223 billionaires.[7]

- The combined net worth of the Forbes 400 topped $885 billion in September 2002, having dropped from a high of $1.2 trillion in 2002).[8]

- Eighty-six percent of stock market gains between 1989 and 1997 flowed to the top ten percent of households while 42 percent went to the most well-to-do one percent.[9]

- Government debt securities are owned dominantly by upper-crust households. The latest figures show that tax-exempt interest was reported on 4.9 million personal tax returns for 1997, about 4 percent of all taxpayers. Total tax-exempt interest income was $48.5 billion in 1997.[10]

- In 1998 the top-earning one percent had as much income as the 100 million Americans with the lowest earnings.[11]

- From 1983-1995, only the top 20 percent of households saw any real increase in their income while the middle-earning 20 percent, if they lost their jobs, had enough savings to maintain their standard of living for 1.2 months (36 days), down from 3.6 months in 1989.[12]

- Economist Robert Frank reports that the top one percent captured 70 percent of all earnings growth since the mid-1970's.[13]

- The Federal Reserve found that "median income between 1989 and 1998 rose appreciably only for families headed by college graduates."[14]

- On an inflation-adjusted basis, the median hourly wage in 1998 was 7 percent lower than in 1973 - when Richard Nixon was in the White House.[15]

- The pay gap between top executives and production workers grew from 42:1 in 1980 to 419:1 in 1998 (excluding the value of stock options).[16]

- Executive pay at the nation's 365 largest companies rose an average 481 percent from 1990 to 1998 while corporate profits rose 108 percent.[17]

- In 1998, Disney CEO Michael Eisner received a pay package totaling $575.6 million, 25,070 times the average Disney worker's pay.[18]

- In the same year (1998) when one American (Bill Gates) amassed more wealth than the combined net worth of the poorest 45 percent of American households,[19] a record 1.4 million Americans filed for bankruptcy — 7,000 bankruptcies per hour, 8 hours a day, 5 days a week.[20]

- Personal bankruptcy filings topped 1.3 million in 1999.[21]

- Since 1992, mortgage debt has grown 60 percent faster than income while consumer debt (mostly auto loans and credit cards) has grown twice as fast.[22]

- The fastest growing segment of the credit card market consists of low-income holders, with the average amount owed growing 18 times faster than income.[23]

- Household debt as a percentage of personal income rose from 58 percent in 1973 to an estimated 85 percent in 1997.[24]

Endnotes

[1] Edward N. Wolff, "Recent Trends in Wealth Ownership," a paper for the conference on "Benefits and Mechanisms for Spreading Asset Ownership in the United States," New York University, December 10-12, 1998. In 1995, the financial wealth of the top one percent was greater than the bottom 90 percent.

[2] Forbes 400, October 11, 1999.

[3] Edward N. Wolff, "Recent Trends in Wealth Ownership," *Ibid*. The period cited was 1983 to 1995, based on the Federal Reserve's 1995 Survey of Consumer Finances.

[4] *Forbes 400* wealth was $624 billion in 1997, $738 billion in 1998 and $1 trillion-plus in 1999. See www.forbes.com.

[5] Federal Reserve Bulletin, January 2000, p. 10.

[6] Median household financial wealth was less than $10,000 in 1995. The $11,700 figure is based on a 12-percent growth projection in Wolff, "Recent Trends in Wealth Ownership," *Ibid.*

[7] *Forbes 400*, September 13, 1982; *Forbes 400*, September 30, 2002.

[8] *Ibid.*

[9] David Wessel, "U.S. Stock Holdings Rose 20% in 1998," *The Wall Street Journal*, March 15, 1999, p.A6.

[10] "Tax Report," *The Wall Street Journal*, July 21, 1999, p. 1

[11] Congressional Budget Office Memorandum, Estimates of Federal Tax Liabilities for Individuals and Families by Income Category and Family Type for 1995 and 1999, May 1998.

[12] Edward N. Wolff, *Ibid.*, p. 10.

[13] Robert Frank, *Luxury Fever* (New York: Simon & Schuster, 1999).

[14] *Federal Reserve Bulletin*, January 2000, p. 53.

[15] Median earnings based on Commerce Department's Bureau of Economic Analysis data reported in *State of Working America* 1998-99; labor's share of non-farm business sector income based on Bureau of Labor Statistics data reported in *Economic Report of the President* (February 1999), at p. 384.

[16] *Business Week*, "49th Annual Executive Pay Survey," April 19, 1999.

[17] *A Decade of Executive. Excess: The 1990s* (Boston: United for a Fair Economy and Institute for Policy Studies, 1999).

[18] It was only after strenuous objection from institutional investors that Eisner agreed to remove his personal attorney from the compensation committee of Disney's board of directors.

[19] Professor Edward N. Wolff cited in "A Scholar Who Concentrates... on Concentrations of Wealth," *Too Much*, Winter 1999, p.8.

[20] Doug Henwood, "Debts Everywhere," *The Nation*, July 19, 1999, p. 12.

[21] *Ibid.*

[22] *Ibid.*

[23] *Ibid.*

[24] *Ibid.*

APPENDIX 6
"DEFINING ECONOMIC AND SOCIAL JUSTICE"

Center for Economic and Social Justice

In pursuing and implementing justice in today's world, the first challenge is to clarify these terms so that everyone can understand them. The next problem is to develop a conceptual framework and practical methodologies for applying universal moral values in a practical way in our daily lives, in order to realize technology's promise of universal abundance, ultimate human liberation and world peace.

Defining Justice.

One definition of justice is "giving to each what he or she is due." The problem is knowing what is "due".

Functionally, "justice" is a set of universal principles which guide people in judging what is right and what is wrong, no matter what culture and society they live in. Justice is one of the four "cardinal virtues" of classical moral philosophy, along with courage, temperance (self-control) and prudence (efficiency). (Faith, hope and charity are considered to be the three "religious" virtues.) Virtues or "good habits" help individuals to develop fully their human potentials, thus enabling them to serve their own self-interests as well as work in harmony with others for their common good.

The ultimate purpose of all the virtues is to elevate the dignity and sovereignty of the human person.

Distinguishing Justice From Charity.

While often confused, justice is distinct from the virtue of charity. Charity, derived from the Latin word *caritas*, or "divine love," is the soul of justice. Justice supplies the material foundation for charity.

While justice deals with the substance and rules for guiding ordinary, everyday human interactions, charity deals with the spirit of human interactions and with those exceptional cases where strict application of the rules is not appropriate or sufficient. Charity offers expedients during times of hardship. Charity compels us to give to relieve the suffering of a person in need. The highest aim of charity is the same as the highest aim of justice: to elevate each person to where he does not need charity but can become charitable himself.

True charity involves giving without any expectation of return. But it is not a substitute for justice.

Defining Social Justice.

Social justice encompasses economic justice. Social justice is the virtue which guides us in creating those organized human interactions we call institutions. In turn, social institutions, when justly organized, provide us with access to what is good for the person, both individually and in our associations with others. Social justice also imposes on each of us a personal responsibility to work with others to design and continually perfect our institutions as tools for personal and social development.

Defining Economic Justice.

Economic justice, which touches the individual person as well as the social order, encompasses the moral principles which guide us in designing our economic institutions. These institutions determine how each person earns a living, enters into contracts, exchanges goods and services with others and otherwise produces an independent material foundation for his or her economic sustenance. The ultimate purpose of economic justice is to free each person to engage creatively in the unlimited work beyond economics, that of the mind and the spirit.

The Three Principles of Economic Justice.

Like every system, economic justice involves input, output, and feedback for restoring harmony or balance between input and output. Within the system of economic justice as defined by Louis Kelso and Mortimer Adler, there are three essential and interdependent principles:

The Principle of Participation, The Principle of Distribution, and the Principle of Harmony.

Like the legs of a three-legged stool, if any of these principles is weakened or missing, the system of economic justice will collapse.

The Principle of Participation.

The principle of participation describes how one makes "input" to the economic process in order to make a living. It requires equal opportunity in gaining access to private property in productive assets as well as equality of opportunity to engage in productive work. The principle of participation does not guarantee equal results, but requires that every person be guaranteed by society's institutions the equal human right to make a productive contribution to the economy, both through one's labor (as a worker) and through one's productive capital (as an owner). Thus, this principle rejects monopolies, special privileges, and other exclusionary social barriers to economic self-reliance.

The Principle of Distribution.

The principle of distribution defines the "output" or "outtake" rights of an economic system matched to each person's labor and capital inputs. Through the distributional features of private property within a free and open market-place, distributive justice becomes automatically linked to participative justice, and incomes become linked to productive contributions. The principle of distributive justice involves the sanctity of property and contracts. It turns to the free and open marketplace, not government, as the most objective and democratic means for determining the just price, the just wage, and the just profit.

Many confuse the distributive principles of justice with those of charity. Charity involves the concept "to each according to his needs," whereas "distributive justice" is based on the idea "to each according to his contribution." Confusing these principles leads to endless conflict and scarcity, forcing government to intervene excessively to maintain social order.

Distributive justice follows participative justice and breaks down when all persons are not given equal opportunity to acquire and enjoy the fruits of income-producing property.

The Principle of Harmony.

The principle of harmony encompasses the "feedback" or balancing principles required to detect distortions of either the input or output principles and to make whatever corrections are needed to restore a just and balanced economic order for all. This principle is violated by unjust barriers to participation, by monopolies or by some using their property to harm or exploit others.

"Economic harmonies" is defined in *The Oxford English Dictionary* as "Laws of social adjustment under which the self-interest of one man or group of men, if given free play, will produce results offering the maximum advantage to other men and the community as a whole." This principle offers guidelines for controlling monopolies, building checks-and-balances within social institutions, and re-synchronizing distribution (outtake) with participation (input). The first two principles of economic justice flow from the eternal human search for justice in general, which automatically requires a balance between input and outtake, i.e., "to each according to what he is due." The principle of harmony, on the other hand, reflects the human quest for other absolute values, including Truth, Love and Beauty.

It should be noted that Kelso and Adler referred to the third principle as "the principle of limitation" as a restraint on human tendencies toward greed and monopoly that lead to exclusion and exploitation of others. Given the potential synergies inherent in economic justice in today's high technology world, CESJ feels that the concept of "harmony" is more appropriate and more-encompassing than the term "limitation" in describing the third component of economic justice. Furthermore, "harmony" is more consistent with the truism that a society that seeks peace must first work for justice.

(For more discussion on these terms, see Chapter 5 of *The Capitalist Manifesto*, by Louis O. Kelso and Mortimer J. Adler (Random House, 1958) and Chapters 3 and 4 of *Curing World Poverty: The New Role of Property*, John H. Miller, ed., Social Justice Review, 1994.)

APPENDIX 7

A COMPARISON OF
CAPITALISM, SOCIALISM AND THE "JUST THIRD WAY"

Center for Economic and Social Justice, © 2003 (updated)

CAPITALISM	SOCIALISM	"JUST THIRD WAY"
Political power accessible to all; economic power concentrated in a wealthy elite	Economic and political power concentrated in a governing elite	Both economic and political power are accessible to all
Capital ownership concentrated in a wealthy elite	Capital ownership concentrated in a collective controlled by a bureaucratic elite	Capital ownership is systematically deconcentrated and made accessible to every person
Capital incomes beyond consumption capacity for a wealthy elite	Adequate and secure incomes from capital for a governing elite	Adequate and secure capital incomes accessible to every person
Individualistic, atomistic system (ignores or trivializes common good)	Collectivist system (denies economic freedom and independence of individual)	System based on sovereignty of every person within institutions embodying principles of social justice
Institutionalizes greed	Institutionalizes envy	Institutionalizes justice
Materialistic ideology and system that ignores the growing income insecurity of non-owning workers facing displacement by technology or lower-paid workers	Materialistic ideology and system based on and fostering the absolute dependency of all citizens on the state for their income security and well-being	Moral philosophy and economic system based on the inherent dignity and sovereignty of each person; which fosters the inalienable right of every person to be a worker and an owner within a society where spiritual values and the respect for all creation transcend material values
Labor-centric, classical laissez-faire economic system (ultimately recognizes that only one factor—labor—produces wealth and creates economic value)	Labor-centric Marxist and Keynesian systems (only one factor—labor—produces wealth and creates economic value)	Kelsonian binary economic system [two interdependent yet distinct factors — human ("labor") and non-human ("capital") — produce wealth and create economic value]
Win-lose, zero-sum, scarcity, "dog-eat-dog" orientation	Lose-lose, zero-sum, scarcity, forced-leveling orientation	Win-win, synergistic, post-scarcity (improving systems and technology to do more with less) orientation
Sacrifices justice for efficiency	Sacrifices efficiency for collectivist "justice"	Justice and efficiency go hand-in-hand
Wage system (jobs for the many, capital ownership for the few)	Wage system (jobs for all, capital ownership for none)	Ownership system (every worker/person a capital owner)
Equality of opportunity to work; inequality of opportunity to own	Forced duty to work and forced equality of results as determined by governing elite	Equality of opportunity to work; equality of opportunity to own
Protects private property rights of the few who own productive wealth, and monopolizes access to future ownership opportunities	Truncates or eliminates rights of private property, putting control over means of production in hands of political elite	Universalizes right to private property and protects rights of property (to extent others are not harmed)

Continued on next page

A COMPARISON OF
CAPITALISM, SOCIALISM AND THE "JUST THIRD WAY"

CAPITALISM	SOCIALISM	"JUST THIRD WAY"
"Hands-off" role of the state regarding monopolization of ownership and control; state ends up redistributing wealth and incomes	Economic power is totally centralized in or regulated by the state; state redistributes incomes	Economic power of the state is limited (e.g., preventing abuses and monopolies, and dismantling barriers to universal participation in capital ownership)
Prices and wages protected from global competition; promotes mercantilism	Prices and wages controlled by government	Prices, wages and profits set by free and open markets with profits spread among many owners
Capital credit available to a few; consumer credit available to the many	All credit controlled by state	Access to capital credit universalized and allocated by local financial institutions
Past savings used to finance future ownership by few	Past savings used to finance future ownership by state	Pure credit, future savings and capital credit insurance used to finance growth linked to future ownership opportunities for all
Technology controlled by a private sector elite, subject to government oversight	Technology controlled by a non-accountable governing elite	Technology owned and controlled by private sector entities that are accountable to many shareholders and stakeholders
"Social safety net" for poor: Trickle-down incomes and social entitlements provided through government transfers of income, institutional charity and personal charity	"Social safety net" for poor: Trickle-down incomes and social entitlements provided through state monopolies, forced redistri- bution of wealth and income by government	"Social safety net" for poor: Connects poor individuals and families to growth dividends, supplemented by personal charity, institutional charity, and government transfers
Indifferent to environmental degradation; economically powerless become victims of development and environmental hazards; the well-being of future generations is sacrificed for short-term profits	Economic inefficiencies lead to inability to finance the most advanced and environmentally sustainable technology; economically powerless become victims of development and environmental hazards	Anticipatory approach to sustainable growth and development; aims to internalize externalities, assigning environmental costs to polluters and passing costs on to consumers; offers means of financing most advanced "green" technologies while economically empowering people to protect themselves against environmental hazards; plans for future generations
Purpose of education is to train people to get jobs	Purpose of education is to train people to get jobs	Purpose of education is to teach people how to become life-long learners and virtuous human beings, with the capacity to adapt to change, to become masters of technology and builders of civilization through their "leisure work", and to pursue the highest spiritual values

APPENDIX 8

"THE ELUSIVE THIRD WAY"

A16 TUESDAY, SEPTEMBER 22, 1998 R

The Washington Post

AN INDEPENDENT NEWSPAPER

LETTERS TO THE EDITOR

The Elusive 'Third Way'

The Post's Aug. 30 editorial "As Russia Abandons Reform" asserts that "there is in fact no 'third way to prosperity.' " Let's examine this point.

On the one hand there is capitalism, an economic system governed by market forces but where economic power is concentrated in the hands of a few who own or control productive capital. On the other hand, socialism, in its many forms, is an economic system governed centrally by a political elite, with even more highly concentrated ownership and economic power. Logically, a "third way" would be a free-market system that economically empowers all individuals and families through direct and effective ownership of the means of production — the best check against the potential for corruption and abuse.

A mistake in the editorial, and one made by many academics and economists today, is to equate democracy and the market system with the top-down, Wall Street capitalist model, with its growing gap of wealth and power between the rich and the poor. That there is excessive corruption under capitalism and socialism, even where governments are democratically elected, should come as no surprise. Lord Acton warned us years ago about systems that concentrate power.

Capitalist theorists such as Milton Friedman pay no attention to concentrated ownership of labor-displacing technology. Marxist theorists do, but conclude that the state should own and regulate all means of production. Keynesians offer a feeble synthesis between these two models of development based on the premise that maldistribution of ownership is acceptable.

The so-called "third way" of Bill Clinton and Tony Blair follows the Keynesian model. As recognized by Bill Greider in Chapter 18 of "One World, Ready or Not: The Manic Logic of Global Capitalism," Louis Kelso in 1958 fathered a real "third way," a comprehensive systems approach to solving the structural problems of Russia and other economies impacted by centralized control over global money and credit.

As Daniel Webster maintained, "power necessarily and inevitably follows property." If Russia still is hoping that the West will offer a true "third way" to help save the Russian economy, it should turn to Louis Kelso, not Bill Clinton or Tony Blair or others unwilling to address the root problem of concentrated ownership in a globalized economy.

NORMAN G. KURLAND
President
Center for Economic and Social Justice
Washington

APPENDIX 9
A NEW MODEL OF NATION-BUILDING
FOR CITIZENS OF IRAQ

Executive Summary

(Center for Economic and Social Justice, updated May 12, 2003)

• The Abraham Federation is a major innovation in democratic nation-building, offering an inclusive, comprehensive plan of economic development called "Capital Homesteading." In contrast with capitalist and socialist models of development being rejected by Third World countries, it starts from a radically new perspective based on universalized citizen access to viable capital ownership and structured democratization of economic power as the basis for political democracy.

• The Abraham Federation strategy was first developed in 1978 to create a new democratic nation state for the Holy Land. Freedom of religion and conscience would be secured by a government that systematically diffuses economic power into the hands of every citizen. This strategy proposed starting with lands now controlled by the Israeli military on the West Bank and Gaza Strip, and offering citizenship to Palestinians and to all Muslims, Jews, Christians and others wishing to settle on this land. Today it also offers a viable and politically unifying framework for rebuilding post-Saddam Hussein Iraq.

• The new model addresses a "fatal omission" in conventional approaches to nation-building that result in a growing exclusionary gap between the rich and poor, concentration of power and ownership within a small elite, corruption and abuses of power at all levels, and instability within society.

• The leading edge of this strategic framework is an economic component that attacks directly the root causes of terrorism and the basis of its support among the populace. It will answer the demands for justice and an end to poverty and oppression of all Iraqi citizens. It will create a unique nation of owners.

• It systematically promotes the growing economic sovereignty (i.e., empowerment) of each citizen — as a worker, as a consumer and as a capital owner. Economic governance and accountability would be diffused through the structured spreading of productive capital assets throughout society. This would enhance the economic well-being and self-determination of the people, and reduce the likelihood of corruption and abuses of power associated with any form of monopoly power.

- It sets up the legal and constitutional framework for moving quickly to a high-growth, free market system. It is based on the four pillars of a just market economy: (1) expanded capital ownership, (2) limited economic power of the state, (3) restoration of free trade and open markets for determining just prices, just wages and just profits, and (4) restoration of private property in all means of production.

- Because of its emphasis on infrastructural re-engineering, particularly with respect to central banking and capital credit, this framework would radically reduce the cost of reconstruction of Iraq, allowing for low-cost internal means of financing the reconstruction. This would reduce the cost to the U.S. taxpayer, the UN and those countries supporting the effort in Iraq.

- It would help Iraq become economically self-sufficient as soon as possible, providing the basis for a stable, independent, and democratic government that would serve as a model for other nations in the Middle East and around the world.

Phases for Applying the Abraham Federation Model in Iraq

PHASE I: Denationalize the oil fields of Iraq, as a catalyst for building a new "Just Third Way" economy. Convert the Iraqi National Oil Company into a professionally managed limited liability corporation. Issue initial shares *at no cost* to every oil worker and Iraqi citizen and guarantee them first-class shareholder rights to the profits and voting control of the company. Encourage preferential oil production leases to competitive operating companies that are broadly owned. To lay the foundations for Iraq's future economy, launch projects to be owned by Iraqi citizens, using advanced U.S. technologies that produce power and water from sea water and waste. Future government revenues would then come from increased citizen incomes, reducing non-accountable political control by a military or political elite, or by foreign oil interests.

Set up individual share accounts (like IRAs) within local banks for each worker and every citizen of Iraq, including those now in exile who return to Iraq. Free, full-dividend payout shares would be distributed equally to these individual accounts, representing the current assets of the denationalized Iraq National Oil Company. These initial shares would be nontransferable for 10 to 20 years, except for inheritance upon death. The tax-sheltered equity accumulation accounts would be given the power to borrow interest-free, nonrecourse productive credit on behalf of the shareholders for future share issuances to meet the expansion and modernization needs of the former state-owned oil company, as well as new enterprises, with the debt secured and repaid by the projected dividends on the newly issued shares.

One cautionary note: Experience with employee stock ownership plans has shown that it is not sufficient merely to give people ownership and expect any significant change in their behavior and value systems. It is essential that management systems be introduced during the planning and implementation phases of Capital Homesteading to offer a new servant leadership philosophy and structures and processes for diffusing economic power and ownership. One such system called "Justice-Based Management" systematically builds internal ownership cultures necessary to educate all members and maintain the continued deconcentration of power and accountability of managers to the worker- and citizen-shareholders.

PHASE 2: Help the Iraqis to establish a written constitution that reflects all the rights contained in the UN Declaration of Human Rights, strengthening Article 17 (acknowledging every person's right to own property individually or in association with others). The new Iraqi constitution would include the provision that as a fundamental right of citizenship every citizen is guaranteed access to the social means (i.e., money and interest-free productive credit) of access for acquiring and possessing income-producing property. All tax, credit, property, corporation, insurance, inheritance and related laws should, if necessary, be reconstituted to conform to the constitution and to establish institutions supporting economic democracy and universalization of the right to private property and protection of the rights of property.

PHASE 3: Restructure the discount power of the central bank in Iraq to create interest-free money for facilitating private-sector growth without inflation, linked to providing more widespread access to capital credit and allocated through local banks and institutions.

PHASE 4: Have the U.S. introduce a resolution into the UN General Assembly to treat Iraq as a "global free trade zone" whose imports and exports would be exempt from all trade barriers and tariffs of other countries. In this way the international community could provide a major catalyst for "Peace Through Justice" in Iraq and throughout the Middle East.

For more information, visit www.cesj.org or www.globaljusticemovement.org, or e-mail thirdway@cesj.org. "Extending the Abraham Federation Model: A Just Third Way for Bringing Democracy to the Iraqi People" is available at http://www.cesj.org/homestead/strategies/regional-global/abrahamfederation-nk.html.

APPENDIX 10

ABOUT CESJ

The Center for Economic and Social Justice (CESJ), established in 1984, promotes a free enterprise approach to global economic justice through expanded capital ownership. CESJ is a 501(c)(3) nonprofit, nonpartisan, ecumenical, all-volunteer organization with an educational and research mission.

CESJ's global membership shares a common set of moral values and works together to transform good ideas into effective action. CESJ's network presently reaches out from the U.S. to people in Argentina, Australia, Bangladesh, Cameroon, Canada, China, Colombia, Costa Rica, Democratic Republic of Congo, the Czech Republic, Denmark, Egypt, El Salvador, England, Finland, France, Guatemala, Hungary, Israel, Japan, Mexico, New Zealand, Nigeria, the Philippines, Poland, Russia and other republics of the former USSR, Saudi Arabia, South Africa, Tanzania, Turkey, and Uruguay. This global network includes leaders from business, labor, government, religion, and academia, and others promoting justice in institutions and societies.

CESJ is a founding member of the emerging Global Justice Movement. Building upon the ideals of the American Revolution—a "New World" revolution to spread political democracy globally—CESJ focuses on extending economic power to all. Going beyond the rhetoric of empowerment, CESJ has developed a common-sense, comprehensive plan—the Capital Homestead Act—to liberate every person economically. To build equity with efficiency at the workplace, CESJ developed a management system for 21st Century corporations, known as "Justice-Based Management^SM" (which CESJ originally called "Value-Based Management"). In 1991 CESJ created a global award (presented to three companies) to recognize business corporations that exemplified this concept and applied principles of economic and social justice in their corporate ownership structures, governance and operations.

CESJ's macro- and microeconomic concepts and applications are derived from the binary economic theories and principles of economic justice developed by the late lawyer-economist Louis Kelso and the Aristotelian philosopher Mortimer Adler. Combined with the ideas of social justice developed by Pope Pius XI and Fr. William Ferree, and the world design science revolution launched by R. Buckminster Fuller, these "post-scarcity intellectual giants offer a new paradigm for global development in the 21st Century. CESJ calls this new paradigm—which transcends the power- and ownership-concentrating wage systems of traditional capitalism and socialism—"the Just Third Way."

CESJ's philosophy starts from the inherent sacredness, and aims for the empowerment, of each person. CESJ holds that political and social democracy is untenable without economic democracy, which requires widespread participation by individuals in the ownership, control and profits of productive enterprises. Toward that end, CESJ has developed practical strategies and social technologies

centered around basic monetary and credit reforms for expanding capital ownership opportunities to every person. Such means include share ownership plans for employees (ESOPs), utilities customers (CSOPs), residents of new and redeveloped communities (Community Investment Corporations), and all citizens through leveraged personal Capital Homestead Accounts (CHAs).

Many of the model ESOPs and the first ESOP laws in the U.S., Egypt, and Central America resulted from the work of CESJ members. In 1985, CESJ members initiated the Congressional legislation which created the Presidential Task Force on Project Economic Justice. This 1986 bipartisan task force offered a bold regional strategy of expanded capital ownership for economic revitalization in Central America and the Caribbean. In 1987, CESJ representatives presented the Task Force report, *High Road to Economic Justice*, to President Ronald Reagan and Pope John Paul II. CESJ's compilation, *Every Worker an Owner*, served as the orientation book for the task force. This book was later translated into Polish and distributed throughout Solidarity channels in Poland, prior to the collapse of the Soviet Union.

In 1994, the Social Justice Review (St. Louis, Missouri) published CESJ's "textbook for change," *Curing World Poverty: The New Role of Property*. This book contains selected articles by leading thinkers on the moral philosophy, systems theory, macroeconomic reforms, and practical applications of the expanded ownership paradigm.

CESJ speakers are distinguished professionals and scholars who have conducted seminars throughout the world for high-level government policy-makers, business executives, and labor officials on the economic democratization model of privatization and development. CESJ's conferences and workshops cover such subjects as "the Just Third Way," binary economics, capital homesteading as national policy, the four pillars of a just free market, the future role of central banking and global currencies for achieving rapid growth without inflation, the democratization of capital credit, tax reform, infrastructural and legal reform in developing and transforming economies, nation-building from the bottom-up, share and asset valuations in nations without active stock markets, creating new leaders and ownership cultures through Justice-Based Management[SM], restructuring global debt, and new sources for financing private sector development.

APPENDIX 11

ABOUT THE AUTHORS

Norman G. Kurland

Mr. Kurland, principal author of *Capital Homesteading for Every Citizen: A Just Free Market Solution for Saving Social Security*, is President of the all-volunteer Center for Economic and Social Justice (CESJ), a nonprofit think tank headquartered in Arlington, Virginia. He cofounded CESJ in 1984 with social justice philosopher Fr. William Ferree and other economic and social justice advocates. Mr. Kurland is a lawyer, empowerment economist, pioneer of employee stock ownership plans (ESOPs), and leading global advocate for "the Just Third Way." This post-scarcity development model transcends traditional capitalism and socialism by combining free markets with the democratization of economic power and capital ownership.

In 1982 he founded Equity Expansion International, Inc. (EEI), which designs expanded ownership financing mechanisms and implements "Third Way" strategies around the world. Mr. Kurland serves as EEI's President and Managing Director. He teaches binary economics and binary policy reforms in privatization seminars at the International Law Institute in Washington, D.C., and has lectured before many private sector and governmental groups.

Mr. Kurland was a close colleague for eleven years of Louis O. Kelso, author of binary economics and inventor of the ESOP. With Kelso, Kurland cofounded the Institute for the Study of Economic Systems. He later became Washington Counsel for Kelso's investment banking firm. Collaborating with Kelso, Mr. Kurland authored and lobbied the first (1973) and subsequent ESOP legislative initiatives in the U.S. Congress. In 1985, President Reagan appointed Mr. Kurland as deputy chairman of the bipartisan Presidential Task Force on Project Economic Justice, to promote economic democratization through ESOP reforms in Central America and the Caribbean.

He is the principal architect of several model ESOPs and legal systems for expanding ownership, including the first ESOP and worker shareholders association in the developing world at the Alexandria Tire Company in Egypt. Mr. Kurland conceived the "Capital Homestead Act" (a comprehensive package of national monetary and tax reforms); the "Community Investment Corporation" (which enables community residents to share in land ownership and profits); and "Justice-Based Management[SM]" (a system he originally called "Value-Based Management" that applies principles of economic justice to create an ownership culture within the business corporation). *Business Week* described him as "the resident philosopher of ESOP in the capital." He was the recipient of

CESJ's first Kelso-Ferree Lifetime Achievement Award, an honor he shares with Senator Russell Long, the legendary champion of ESOP on Capitol Hill.

Before joining Kelso, Mr. Kurland was director of planning of the Citizens Crusade Against Poverty, a national coalition headed by the labor statesman Walter Reuther. Previously Mr. Kurland, as a Federal government lawyer, was deeply involved as a civil rights investigator in the Mississippi "one-person, one-vote" movement and later with the core group shaping economic empowerment initiatives in President Johnson's "War on Poverty." He came to Washington in December 1959 after receiving a Doctor of Laws degree from the University of Chicago, where he studied law and economics, following five years as an officer on flying status in the U.S. Air Force.

Dawn K. Brohawn

Ms. Brohawn, chief editor of *Capital Homesteading for Every Citizen*, is a co-founder, Executive Committee member, and volunteer Director of Communications of the Center for Economic and Social Justice (CESJ). She edits CESJ's publications and manages CESJ's volunteer, internship and membership programs, and internal operations. She has conceived and organized CESJ seminars (including CESJ's "Information and Education" and "Great Ideas" series), international roundtables, syntegrations℠, and conferences. At CESJ's Vatican conference in 1991, she was honored with the annual "Soldier of Justice" Award. She serves as CESJ's liaison to the Institute for Economic and Social Justice at the University of the District of Columbia, launched as part of CESJ's mission to establish an academic base for the study of economic and social justice, binary economics, Capital Homesteading, and Justice-Based Management℠.

Ms. Brohawn was the editor of *Every Worker an Owner*, which served as the orientation book for the 1986 Presidential Task Force on Project Economic Justice. She was a contributing author to and editorial advisor for CESJ's *Curing World Poverty: The New Role of Property*. She also serves as Secretary-Treasurer and board member of Equity Expansion International (EEI), which she co-founded in 1982. As EEI's Director of Justice-Based Management℠ Services, Ms. Brohawn designs employee ownership education and participation programs for ESOP companies.

Since 1989 she has been a member of The ESOP Association's Advisory Committee on Ownership Culture (formerly Competitiveness, Communications and Participation), and served twice as a judge for The ESOP Association's national competition for excellence in employee ownership communications. Ms. Brohawn was editor of *Journey to an Ownership Culture* published in 1997 by Scarecrow Press. Ms. Brohawn received her B.A. in 1979 from Georgetown University, where she was selected for the English Honors Program and Liberal Arts Seminar.

Michael D. Greaney

Mr. Greaney, researcher for *Capital Homesteading for Every Citizen*, is Secretary, executive committee member and volunteer Director of Research of the Center for Economic and Social Justice. A Certified Public Accountant, he has audited profit and nonprofit organizations throughout the world with the American Red Cross, Georgetown University Medical Center, and the U.S. Federal Election Commission. In his consulting work in ESOP administration, Mr. Greaney authored the ESOP Administration and Accounting Manual for the Alexandria Tire Company of Egypt, the first employee stock ownership plan in a developing country.

Mr. Greaney has authored numerous articles on expanded ownership, money and credit, and social development. He was a contributing author and the associate editor of *Curing World Poverty: The New Role of Property*, published in 1994 by the Social Justice Review in collaboration with CESJ. In 2002 he was awarded first place by the American Numismatic Association for his series on "A Millennium of Irish Coinage, AD 1001-2002" published by *World Coin News*.

He received CESJ's Soldier of Justice Award in 1994. Mr. Greaney is also a board member and Director of ESOP Administration Services of Equity Expansion International, which provides ESOP investment banking and consulting services worldwide. He has consulted and lectured on expanded capital ownership in the U.S., Canada, Denmark, Russia and Kazakhstan. Mr. Greaney received his B.B.A. in Accounting from the University of Notre Dame in 1977 and his M.B.A. from the University of Evansville in 1979.

INDEX

Printed in the United States
16291LVS00002B/145-241